American Federalism

American Federalism

Competition Among Governments

Thomas R. Dye
Florida State University

Lexington Books
D.C. Heath and Company/Lexington, Massachusetts/Toronto

Library of Congress Cataloging-in-Publication Data

Dye, Thomas R.
    American federalism : competition among governments / Thomas R.
Dye.
        p.   cm.
    Includes bibliographical references.
    ISBN 0-669-21475-2 (alk. paper).—ISBN 0-669-21474-4 (pbk. :
alk. paper)
    1. Federal government—United States.   2. State-local relations-
-United States.   3. Intergovernmental fiscal relations—United
States.   I. Title.
JK325.D94   1990
321.02′0973—dc20   89-37585
                                                                                              CIP

Published simultaneously in Canada
Printed in the United States of America
Casebound International Standard Book Number: 0-669-21475-2
Paperbound International Standard Book Number: 0-669-21474-4
Library of Congress Catalog Card Number: 89-37585

The paper used in this publication meets the minimum requirements of
American National Standard for Information Sciences—Permanence of
Paper for Printed Library Materials, ANSI Z39.48-1984. ∞™

Year and number of this printing.

        92   10 9 8 7 6 5 4 3

Contents

Figures

Tables

Preface

> In framing a government which is to be administered by men over men, the great difficulty lies in this: you must first enable the government to control the governed; and in the next place oblige it to control itself."
>
> ——James Madison, *Federalist,* Number 51

The founders of the American nation understood that democratic political processes alone could not be depended upon to restrain governmental power and protect the liberties of individuals. They believed that "auxiliary precautions" were essential in controlling government and restraining "unjust and interested" majorities. The founders also understood that written constitutional limits on government, "parchment barriers," would not enforce themselves and that the solution to controlling government power lay in creating "opposite and rival interests" within government itself. Federalism is not only competition between the national government and the states, the topic of most modern scholarship; it is also competition among state and local governments.

American Federalism: Competition Among Governments sets forth a theory of competitive federalism: the encouragement of rivalry among state and local governments to offer citizen-taxpayers the best array of public services at the lowest costs. It argues that eighty thousand governments are better than one—that intergovernmental competition was recognized by the founders as an auxiliary precaution against the monopoly abuse of power by a single centralized government. It develops arguments for truly federal, competitive, and decentralized government: greater overall satisfaction of citizen preferences, incentives for government to become efficient and provide good-quality services at their lowest costs, restraints on the size of the public sector and the tendencies of governments to oversupply goods and services, greater responsiveness to the policy preferences of consumer-taxpayers, restraints on the overall burdens of taxation and the imposition of nonproportional taxes, encouragement of economic growth, and experimentation in policies designed to improve the well-being of citizens.

Competitive federalism is different from past popular conceptualizations of federalism, most of which focused on nation-state relationships rather than competition among state and local governments. Federalism is not merely decentralized national government, and it is certainly not an effort to achieve cooperation among national, state, and local governments in carrying out national policy.

Competitive federalism requires that state and local governments have significant and independent responsibilities for the welfare of people living in their jurisdictions. These governments cannot be truly competitive if the federal government determines national priorities and assigns responsibility to state and local governments for policy implementation. Nor can state and local governments be truly competitive if the costs of their decisions can be externalized—shifted through federal grants-in-aid to the national government and to taxpayers throughout the nation. Competitive federalism requires that voter-taxpayers within the states bear the burdens, as well as the benefits, of their own choices.

This book shows that state and local government is still a significant sector of the economy and responsive to the demands of citizen-taxpayers. It argues that in the performance of their major functions, especially education, state and local governments are generally responsive to demands of consumer-taxpayers. Despite a nationalization of the economy, policy differences among the states are not diminishing; both the benefits and burdens of government vary considerably from state to state. Political competition within the states is shown to have little policy relevance. Even in competitive states, a change in party control of state government seldom results in significant policy alterations. Competitive federalism operates independently of the types of political systems within the states to insure responsiveness.

The book also shows that public policy in the states makes a difference in the economic well-being of their citizens. Both the taxing and spending decisions of these governments have economic consequences—identifiable effects on the personal income of individuals. The wealth of states, like the wealth of nations, is affected by government policies.

The book concludes with a discussion of the values of federalism and intergovernmental competition, the implication of competitive federalism for public policy, and specific constitutional and legislative prescriptions designed to strengthen competitive federalism in the U.S. system of government.

The ideas set forth in this book challenge fifty years of scholarship on American federalism. The academic euphemisms used to legitimize centralized government—"partnership," "cooperation," "sharing"—are explicitly rejected in favor of the founders' original notion of encouraging "opposite and rival interests" within the structure of government. Many in the academic establishment will feel threatened by ideas that challenge centralized monopoly government, and many political scientists will feel uncomfortable with ideas derived from market analogies. Indeed, the "public choice" model, which inspires much of the analysis in this book, will confound those who confuse rational choice with conservatism. But we hope that even the most devoted centralists will at least consider the arguments set forth here and allow their students to confront them. We hope to convince readers that our notion of competitive federalism better reflects the founders' original concept of American federalism than most current scholarship on the topic.

Acknowledgments

We wish to express appreciation to the Lynde and Harry Bradley Foundation for the financial support that made this work possible. We also wish to acknowledge the many comments and suggestions made by colleagues in various stages of this work, notably the assistance rendered by William C. Mitchell, University of Oregon; Aaron Wildavsky, University of California, Berkeley; Robert Bish, University of Victoria; Susan A. MacManus, University of South Florida; and Beverly A. Cigler, Pennsylvania State University. We are grateful to Paul O'Connell of Lexington Books for his willingness to publish a book that challenges the accepted academic orthodoxy.

1
Federalism as Competition

I put for a general inclination of all mankind, a perpetual and rest-
less desire for power after power, that ceaseth only in death.
—Thomas Hobbes, *Leviathan,* 1651

The very principle of constitutional government requires it to be
assumed that political power will be abused to promote the particular purposes of the holder; not because this has always been so,
but because it is the natural tendency of things, to guard against
which is the especial use of free institutions.
—J.S. Mill, *Considerations on Representative Government,* 1861

Chaining Leviathan

All governments, even democratic governments, are dangerous. They wield
coercive power over the whole of society. They tax, penalize, punish, limit,
confine, order, direct, and regulate. They seize property, restrict freedom, and
even take lives, all under the claim of legitimacy. Governments expect people
to accept these vexations as rightful. Thomas Hobbes justified the creation
of such a dangerous institution by arguing that it was the only alternative to
anarchy—a war of all against all, "where every man is enemy to every man"
and life is "solitary, poor, nasty, brutish and short." Only the "continual fear
and danger of violent death" justified the establishment of a Leviathan.

Democracy offers little protection to individuals. The founders of the
American nation were acutely aware of the vulnerability of the individual to
majority rule: "Such democracies have ever been spectacles of turbulence and
contention; have ever been found incompatible with personal security or the
rights of property and have in general been as short in their lives as they have
been violent in their deaths" (*Federalist*, Number 10). We do not have to view
popular majorities as incurably "factious," "mischievous" "passionate," or
selfish, as the founders did. It is a sufficient worry that the awesome powers
of government may be abused by selfish majorities. The Constitution itself,
by specifically denying some powers to the majority, is evidence that the
founders understood that "republican principles" alone could not restrain
government.

Yet we must still be concerned with the "general inclination of all mankind" for power (Hobbes) and with the "natural tendency" of political power

"to be abused to promote the particular purposes of the holder" (J.S. Mills). Like Adam Smith, we may acknowledge that our butcher and our baker are benevolent people, but we would still feel more secure if the marketplace were organized so that their self-interest coincided with the public good. So also in government: we may acknowledge that great wisdom resides in the American people and that statesmen frequently pursue the public welfare without regard to personal gain. But we would still feel more secure if government were organized so that official pursuit of self-interest coincided with the public good.

Democratic political processes alone cannot restrain Leviathan. The founders understood that "republican principles," while they should be nurtured and cherished, would not be sufficient in themselves to protect individual liberty. Periodic elections, party competition, voter enfranchisement, and political equality may function to make governing elites more responsive to popular concerns, but these processes do not protect minorities or individuals, "the weaker party or an obnoxious individual," from government deprivations of liberty or property. Indeed "the great object" of constitution writing was to preserve popular government and at the same time to protect individuals from "unjust and interested" majorities. "A dependence on the people is, no doubt, the primary control of government; but experience has taught mankind the necessity of auxiliary precautions" (*Federalist*, Number 51).

"Opposite and Rival Interests"

Among the most important "auxiliary precautions" the founders devised to control government is federalism, which they viewed as a source of constraint on Leviathan. Governments and government officials were seen as likely to act in their own self-interest:

> No man is allowed to be a judge in his own cause, because his interest would certainly bias his judgement, and not improbably, corrupt his integrity. With equal, nay with greater reason, a body of men are unfit to be both judges and parties at the same time; yet what are many of the most important acts of legislation, but so many judicial determinations, not indeed concerning the rights of single persons, but concerning the rights of large bodies of citizens? And what are the different classes of legislators but advocates and parties to the causes which they determine? (*Federalist*, Number 10)

Therefore constitutional arrangements must be devised so that the personal interest of government officials coincides with the interest of society.

The solution to the problem of adjusting the self-interests of government officials to interests of the larger society is competition. Rather than rely on the "better motives" of statesmen, the founders sought to construct a governmental system incorporating the notion of "opposite and rival interests." Governments and government officials can be constrained by competition with other governments and other government officials:

> Ambition must be made to counteract ambition. The interest of the man must be connected with the constitutional rights of the place. It may be a reflection on human nature, that such devices should be necessary to control the abuses of government. But what is government itself, but the greatest of all reflections on human nature? (*Federalist*, Number 51)

Constitutional limits on governmental power do not enforce themselves. Regardless of how explicitly a constitutional protection may be stated in a document, it will not give much protection to individuals unless government officials are provided with personal motives to enforce it. Those motives must be supplied by constitutional arrangements that encourage competition within and among governments. The solutions the founders advanced were federalism and the separation of powers within the national government:

> In the compound republic of America, the power surrendered by the people is first divided between two distinct governments, and then the portion allotted to each subdivided among distinct and separate departments. Hence a double security arises to the rights of the people. The different governments will control each other, at the same time that each will be controlled by itself. (*Federalist*, Number 51)

Federalism is the creation of "opposite and rival" interests among governments. Understanding U.S. federalism is recognizing the paramount importance of competition among governments. Federalism is not only competition between the national government and the states, the topic of most modern scholarship and federalism; it is also competition between the states. Indeed, it is also, by extension, competition among the nation's eighty-three thousand local governments. The founders themselves recognized the importance of "the system of each state within that state" as a component of federalism (*Federalist*, Number 33).

Federalism in Search of a Definition

Federalism has fallen on hard times. It has lost its meaning in American politics not only as a result of centralizing tendencies in government but also as a result of the failure of scholars to nourish the idea of it. A survey of contemporary scholarship on the topic concludes that "the theory of federalism has fallen into disrepair" (Beam, Conlan, and Walker, 1983). Indeed, the notion of federalism has fallen on such hard times that some leading scholars have urged its replacement with simple descriptions of "intergovernmental relations" (Wright 1978). Rather than search for a viable analytic or normative model of federalism, it seems easier to provide empirical descriptions of current relationships among national, state, and local governments.

The centralizing forces in the American political system have discouraged all but the most devoted scholars of federalism. Political scientist Daniel Elazar laments:

> We have moved to a system in which it is taken as axiomatic that the federal government shall initiate policies and programs, shall determine their character, shall delegate their administration to the states and localities according to terms that it alone determines, and shall provide for whatever intervention on the part of its administrative agencies as it deems necessary to secure compliance with those terms. . . . Not only has the Constitutional theory of federalism been replaced by a half-baked theory of decentralization, but it is a vulgar and, at times, vicious theory as well. (Elazar 1980, pp. 84–85, 86)

Federalism is not merely a decentralized national government. Although it is undoubtedly true that decentralization makes government more manageable and assists in the implementation of national policy, federalism is not the existence of administrative units of the national government. The states are not "middle managers" (Elazar 1981b).

Federalism is not intergovernmental relations. It is not an effort to achieve cooperation between the national government and state and local governments in carrying out national policy. Regrettably the disciplines of political science and public administration have generally treated federalism as an administrative problem to be overcome in the implementation of national policy. Federalism is equated with efficient government administration, with improving the management of federal programs. But federalism is not an administrative or managerial concept.

Federalism is not representation of state or local units of government in the national government. This is the definition of federalism implicit in the U.S. Supreme Court's *Garcia* decision (1985): a federal system is one in which the legislature of the national government is composed of individuals elected from subnational units of government. There are few governments in the world that are not federal by such a vacuous definition.

State and local governments are political systems, not administrative units of the national government. Their primary function remains political, not managerial. Daniel Elazar has endeavored to preserve our understanding of federalism by stressing the states' role as "polities." Consider his definition of federalism: "The mode of political organization that unites smaller *polities* within an overarching political system by distributing power among general and constituent governments in a manner designed to protect the existence and authority of both national and subnational political systems enabling all to share in the overall system's decision-making and executing processes" (Elazar 1966, p. 2). His key descriptive term for state and local governments is "polities"; the principal task of these units is to govern, not simply administer or manage programs devised by the federal government.

Political scientist Paul E. Peterson has provided an excellent starting place for rebuilding a meaningful notion of federalism: "Federalism is a system of government in which powers are divided between higher and lower levels of government in such a way that both levels have a significant amount of separate and autonomous responsibility for the social and economic welfare of those living within their respective jurisdictions" (Peterson 1981, p. 67). Moreover, says Peterson, the responsibilities of the subnational governments must include, at a minimum, the recruitment of their own political and administrative leaders and the power and responsibility to tax their citizens to provide whatever services their citizens demand. We would add another minimal condition: the autonomy of the subnational governments must be given exceptional legal protection, such as a written constitution that cannot be amended without the consent of both national and subnational populations. In other words, subnational governments cannot be dependent on the national government politically or financially if the system is to retain a genuine federal character.

Federalism must grant some political and financial independence, some responsibility for deciding about policy and paying for these policy decisions, to state and local governments if they are to be truly competitive. These governments must be able to pursue a range of public policies, to provide a variety of public services, and to vary the level of these services. The costs of these policy decisions must be borne by the people in these jurisdictions. State and local governments cannot be truly competitive if the national government determines national priorities and treats state and local governments as administrative units, assigning them responsibilities for policy implementation. Nor can state and local governments be truly competitive if the costs of their decisions can be externalized—shifted to the national government and to taxpayers throughout the nation. Competition requires that voter-taxpayers within states and communities bear the burdens as well as the benefits of their own choices.

Federalism in Search of a Theory

Federalism is a defense against tyranny. The political argument for it centers on preventing the abuse of power. Creating "opposite and rival interests" within government protects minorities and individuals from abuse by partic- ular governing elites or popular majorities, either within the states or in the nation as a whole. A federal system, with many rival and competitive gov- ernments, better protects individual liberty than a single government.

But to defend against tyranny, governments within a federal system, all eighty-three thousand of them, must indeed be rivals. Only a truly competi- tive federalism offers protection against abusive government. Most of the models of federalism advanced in the scholarly literature of modern political science, either as descriptions of the historical evolution of federalism in the United States or as normative ideals for a federal system, are noncompetitive and offer little protection against tyranny.

Dual Federalism

Consider, for example, the model of dual federalism, which was said to de- scribe federal-state relations during the nation's first hundred years. In this model, states and nation, functioning in the same territory, divide govern- mental functions. The national government deals exclusively with its enumer- ated powers in Article I, section 8, principally national defense, international affairs, money and credit, and foreign and interstate commerce, and the states deal with the most important domestic issues, including education, welfare, health, and criminal justice.

This was the founders' understanding of federalism, as evidenced, for example, in Madison's explanation:

> The powers delegated by the proposed Constitution to the federal govern- ment are few and defined. Those which are to remain in the State govern- ments are numerous and indefinite. The former will be exercised principally on external objects, as war, peace, negotiation, and foreign commerce; with which last the power of taxation will, for the most part, be connected. The powers reserved to the several States will extend to all objects which, in the ordinary course of affairs, concern the lives, liberties, and properties of the people, and the internal order, improvement, and prosperity of the States. (*Federalist*, Number 45)

Under the federal system contemplated by the Constitution, the states would "form distinct and independent portions of the supremacy, no more subject within their respective spheres to the general authority than the general au- thority is subject to them within its own sphere" (*Federalist*, Number 39). Even Alexander Hamilton, an ardent spokesman of national power, acknowl- edged that "the state governments would clearly retain all the rights of sov- ereignty which they before had, and which were not, by that act, *exclusively* delegated to the United States" (*Federalist*, Number 32). In 1871 the U.S.

Supreme Court in *Tarbel's Case* defined American federalism in this same fashion:

> There are within the territorial limits of each state two governments, re-stricted in their sphere of action, but independent of each other, and supreme within their respective spheres. Each has its separate departments, each has its distinct laws, and each has its own tribunals for their enforcement. Nei-ther government can intrude within the jurisdiction of the other or authorize any interference therein by its judicial officers with the action of the other.

If taken seriously, however, "dual federalism" would prevent competition between the national and state governments. In this "layer cake" model (Grodzins 1966), each level of government would exercise unchecked power in its own policy domain. However, we know that in fact this model never described federal-state relations well. From the earliest days, the national government involved itself in public activities reserved to the states and peo-ple (Elazar 1962).

Cooperative Federalism

The model of cooperative federalism, which was said to describe federal-state relations in the first half of the twentieth century, at least allowed for the possibility of federal-state rivalry. This "marble cake" federalism mixed fed-eral and state policy responsibilities: "As the colors are mixed in a marble cake so functions are mixed in the American federal system" (Grodzins 1966, p. 265). Yet even in this model of shared nation-state responsibilities, the normative bias was clearly toward cooperation rather than competition—and the cooperation expected of states and communities was in achieving goals determined by the national government. Congress acknowledged it had no direct constitutional power to regulate public health, safety, or welfare. It therefore relied upon its power to tax and spend for the general welfare to establish a system of financial rewards and punishments—giving or with-holding grants-in-aid—in order to achieve national goals. The normative bias of this model was toward cooperation; rivalry or competition from state and local governments was viewed as parochial, backward, unresponsive, or worse.

Centralized Federalism

Centralized federalism drops all pretense to federal, state, and local sharing in policymaking for the nation. When President London B. Johnson launched the Great Society in 1964, the federal government assumed the power to define national problems and set national goals in virtually all areas of public policy: education, health, and welfare, water and air pollution, consumer safety, home insulation, noise abatement, highway beautification, and even metric conversion. This model of "federalism" is indistinguishable from a centralized government. State and local governments are viewed as adminis- trative instruments of the national government. If flexibility is permitted at all, it is only better to implement national goals in a local environment. Con- gress legislates directly on whatever matter it chooses, without regard to its enumerated powers and without even pretending to rely on financial incen- tives. As for the cake analogies, one commentator observed: "The frosting had moved to the top, something like a pineapple upside down cake" (Reese 1979, p. 78).

Liberal scholars rushed to defend this theory of federalism. James Sundquist (1969) of the Brookings Institution explained that "the nation for decades has been steadily coalescing into a national society" (p. 10); "the Great Society is, by definition, one society; the phrase is singular, not plural" (p. 12); and effective governance requires "close federal supervision and con- trol to assure that national purposes are served" (p. 3).

Not much is left of federalism under such a theory, but the proponents of this view still claim the federalism label. Their claim rests on the represen- tational idea: the United States is said to retain a federal system because na- tional officials—the president, through the operation of the electoral college, and the Congress, through the allocation of two Senate seats per state and the appointment of representatives to states based on population—are se- lected from subunits of government.

Representational Federalism

The U.S. Supreme Court appears to have adopted this notion of "represen- tational federalism." According to the Supreme Court's *Garcia* decision (1985), there are no constitutionally protected powers of the states, no "a priori definitions of state sovereignty," no "discrete limitations on the objects of federal authority," other than the provision granting the states a role in the selection of Congress and the president. (The constitutional provisions spe- cifically dealing with the federal division of powers and with federal repre- sentation are shown in table 1–1.) The Court rhetorically endorsed a federal system but left it up to the national Congress, rather than the Constitution or the courts, to decide what powers the states and the national government should exercise. But if federalism is to retained, the Constitution, not the Congress, must divide powers. "The states role in our system of government is a matter of constitutional law, not legislative grace." And the courts must interpret the Constitution, protecting the powers of the states and defining the powers of the national government. In the words of the Supreme Court's dissenting members in *Garcia*, "The extent to which the states may exercise

Table 1–1
Federalism in the Constitution

Guarantees to the States	*Limits on the States*
1. General	
Powers not delegated to the U.S. by Constitution, or prohibited by it to the states, are reserved to the states (Amend. X)	States cannot enter into treaties, alliances, or confederations (Art. I, sec 10)
	No separate coinage (Art. I, sec. 10)
States cannot be sued by citizens of another state or a foreign nation (Amend. XI)	No interstate or foreign compacts without congressional consent (Art. I, sec. 10)
No division or consolidation of states without state legislative consent (Art. IV, sec. 2)	Constitution, all laws and treaties made under it, to be the supreme law of the land, binding on every state (Art. VI)
Republican form of government (Art. IV, sec. 2)	Slavery forbidden (Amend. XIII)
Protection against invasion (Art. IV, sec. 2)	All state legislative, executive, and judicial officers and state representatives in Congress to be bound by Constitution (Art. IV)
Protection against domestic violence on application of proper state authorities (Art. IV, sec. 2)	
2. Military	
Power to maintain militia and appoint militia officers (Art. I, sec. 8, Amend. II)	No letters of marque and reprisal (Art. I, sec. 10)
	No maintenance of standing military forces in peacetime without congressional consent (Art. I, sec. 10)
	No engagement in war without congressional consent, except for the purpose of repelling invasion (Art. I, sec. 10)
	Congress may provide for organizing, arming, and disciplining the militia when it is not in federal service and for governing it when it is in federal service (Art. I, sec. 8)
3. Commerce, Money, and Taxation	
Equal apportionment of direct federal taxes (Art. I, sec. 2, 9)	No levying of duties on vessels of other states (Art. I, sec. 9)
No federal export duties (Art. I, sec. 9)	No legal tender other than gold or silver (Art. I, sec. 10)
No preferential treatment for ports of one state (Art. I, sec. 9)	No impairment of obligations of contracts (Art. I, sec 10)
Reciprocal full faith and credit among states for public acts, records, and judicial proceedings (Art. IV, sec. 1)	No levying of import or export duties without consent of Congress except the levying of reasonable inspection fees (Art. I, sec. 10)
Reciprocal privileges and immunities for citizens of the several states (Art. IV, sec. 2)	No tonnage duties without congressional consent (Art. I, sec. 10)

Table 1–1 continued

Guarantees to the States	Limits on the States

4. Justice

Guarantees to the States	Limits on the States
Federal criminal trials to be held in state where crime was committed (Art. III, sec. 2)	No bills of attainder (Art. I, sec. 10)
Extradition for crimes (Art. IV, sec. 2)	No ex post facto laws (Art. I, sec. 10) Supreme Court has original jurisdiction over all cases in which a state shall be a party (Art. III, sec. 2)
Federal criminal juries to be chosen from state and district in which crime was committed (Amend. VI)	Judges in every state bound by the Constitution and all laws and treaties made under it, notwithstanding the constitutions or laws of any state (Amend. VI)
Federal judicial power to extend to controversies between two or more states, between a state and citizens of another state when state is plaintiff, and between foreign nation or its citizens, with original jurisdiction vested in the Supreme Court (Art. III, sec. 2)	No denial of life, liberty, or property without due process of law (Amend. XIV)
	No denial of equal protection of state laws to person within its limits (Amend. XIV)
	No abridgement of privileges and immunities of U.S. citizens (Amend. XIV)

5. Representation
Congress

Guarantees to the States	Limits on the States
Members of House of Representatives chosen by voters, those qualified to vote for most numerous house of state legislature in the several states (Art. I, sec. 2)	Representatives must be 25 years old and U.S. citizens for seven years (Art. I, sec. 2)
At time of election, representatives must be inhabitants of states from which they are elected (Art. I, sec, 2)	Senators must be 30 years old and U.S. citizens for nine years (Art. I, sec. 3)
Representatives to be apportioned among the states according to population every ten years (Art. I, sec. 2)	Congress may make or alter regulations as to the times, places, and manner of holding elections for senators and representatives (Art. I, sec. 4)
State executive has authority to fill vacancies (Art. I, sec. 2)	Each house shall be the judge of the elections, returns, and qualifications of its own members, shall punish its members for disorderly behavior, and shall expel a member by two-thirds vote (Art. I, sec. 5)
Each state shall have at least one representative (Art. I, sec. 2)	Basis for appointment of representation in House of Representatives may be reduced proportionate to state deprivation of the right to vote of otherwise qualified citizens (Amend. XIV, sec. 2)
Senate shall be composed of two senators from each state (Art. I, sec. 8) who are chosen by the people qualified to vote for the most numerous house of the state legislature (Amend. XVII), with vacancies to be filled as prescribed by state legislation (Amend. XVII)	Without express consent of two-thirds of Congress, states cannot be represented by persons who have taken an oath to support the Constitution and have since engaged in insurrection (Amend. XIV, sec. 3)
At time of election, senators must be inhabitants of the states from which they are chosen (Art. I, sec. 3)	

Table 1–1 continued

Guarantees to the States	Limits on the States
Times, places, and manner of holding elections for senators and representatives shall be prescribed for each state by its legislature (Art. I, sec. 4)	
No state to be deprived of equal representation in the Senate without its consent (Art. V)	

President

Guarantees to the States	Limits on the States
To be selected by the electors of the several states, with each allotted a number of electors equal to the total number of its senators and representatives (Art. II, sec. 1)	Congress may determine the time of choosing electors and a uniform day on which they shall cast their votes (Art. II, sec. 1)
Each state to have one vote if presidential election is decided in House of Representatives (Art. II, sec. 1)	
Approval of presidential appointees by the Senate as Congress shall prescribe (Art. II, sec. 2)	

Amendments to Constitutioin

Guarantees to the States	Limits on the States
Amendments must be ratified by three-fourths of the states (Amend. V)	
Amendments can be proposed by two-thirds of the states (Amend. V)	

Voting

Guarantees to the States	Limits on the States
	on grounds of race, color, or previous condition of servitude (Amend. XV, sec 1)
	Cannot be denied or abridged on account of sex (Amend. XIX, sec. 1)
	No poll tax may be levied as requirement to vote in federal elections (Amend. XXIV)
	Cannot be denied or abridged for citizens 18 years of age or older on account of age (Amend. XXIV)

Foreign Affairs

Guarantees to the States	Limits on the States
Treaties must be ratified by two-thirds of Senate (Art. II, sec. 2)	Treaties binding on states as supreme law of the land (Amend. VI)
Appointment of foreign service officers subject to Senate confirmation (Art. II, sec. 2)	

their authority . . . henceforth is to be determined by political decisions made by members of the federal government, decisions the Court says will not be subjected judicial review. It does not seem to have occurred to the Court that it—an unelected majority of five justices—today rejects almost 200 years of the understanding of the constitutional status of federalism."

Fiscal Federalism

Economists have developed the notion of fiscal federalism based on spatial efficiency in the provision of government goods and services. They have sought to determine which level of government can minimize spillover benefits and costs in the provision of a public service and which level of government can achieve the greatest economy of scale. Thus, fiscal federalism has generally dealt with the assignment of various government functions and sources of revenues to different levels of government. (See, for example, Musgrave 1969 and especially Oates 1972.) These economists acknowledge that decentralization can result in a better fit between citizen demands and public policy, but "if the central government can achieve cost savings by providing a uniform service level across localities, then this must be weighed against the potential welfare gains from diversified local outputs to ascertain the appropriate level of government to provide the service" (Oates 1972, p. 6).

Fiscal federalism models largely ignore the political problem of controlling Leviathan. Creating "opposite and rival interests" within government itself, that is, ensuring competition within and between levels of government, is not the principal concern of the fiscal federalists. On the contrary, by assigning specific governmental functions to a single level of government based on considerations of scale, the fiscal federalists would weaken the most attractive feature of federalism: competition among governments.[1] The fiscal federalists would create government monopolies in various public goods based on their criteria of minimizing externalities and maximizing economies of scale. Wallace Oates describes fiscal federalism: "In this model there is a clear division of functions among levels of government that leads to the attainment of a welfare optimum" (p. vii). Thus the fiscal federalism model leads to a system of government monopolies, not to a competitive system of rival governments.

New Federalism

New federalism models seek to reverse centralizing tendencies in American government, to restore a balance of power between nation and states, to revitalize the powers of state and community governments. According to President Reagan:

> Our citizens feel they have lost control of even the most basic decisions made about the essential services of government, such as schools, welfare, roads, and even garbage collection. They are right. A maze of interlocking jurisdictions and levels of government confronts the average citizen in trying to solve even the simplest of problems. They do not know where to turn to for answers, who to hold accountable, who to praise, who to blame, who to vote for or against. (State of the Union Message, 1982)

The phrase *new federalism* originated in the administration of President Richard M. Nixon, who used it to describe general revenue sharing—the national government's sharing of its own tax revenues with state and local governments with few strings attached. Later President Ronald Reagan used the phrase to describe a series of proposals designed to reduce federal spending for domestic programs and encourage states to undertake greater policy responsibilities themselves.

But these new federalism models do not amount to a coherent theory of federalism—a theory of "opposite and rival interests" as protection against tyranny. On the contrary, they emphasize a division of revenues and responsibilities. They recognize that the national government has grown too large and too intrusive, but they envision a separation of national and state functions rather than competition among state governments and between state and national governments.

None of these models of American federalism gives much attention to competition, either normatively or analytically. Yet fostering competition, creating "rival and competing interests," was the principal concern of the founders in their effort to oblige government "to control itself."

Competitive Federalism as Marketplace

Traditionally political science gave little attention to market solutions to questions of government. Concentrations of political power were not perceived in the same fashion as concentrations of wealth. Centralized government was not explicitly described as a monopoly problem. Yet it is not difficult to view Hobbes's Leviathan as a monopoly problem or to envision competition among rival governments for the voluntary affiliation of freely choosing individuals as the solution.

A market economy depends on voluntary exchange. Individuals choose whether to enter into agreements based on their own calculations of net benefits to themselves. They affect the market both when they enter into agreements and when they decline to do so. Individuals are assumed to act in their own self-interest. Competition stimulates them to offer more to others at lower costs. The combination of personal incentives and competition creates efficiency in society as a whole, raising output and lowering costs. The market process works best when there are many buyers and sellers, freedom of entry and exit, good information, and protection of private property. Markets maximize individual choice, rely on voluntary exchange rather than coercion, and provide personal incentives for societal progress.

Competitive federalism envisions a marketplace for governments where consumer-taxpayers can voluntarily choose the public goods and service they prefer, at the cost they wish to pay, by locating in the governmental jurisdiction that best fits their policy preferences. In this model of federalism, state and local governments compete for consumer-taxpayers by offering the best array of public goods and services at the lowest possible costs. The preferences of all individuals in society are better met in a system of multiple governments offering different packages of services and costs than of a single monopoly government, even a democratic one, offering a single package reflecting the preferences of the majority. The greater number of governments to select from, and the greater the variance in public policies among them, the closer each consumer-taxpayer can come to realizing his or her own preferences.

Matching public policy to citizen preferences is the essence of responsive government. Competitive elections and political parties were designed to achieve this goal. But decentralized government is also a way to match citizen preferences with public policies. Given variation in policy preferences across the nation and given independent governments with the authority to offer a wide range of policies at different costs, a truly federal government can achieve a far better match between preferences and policies than a centralized government imposing uniform policies throughout the nation.

Competitive federalism forces governments to improve services and reduce costs, that is, to become efficient. It forces governments to make better estimates of citizen preferences for public goods. Indeed, it provides a market solution to the problem of accurately assessing the demand for public goods. The ability of government to know the true demand for public goods is perceived by many market-oriented economists as the core problem of government. The absence of a market and a price system makes information about the true value of government activities difficult to assess. But competition among governments, offering different types and levels of public goods at different costs, provides a rough market solution to the information problems confronting public officials.

Competition in the private marketplace forces sellers to become sensitive to preferences of consumers. Competition among governments forces public officials to become sensitive to the preferences of citizens. Lessened competition in the marketplace results in higher prices, reduced output, and greater inefficiency in production. Lessened competition among governments results in higher taxes, poorer performance, and greater inefficiencies in the public sector. Competition in the marketplace promotes discoveries of new products. Competition among governments promotes policy innovation.

Competitive federalism, viewed as a marketplace model, is an extension of the "pure theory of local expenditures" described by economist Charles M. Tiebout many years ago (Tiebout 1956). Automobiles and expressways had only recently extended the mobility of significant segments of the metropolitan population. The Tiebout model was designed for local governments and metropolitan locational decisions. According to Tiebout, "The consumer voter may be viewed as picking that community which best satisfies his preference pattern for public goods. This is a major differences between central and local provision of public goods. . . . The consumer-voter moves to that community whose local government best satisfies his set of preferences. . . . The greater the number of communities and the greater the variance among them, the closer the consumer will come to fully realizing his preference position" (p. 418). The Tiebout model not only better satisfies the preferences of consumer-taxpayers; it also forces local governments to compete and thereby become more efficient. "On the production side it is assumed that communities are forced to keep production costs at a minimum either through the efficiency of city managers or through competition from other communities" (p. 422).

Mobility

According to Tiebout, the assumption of mobility is critical to the marketplace model: "The act of moving or failing to move is crucial. Moving or failing to move replaces the usual market test of willingness to buy a good and reveals the consumer-voter's demand for public services" (p. 420). "Spatial mobility provides the local public-goods counterpart to the private market's shopping trip" (p. 422).

The mobility assumption is often viewed as the weakness of the Tiebout model. It is more difficult to "shop" from one municipality, school district, or state to another than it is to go from store to store in search of bargains. But Americans are the most mobile people in the world, and mobility is much greater today than when Tiebout constructed his model. Between 1980 and 1985, 40 percent of Americans moved their residences, and nearly 10 percent moved to a different state. Family mobility is important; families are consumer-taxpayers. But perhaps even more important is the mobility of capital investment. Business and industry are also consumer-taxpayers, and there are many reasons to believe that industry and capital are more mobile today than at any other time in the nation's history. Heavy industry, with bulky raw materials and finished products, is dependent upon water and rail transportation. But heavy industry has been replaced by light industry as the driving force in the American economy. And light industry—high-tech enterprise, trade and services, and finance and administration—is much more mobile. As transportation and communication systems have improved, mobility has increased. Thus, capital as well as labor, people as well as enterprise, are increasingly mobile.

The competitive federalism model does not require that every household or firm in the United States be prepared to move in response to government policy change. That is a caricature of the model. Markets are determined by the actions of marginal buyers and sellers. All that is required is that a significant number of households and firms, families and business, and investment capital be mobile and responsive to government policies.

Information

Information is even more critical than mobility to the competitive government model. Here we diverge somewhat from the emphasis Tiebout placed on mobility. Multiple governments offering a range of public services at various costs provide comparative information to both officials and taxpayers about government services and their costs. This information itself is valuable because it enables citizens to compare governmental performances. Citizens are not only consumer-taxpayers; they are also voters and as such can exert influence on their own governments to match or exceed the performance of other governments.

The amount of information now available to people and firms, and the speed with which the information reaches them, is vastly greater than only a few decades ago. Again, not all voters must have information about the performance of governments in other jurisdictions in order to influence public officials. Governments respond to small attentive publics, and many public officials may welcome comparative information on public services and costs in other cities and states.

Competitive federalism offers dissatisfied citizens two separate options when they find themselves in a minority position on policy issues. These options correspond to traditional market and political responses to dissatisfaction. Market models rely on the exit response (Hirschman 1970). Dissatisfied consumers of certain products cease buying them and find other products in the marketplace; dissatisfied employees quit their jobs and find employment elsewhere. But democratic governments offer another option to dissatisfied citizens, that of voice. Citizen-voters can complain and threaten elected officeholders with ouster. (Actually, the voice and exit mechanisms are available in both government and private markets. Exit may be more commonplace in the private market, but dissatisfied consumers sometimes complain to business and demand refunds. Voice may be more commonplace in government, but dissatisfied citizens sometimes do withdraw their children from public school or move to states with lower taxes.) The combination of exit and voice responses strengthens the power of citizens in relation to their government. The exit responses provide the "auxiliary precaution" against tyranny that the founders sought to provide through federalism.

Dealing with Externalities, Especially Welfare

Markets are limited in the types of goods and services they can provide. Indeed, even in a free market economy it is recognized that some public goods cannot be supplied by markets but must instead be supplied by governments. Public goods are defined as services, activities, or functions that are nonexclusive; once they are provided to anyone, no one can be excluded from their benefits. The nonexclusive character of public goods recognizes the free-rider problem: these goods cannot be provided on the free market because nonbuyers would benefit just as much as buyers even through the nonbuyers paid none of the costs. National defense is the familiar example of a public good. Once it is provided, it is provided for all; it cannot be provided by the market because nonbuyers would free ride on the purchases of buyers.

The logic of public goods can be extended to federalism. In a system of multiple competing governments, the free-rider problem inhibits governments from providing a nonexclusive service—one that citizens in their jurisdictions could benefit from without paying the cost. Some governments would let other governments provide the nonexclusive service, encouraging their own citizens to consume it without contributing to its costs. The providing governments would soon be dissuaded from offering the service at all as their own citizens observe the free-riding beneficiaries pouring into their jurisdiction and confront costs not borne by citizens of other jurisdictions.

It is frequently argued that state and local governments, in a competitive environment in which citizen-taxpayers can move freely from one jurisdiction to another, cannot provide adequate welfare services. The reasoning is that any government that raises welfare benefits may be flooded with poor people fleeing more miserly jurisdictions, which would free ride on the compassionate decision of their neighbor. Moreover, the increased taxes required to pay for higher welfare benefits might encourage affluent citizens and business to relocate to jurisdictions that did not impose these welfare burdens. Thus, competition among governments might result in the underprovision of welfare services.

It is certainly true that the principles of efficiency and equity are frequently in conflict in political and economic affairs (cf. Okun 1975). Competitive federalism may involve some trade offs between these values: protection against tyranny and the overall satisfaction of individual preferences versus the underproduction of welfare services. The political and economic benefits of competitive federalism may come at the costs of some equity considerations. If this is true, it should not necessarily doom the idea; society makes many such trade-offs. Indeed it is frequently argued that our society has traded off efficiency in so many of its redistributional programs that it threatens to impoverish both rich and poor. But let us examine the equity effects of competitive federalism more closely. Perhaps it does not require a trade-off of equity after all. Perhaps the poor will benefit from competitive federalism or at least not be adversely affected by it.

The reason that efficiency and equity principles are generally perceived as conflicting is that efficiency is seen in a very narrow sense. That is, individuals, families, and firms are seen as exclusively motivated by monetary benefits to themselves and exclusively interested in their own material well-being. But this assumption—*homo economicus*—does not describe many of us. Our personal "utility functions" more often include some concerns for the well-being of our fellow citizens. We feel better when others are ensured of a decent existence—some minimum standards of nutrition, housing, health care, education, and other necessities of life. We are even willing to pay some portion of our own incomes, reducing our own consumption, in order to mitigate the suffering of others. A comprehensive assessment of the preferences of consumer-voters must include their equity preferences.

If the welfare policies of the national or state governments depended exclusively on the voting power of the poor, there would be very few welfare services in the United States. Welfare policies in the United States are primarily an expression of the equity preferences of middle-class Americans, not a response to the demands of the poor themselves. Indeed, when we examine the welfare policies of the states in chapter 2, we will find that the states with the greatest numbers and percentages of poor people provide the least in the way of welfare services. The states with the most generous welfare programs, in both absolute terms and in proportion to their incomes, are those with the larger personal incomes. The most important determinant of public welfare benefit levels is the income level of the population (Dye 1966). Our equity preferences increase with increases in personal income. It is better to be poor in a rich state than in a poor one.

If multiple competing governments are seeking to maximize the true preferences of consumer-taxpayers, they must do so in the provision of welfare services as well as any other public goods. Compassionate welfare policies will attract middle-class families and wealthy firms. Is it reasonable to assume that migrating families and firms would wish to locate in areas of squalor, poverty, homelessness, and human degradation simply to avoid the costs of welfare services? The cross-sectional evidence—that wealthy states provide more welfare service than poorer states—suggests that welfare services are preferred by many middle-class residents and wealthy firms.

The view that competitive federalism would result in the underproduction of welfare services rests largely on the belief that the poor will migrate to the most generous jurisdictions. But the poor are the least mobile segments of society. Whatever their impact on state welfare services, it is certainly less than the impact of mobile upper-middle-class Americans and wealthy firms. Under competitive federalism, the most mobile sectors of the population and the economy exercise the greatest influence over public policy. But there is convincing evidence that these affluent segments of the population are more likely to support welfare services than society generally.

In short, competitive federalism tends to ensure policy responsiveness. Admittedly, it is not designed to maximize equity, that is, to encourage redistributional policies. But the preferences of consumer-taxpayers are not necessarily narrow and selfish. Competitive federalism ensures responsiveness to redistributional preferences, as well as other policy preferences.

Competitive Federalism and Responsive Government

Competitive governments ought to be more responsive than monopoly government to citizen preferences. Democracy itself, with competing parties and periodic free elections, is a powerful inducement to policy responsiveness, at least to majority policy preferences, even in a monopoly government. But if multiple governments are both democratic and competitive, citizens have two separate mechanisms to help achieve congruence between their preferences and public policy. If people can "vote with their feet," as well as cast ballots in contested elections, they have two separate potential responses to policies they do not like. Elections offer people periodic opportunities to change governmental leadership and public policy as well. Moving to rival cities or states offers people the continuing opportunity to choose alternative policies. Individuals with differing policy preferences can choose to live in states and communities where policies most closely match their preferences. Rival cities and states, realizing that people can choose among them, are forced to be sensitive to the preferences of mobile consumer-taxpayers. Thus, competitive federalism ensures responsive government and a closer match between citizen preferences and public policy.

Competitive federalism depends upon state and community governments' providing different packages of services and taxes. These governments must not be coerced or bribed by the national government into policy uniformity. There is no real competition, and hence no true responsiveness to individual preferences, if state and local governments are not free to pursue a wide range of policies. Policy variation among government is a requirement for genuine competitive federalism.

Competitive Federalism and Policy Innovation

Traditional defense of federalism frequently cited the opportunity it provides for policy experimentation. According to this argument, states can serve as laboratories where solutions to public problems can be tried and tested. Policy innovation and initiative are encouraged by federalism.

Federalism may be perceived today as a conservative idea, but it was once viewed as the instrument of progressivism. A strong argument can be made that the groundwork for the New Deal was built in state policy experimentation during the progressive era. Federal programs as diverse as the income tax, unemployment compensation, countercyclical public works, social security, wage and hour legislation, bank deposit insurance, and food stamps all had antecedents at the state level. Indeed, much of the current neoliberal agenda—mandatory health insurance for workers, child care programs, notification of plant closings, government support of industrial research and development—has been embraced by various states. Indeed, the compelling phrase "laboratories of democracies" is generally attributed to the great progressive jurist, Supreme Court justice Louis D. Brandeis, who used it in defense of state experimentation with new solutions to social and economic problems (Osborne 1988, p. 2). But the states cannot serve as laboratories, and the innovative potential of federalism cannot be realized if the states are not free to pursue a wide range of policies.

Competition is the driving force behind innovation. This is true in government as in the marketplace. Just as economists are becoming increasingly aware of the central role of the innovative entrepreneur in the creation of wealth (Brenner 1987), political scientists must understand that intergovernmental competition inspires policy innovation. The politician is an entrepreneur. We know that competition for public office inspires the search for new policy proposals. But competition among governments provides additional incentives for inventiveness and innovation in public policy. Yet intergovernmental policy competition is more responsible and restrained than electorial competition.

Competition among governments, like competition in the marketplace, produces a rough policy equilibrium. That is, states and cities will be restrained by competition from pursuing policies that diverge sharply from the national policy "market." We might borrow a metaphor from political scientist John Shannon, who portrayed the fifty states as a naval convoy:

> If a state moves out too far ahead of the convoy on the tax side, it becomes increasingly vulnerable to tax evasion, taxpayer revolts and, most importantly, to tax competition for jobs and investments from other states. If a state-local system lags too far behind the convoy on the public spending side, it becomes increasingly vulnerable to quality of life and economic development concerns—poor schools, poor roads, and inadequate support for high-tech operations. (Shannon 1987, p. 4)

The metaphor can be extended beyond tax and spending policies to virtually any other major policy arena. Competition encompasses both dynamic and stabilizing forces.

Competitive Federalism: Checking Government Growth

Restraining Leviathan is a problem of checking its growth as well as controlling its power. Governments insufficiently constrained will grow very large. Competitive federalism promises a potential constraint on the growth of government.

Governmental growth may not always represent the true preferences of citizen-taxpayers. Many explanations of growth focus on the oversupply of public goods and services originating from the imperfections of political processes. Governments may grow in response to the accumulated demands of interest groups, each of which seeks a concentrated benefit for itself knowing that its costs can be diffused throughout society (Downs 1957; Buchanan and Tullock 1962; Lewis-Beck and Rice 1985). Government may grow as a result of bureaucratic expansionism (Niskanen 1971), as well as the persistent demands of public employees backed up by the exercise of their vote (Buchanan and Wagner 1977). Government may grow because citizens can discount the future costs of public goods and services through deficit spending. Citizens may demand more public services because of the "illusions" of low costs created by withholding taxes and indirect taxes (Buchanan and Wagner 1977). Governments may grow because of productivity lags in public sector

(Baumol 1967) and the cumulative unintentional consequences of past policy decision (Wildavsky 1964).

Determining the optimal size of government—the level of public goods and services that best fits the preferences of all individuals in society—is a difficult task, both theoretically and practically. Indeed, we do not even know whether conventional measures of the size of government—such as total government expenditures as a percentage of the gross national product—actually measure the costs imposed on society by government activity. Regulatory activity prevents people from doing what they otherwise would do and thus imposes costs on society. Yet these costs are unmeasured by conventional taxing and spending figures.

Public sector economics (e.g., Haveman 1970) posits the "maximum social gain" rule for determining public sector activity: Governments should chose policies which result in gains to society which exceed costs by the greatest amount, and governments should refrain from policies if costs are not exceeded by gains. Let us agree on the principle itself: no policy should be adopted if its costs exceed its benefits, and in choosing policy alternatives, officials should opt for the one that produces the greatest benefit over costs. Let us even accept its many assumptions: policymakers are motivated to make decision on the basis of maximum societal benefits and minimum societal costs. Policymakers are rational, as well as farsighted, public spirited, and comprehensive in their judgment. They are not distracted by elections, party competition, interest group pressures, bureaucratic lobbying, or narrow self-interests. Let us assume public officials want to do what is right.

Government and public officials still lack the information necessary to implement the maximum social gain rule for determining public sector size. If they err, it is not their fault. They have no way of knowing every individual's preferences. They have no accurate mechanism for weighing these preferences, for finding the preferred balance between benefits and costs, for estimating the equilibrium level of government activity.

Markets provide this information to producers of private goods and services. Despite many imperfections, markets make known to producers the preferences of consumers. Price movements signal their tastes, the intensities of their desires, and their willingness to sacrifice all other goods for any particular product. The market records this information continuously—whenever people choose to buy goods and when they choose not to do so. The market mechanism ensures that goods will not be produced if their costs exceed their value to society.

Competitive federalism, insofar as it creates a "marketplace" for government goods and services, provides a rough informative guide to the true preferences of citizens for government activity. It allows officials and voters to compare governmental performances by observing the services that are offered, and their costs, in various states and communities. This comparative information is valuable itself, but the potential mobility of citizens gives the system its driving force. Consumer-taxpayers have the opportunity to register their policy preferences by moving into or out of government jurisdictions or simply staying put. Governments and their officials can watch the growth of their states and communities—the movement of people, labor, enterprise, capital, and wealth. States and communities that become more productive over time signal to decision makers that their policy packages are preferred. A loss of people and capital over time—a decline in productivity and income, a loss of jobs, and a decline in the revenues of government—signal decision makers that they should search for alternative government policies.

Admittedly, the information conveyed to state and local government officials by these population and economic changes is imperfect. Moreover, government policies are only one of the many potential influences on the movement of people, jobs, industry, and investments. Nevertheless, some information is better than none. Monopoly government receives little information about the preferences of consumer-taxpayers beyond that provided by the electoral process. Competitive governments receive information from both the electoral processes and the movement of families and firms.

It is our argument that competitive federalism provides additional sources of information to decision makers about the true preferences of citizens. If public goods and services are oversupplied by public officials, then competitive federalism can provide a check against excessive government. It is sometimes argued, of course, that government goods and services are not in oversupply. "Perhaps, after all, Leviathan is a mythical beast" (Oates 1985). Competition promises only to make governments more responsive to the preferences of consumer-taxpayers. It can be expected to reduce the size of government only if monopoly government has in fact been oversupplying public goods and services. Competitive federalism is really only a check against the *potential* for excessive government. Competitive federalism introduces the discipline of the marketplace to government decision making.

Incentives for Government to Compete

A viable theory of competitive federalism must set forth some reasons why states and communities might be expected to compete among themselves. What are the incentives to governmental competition?

States and communities—their citizens as well as their leaders—benefit economically from the inflow of resources: labor, capital, and technology. Jobs, income, homes, businesses, and the amenities of life, all derive from economic productivity.

The nation's economic resources—its "factors of production"—are increasingly mobile. Indeed, labor, capital, and technology are increasingly mobile worldwide. These resources are controlled by large national and multi-national institutions: industrial corporations, banks, insurance companies, investment firms, and national governments.

But there is one factor of production—land—which is not mobile. It stays in one geographical location. Land is a valuable resource, a necessary factor of production. Capital must be placed somewhere. Labor and technology must be located somewhere. People and industry can come and go, but land stays in particular states and communities.

State and local economic elites have strong financial incentives to try to attract labor and capital to their areas. Capital investment raises land values, expands the labor force, and generates demand for housing and commercial services. Corporate plants and offices, federal civilian and defense facilities, and universities and colleges contribute to increased land values—not only on the parcels these facilities use but also on neighboring parcels. Mortgage lending banks, real estate developers, builders, and landowners are direct beneficiaries of decisions to locate in their communities. They are usually joined by local utilities, commercial establishments, communications media, attorneys, and other professionals, whose business volume is expected to increase.

Masses as well as elites benefit from economic growth. Growth creates jobs and incomes. The export industries may bring with them a substantial portion of their own educated, technically trained work force, thereby limit-ing the number of new job openings for the local work force. But more im-portant for most prior residents, new industries create jobs in the local econ-omy—in construction, housing, transportation, trade, and service sectors. The multiplier effect of export industry investment affects employment as well as income.

Governments also have direct incentives to try to attract investment to their communities. State and local government elites generally understand that their powers and functions depend primarily on local fiscal resources. Growth in local budgets and public employment, as well as governmental services, depends upon growth in local economy. Governmental growth ex-pands the power, prestige, status, and often the salary of government offi-cials. It is true that federal revenues tend to diminish these ties; one-sixth of all state and local government revenue comes from the federal government. But taxes from local sources and charges for local services remain the major sources of funding for state and local governments. These revenue sources depend on the economic prosperity of the state and community. The most important determinant of the level of government activity in states and com-munities is their level of economic development (Dye 1966). Thus, if govern-ments or governmental elites behave as rational actors, they will seek to max-imize economic resources within their jurisdictions because these resources form the support base for their governmental powers.

State and local communities, then, can be expected to compete to add to their wealth by making their jurisdictions attractive to productive workers, entrepreneurs, and capital investors. "Quite apart from any effects of economic prosperity on governmental revenues or local voting behavior, it is quite reasonable to posit that local governments are primarily interested in maintaining the economic vitality of the area for which they are responsible" (Peterson 1981, p. 291). Thus we are encouraged to believe that states and communities themselves, apart from the specific interests of individual and groups within them, have a general interest in maintaining and increasing their aggregate economic well-being.

Opposition to Economic Growth

There will be many consumer-taxpayers in various states and communities who will oppose additional economic growth. No-growth movements (or to use the current euphemism, growth-management movements) are found in many localities.

There are good theoretical reasons for expecting some opposition to growth. Tiebout argues that "the preferences of the older residents of the community" may support an optimum city size—the population for which public services can be produced at the lowest average cost. This implies that there are some scarce resources in a state or community, perhaps open land, green space, clean air or water, that are fixed. "Communities below the optimum size seek to attract new residents to lower average costs. Those above optimum size do just the opposite. Those at an optimum try to keep their populations constant." (Tiebout 1956, p. 420.) Perhaps Tiebout's focus on the dollar costs of city services makes his analysis appear implausible; few states or cities consciously strive for lower average cost of public goods. But if we think of public goods as environmental amenities—quiet streets, free-flowing traffic, natural beauty, trees, and so on—then we can more easily visualize an optimal size.

Indeed, it has become fashionable in upper-middle-class circles to complain loudly about the problems created by growth: congestion, pollution, noise, unsightly development, the replacement of green spaces with concrete slabs. People who own their houses and do not intend to sell them, people whose jobs are secure in government bureaucracies or tenured professorships, people who may be displaced from their homes and neighborhoods by new facilities, people who see no direct benefit to themselves from growth, and business or industries that fear the new competition that growth may bring to the community combine to form a potentially powerful counterelite.

No-growth movements are not mass movements. They do not express the aspirations of workers for jobs or renters for their own homes. Instead they reflect upper-middle-class aesthetic preferences—the preferences of educated, affluent, articulate home owners. Growth brings ugly factories, cheap commercial outlets, hamburger stands, fried chicken franchises, and "undesirable" residents. Even if new business or industry would help to hold down local taxes, these affluent citizens would still oppose it. They would rather pay the higher taxes associated with no growth than change the appearance or life-style of their community. They have secure jobs and own their homes; they are relatively unconcerned about creating jobs or building homes for less affluent citizens.

The great advantage of multiple governments and mobile people is the opportunity provided to discontented consumer-taxpayers. Competitive federalism focuses attention on the preferences of potentially migrating consumer-taxpayers. It stresses the exit option. This contrasts with political models that focus on the preferences of the median voter. These models portray the voice option. Competitive federalism is concerned with people who vote with their feet, as well as those who vote with ballots.

Rules and Referees

Competition is not anarchy; it is restrained, disciplined, orderly behavior. Just as the marketplace requires rules—protection of property rights, enforcement of contracts, recognized rules of exchange, and a stable monetary system—so also intergovernmental competition requires rules.

Without question the most important limits on government activity are the guarantees of individual liberty provided by the U.S. Constitution. Over the years the United States has fashioned a national system of civil rights through (1) U.S. Supreme Court decisions under the Fourteenth Amendment extending the Bill of Rights to protection against state and local government infringements, (2) Court decisions guaranteeing due process and equal protection of the laws, and (3) congressional acts prohibiting discrimination in voting, employment, education, housing, and public life. All governments— national, state, and local—are obliged to enforce constitutional liberties. The national government has the special responsibility for implementing the most basic of all mandates in the U.S. Constitution: "This Constitution and the laws of the United States which shall be made in pursuance thereof . . . shall be the Supreme Law of the Land . . . any Thing in the Constitution or Laws of any State to the Contrary notwithstanding" (Art. VI).

Federalism has a dark history to overcome. For nearly two hundred years, states' rights have been asserted to protect slavery, segregation, and discrimination. This history casts a shadow over any effort to defend state or local government autonomy and responsibility. Indeed, only now that a national system of constitutional and legal guarantees of personal liberty and equal protection of the law is in place is it possible to reassert the values of the federal system. Having established that federalism will not be allowed to protect violations of personal liberty and dignity, we are now free to explore fully the true merits of decentralized competitive government. Those who wish well for the notion of federalism must endeavor above all else to ensure that it never again becomes a cover for depriving Americans of their personal liberties.

The nation's founders were acutely aware that interstate competition must be restrained. Indeed, the Constitutional Convention of 1787 was inspired in part by a desire to limit interstate rivalry. Alexander Hamilton worried that the states "if disunited" might "make war upon each other" (*Federalist*, Number 7). He was especially concerned with conflicts over western territories, commercial competition, and disputes over state shares of the public debt. So the Constitution itself set forth a series of basic rules of competition among the states:

1. No state shall "lay any Imposts or Duties on Imports or Exports" (Art. I, sec. 10). The creation of a common market prevents trade barriers and guarantees mobility of products.

2. No state shall "coin money" or "emit Bills of Credit" (Art. I, sec. 10). A uniform monetary system facilitates trade and capital mobility.

3. No state shall pass any "Law impairing the Obligation of Contract" (Art. I, sec. 10). The intent was to guarantee that all states would protect private property, enforce contracts, and thus provide the constitutional framework for a free enterprise system.

4. Congress is given the power to "regulate Commerce with foreign Nations and among the several States" (Art. I, sec. 8). While the interstate commerce clause is phrased in terms of power given to Congress, it also been interpreted to restrict states in burdening interstate commerce.

5. States must give "Full Faith and Credit . . . to the public Acts, Records, and judicial Proceedings of every other State" (Art. IV, sec. 1). The full faith and credit clause seeks to ensure legal comity among the states and thus facilitate the mobility of people and business.

6. "The Citizens of each State shall be entitled to all Privileges and Immunities of Citizen in the several States" (Art. IV, sec. 2). The privileges and immunities clause is designed to prevent state discrimination against citizens of other states and thus facilitate personal mobility.

7. The jurisdiction of the federal courts is extended "to controversies between two or more states" and "between citizens of different states" (Art.

III, sec. 2). The federal court system is designated as the arbiter of disputes between states.

8. No state shall "engage in War, unless actually invaded," either with another state or a foreign power, without the consent of Congress (Art. I, sec. 10). States are not supposed to make war on each other, although they did so from 1861 to 1865. They are supposed to resolve their disputes through the federal court system.

Because these rules have been in effect for two hundred years, it is easy for Americans to overlook their importance. However, consider the difficulties that independent nations encounter because these rules are not in effect. Tariff barriers, trade wars, currency restrictions, threats to nationalize private property, restrictions on personal travel, witless bureaucratic interventions, human rights violations—all combine to thwart human enterprise worldwide. It is a tribute to the wisdom of our constitutional forbears that they sought to establish rules of competition among united states.

Rules require referees. The supremacy clause of the Constitution is the heart of the document; it makes the federal court system the ultimate referee in the American federal system. Under Chief Justice John Marshall, who presided over the Supreme Court from 1801 to 1835, the Court assumed the role of the interpreter of the Constitution and arbiter in disputes between states and nation. Federal courts have struck down fewer than one hundred congressional enactments in two centuries, but uncounted thousands of state and local enactments have been voided under federal judicial review.

Unquestionably a strong federal court system is required to make intergovernmental competition restrained and workable. But the fact that the ultimate referee in disputes between states and the national government has been the national Supreme Court has had a profound effect on federalism. Since the Court is a national institution, one might say that in disputes between nation and states, one of the members of the contending teams is also serving as umpire. Only a very strong tradition of adherence to the original intent of the Constitution by the Supreme Court would have avoided the bias toward centralization inherent in such an arrangement. And regrettably the Supreme Court has explicitly rejected the original constitutional formulation of federalism (*Gracia* v. *San Antonio Metropolitan Transit Authority*, 1985). However, the Supreme Court, and the federal court system generally, have been much more willing to retain the rules of interstate competition—to remove barriers to mobility, to remove restrictions on interstate commerce, and to guarantee all persons due process and equal protection of the law wherever they go in the United States.

No Model Is Perfect

Eighty thousand governments are better than one. Multiple competitive governments more closely approximate citizen preferences than monopoly government. Nonetheless, there are serious obstacles to an ideal market for government goods, where citizens can purchase their desired public services at costs they wish to pay. Competitive federalism may resemble a marketplace, but it fails to achieve the efficiency of a market for several reasons.

First, state and local government are themselves monopolies within their respective jurisdictions. Citizens living within specific jurisdictions cannot choose which government services to purchase and which taxes to pay. Government services—education, health, welfare, streets and highways, parks and recreation, police and fire protection—cannot be tailored to suit the tastes of every consumer-taxpayer. These services are, after all, public goods—goods that cannot be provided to some without being provided to others. Otherwise these goods would be marketed in the same fashion as private goods. In a private supermarket, shoppers can fill their baskets with the goods they want. In the government marketplace, mobile citizens and firms must choose between market baskets of public goods that are already full. No two households can be expected to have the same preferences for government services. Even if people migrate to jurisdictions with like-minded citizens, there will still be significant differences in preferences for public policies among these people—differences over levels of public services and taxes, the desired mix of services (for example, education versus welfare versus public safety) at any given tax level, and specific issues within policy areas (for example, whether schools should undertake sex education or whether health programs should include abortion counseling). Not everyone's policy preferences can be completely satisfied, even with multiple governments and varied public policies.

Moreover, government cannot vary taxes according to the amount of public services particular individuals, households, or businesses consume. Constitutionally, taxes must be uniform. This means that individuals or businesses with the same incomes, the same consumption patterns, the same properties, should pay the same taxes. Although state and local government tax codes, like the federal tax code, are filled with special treatments, privileges, and exemptions, nonetheless, some people who pay equal taxes will not benefit equally from government services. Government user charges offer a potential remedy to this mismatch of benefits and burdens, and they are growing as a proportion of total state and local government revenue. But some public goods cannot be provided on a user charge basis; not every street can have a toll booth. Some people will always be paying for services they do not consume.

These "failures" of state and local governments mean that every consumer-taxpayer will pay for some public service he or she does not want and at the same time will be denied some other public services he or she would be willing to pay for. But this is a problem confronting all governments; it a problem in the provision of public goods at any level. This problem, which economists recognize as an "efficiency" problem, is worse when all consumer-taxpayers are lumped together under a single monopoly government. Multiple competing governments with varied public policies provide opportunities for more closely matching the preferences of citizens with the policies of government.

Finally, mobility is not cost free. Families, businesses, and investors must consider the costs of searching for and moving to a state and community that more closely matches their preferences. If these costs—information and mobility costs— exceed the differences in value between the jurisdiction in which one is already residing and any other jurisdiction, then it is rational to stay put and tolerate unfavorable policies. The higher are the costs of information and mobility in the American federal system, the more people will be obliged to tolerate unfavorable government policies, the higher the ratio of costs to benefits people will be forced to bear, and the less efficient state and local governments will become. The benefits of competitive federalism will be minimal if the costs of migration are high.

Thus, like the simple model of the private economy after which it is fashioned, the competitive federalism model relies on a series of assumptions that are only partially realized in the world. It assumes that state and local governments have a significant and autonomous responsibility for the welfare of the people living in their jurisdiction. It assumes that these governments are free to pursue a range of public policies, to provide a variety of public services, and to vary the level of these services. The model assumes that the costs of government goods and services provided by states and communities are fully reflected in the revenues collected from their residents. To the extent that the national government restricts the policies of state and local governments or offsets the costs of the goods and services they offer by intergovernmental transfers, the model's assumptions are violated.

The model also assumes that there are few externalities associated with the policy responsibilities assigned to state and local governments. It assumes that there is no collusion among state and local governments, no attempt to restrain competition. To the extent that state or local government officials form cartels and enter into agreements to restrict competition or seek federal regulations prohibiting interstate competition, they violate the assumptions of the model.

The model assumes that consumer-taxpayers are mobile, that they have information about the policies and public services of governments, and that they employ this information in their locational decisions. Competitive federalism depends on the behavior of the potentially migrating consumer-taxpayer. State and local government policies in the competitive federalism model would be shaped by the preferences of the mobile segments of the populations and the economy. Yet we know that not everyone is mobile, not everyone knows about the policies of governments, and even among knowledgeable and mobile people and businesses, the policies of government may not rank very high in their locational priorities.

In short, the assumptions of our model are seldom fully met in the American federal system. But such an observation does not destroy the utility of the competitive federalism model itself anymore than the market model is rendered useless by observing externalities, monopolies, immobilities, and imperfect information in real markets. Models are useful when they succeed in directing attention to real-world conditions that obstruct their functioning. An "unrealistic" model is useful when it make us realize how far real-world conditions deviate from the model.

In Search of Competitive Federalism

Competitive federalism, like any other analytic model, is an abstraction or representation of a governmental system. Its purpose is to order and simplify the real world of government and politics so that we can think about it more clearly. It should identify significant characteristics of government and suggest relationships between these characteristics and their consequences. It need not be fully congruent with the real world of government, but it must have some empirical referents. It must be able to direct our inquiries and research into government. If a model's assumptions are unrealistic, if its postulated relationships are totally untestable, then it is not useful for analysis or prescription.

This book will explore many of the assumptions and propositions of the competitive federalism model. We do not intend to prove the model, validate all of its assumptions, or demonstrate its superiority to any other model of government. Rather we intend to examine American state and local government over the past three decades to learn whether the assumptions and propositions of this model have any empirical referents. We hope to identify both the strengths and weaknesses of the model in the American federal system. We want to specify the obstacles to the functioning of the model, as well as the conditions facilitating its operation.

We expect to show, first, that American state and local governments comprise a significant segment of our political economy; it is worthwhile to consider how these governments are structured, what they do, why they do it, and what difference it makes to us. More important for the competitive federalism model, we expect to show that these governments are responsive to the demands of their consumer-taxpayers (chapter 2). They expand and contract in response to identifiabe demands. We are especially interested in the contraction of the state and local government sector because we believe that contraction is evidence of responsiveness to citizens' demands. In the case of the national government, we can never know whether its relentless expansion is a product of citizen demand or bureaucratic expansionism, interest group effects, fiscal illusion, or other supply factors. But when governments contract and their contraction is related to an identifiable reduction in the demand for a government service, we are in a better position to infer that these governments are indeed responsive to public demands.

We expect to show that American state and local governments offer a wide variety of public policies, a greatly varied mix of public benefits, costs, and burdens. It is true that the economy is becoming "nationalized"—that income, employment, and investment levels are becoming more equal among the states over time. Even political life is becoming nationalized in the sense that differences among the states in party competition and voter participation are declining over time. But we expect to show that policy differences among the state are not diminishing; rather, differences among the states in the benefits of education, welfare, health, highways, and other public goods are large and continuing (chapter 2), and so are the burdens of taxation (chapter 3). These policy differences are a necessary condition for the operation of the competitive federalism model.

We also expect to show that federal interventions reduce the responsiveness of state and local governments; federal financial aid expands state and local government services independently of any citizen demand factors (chapter 4). We expect to demonstrate that federal aid distorts the relationship between demands of consumer-taxpayers and the policies of state and local governments.

We expect to show that the responsiveness of state governments is not a product of competitive, policy-relevant party politics in the states. The "responsible party model" is rarely encountered in the states. Electing Democrats or Republicans to state office seldom results in significant policy change (chapter 5). Fortunately, however, competitive federalism operates independently of the type of political system to encourage responsiveness. Theoretically, even authoritarian governments, if they were forced to compete with each other and if citizens could migrate to the government of their choice with little cost to themselves, would be responsive to citizen preferences.

Finally, we expect to show that state and local governments make a difference in the economic well-being of their citizens. These governments affect not only safety and amenities but income and earnings, interest and rents, contracts and jobs. The spending and revenue policies of state and local governments have economic consequences (chapters 6 and 7). It is true that these policies are felt at the margins of economic activity; many other factors affect the economic fortunes of citizens in the states. We must try to observe the effects of the policies all other things being equal. But we expect to show that "the wealth of states," like "the wealth of nations," is affected by government actions. If government policies were irrelevant to the economic well-being of citizens, then competitive federalism would offer little in the way of direct economic benefit. It might still offer protection against the political tyranny of monopoly government, but it would fail to protect against the economic inefficiency of monopoly government.

We do not pretend that competitive federalism, or any other serious model of government or politics, is value free. Competitive federalism is a normative as well as an analytical model (chapter 8). It prescribes how federalism should work, as well as describes how it would work under specified conditions. We conclude the discussion with some specific constitutional prescriptions designed to bring competitive federalism to the American system of government.

Note

1. On this point Robert L. Bish (1987) writes: "Historically the subject matter of fiscal federalism has been tax coordination and competition; more recently it has been grant programs and functional responsibilities for different layers of government. These latter analyses have been facilitated by the theory of public goods and externalities and recognition that most public goods and externalities have effects over areas smaller than the entire country. This work, however, poses interesting problems for conclusions based on market economics and federalist models because fiscal federalism studies emerge with conclusions directly contgrary to conclusions based on market economics and the political theory of federalism. And not only are conclusions of the fiscal federalism literature different, but their normative recommendations would *eliminate* the most distinguishing feature of a federal system, competition among different government."

2
Public Policy in the States

> Many considerations seem to place it beyond doubt that the first
> and most natural attachment of the people will be to the govern-
> ments of their respective states.
> ——James Madison, *Federalist*, Number 46

What are the policy responsibilities of state and local governments? What public goods and services are provided by these govern- ments, and how are they paid for? Are there significant variations among the states in the levels of public goods provided, in the priorities ac- corded different public services, and in the burdens imposed on citizens? Are public policies in a state responsive to the demands of its citizens?

Our theory of competitive federalism requires that we explore these ques- tions. Competitive federalism assumes that states offer valuable public goods and services, that the mix of benefits and costs the states offer varies from state to state, and that these variations in benefits and costs be responsive to the demands of consumer-taxpayers. We want to explore all of these assumptions.

Shrinking Government?

What is the role of state and local government in the national economy? Most Americans tend to focus their attention on spending decisions in Washington, but eighty-three thousand other governments in the United States—states, counties, municipalities, townships, school districts, and special districts (table 2–1)—are spending significant sums of their own. Spending by these governments currently amounts to about 13 percent of nation's gross national product (GNP). While it is true that all of these state and local governments combined spend less than the government in Washington, which is spending about 24 percent of GNP, the state-local public sector is still an important force in the national political economy.

Nothing is so rare as shrinking government. Total public sector spending in the United States—federal, state, and local government combined—has grown continuously throughout the twentieth century. Before the New Deal, aggregate government spending accounted for only 10 percent of GNP. State

Table 2–1
Governments in the United States

U.S. government	1
State governments	50
Counties	3,041
Municipalities	19,205
Townships and towns	16,691
School districts	14,741
Special districts	29,487
Total	83,217

Source: U.S. Department of Commerce (1987).

Table 2–2
Government Spending as a Percentage of the GNP

	Total Public Sector	Federal Government	State-Local Government	State Government	Local Government
1929	10.0%	2.5%	7.5%	2.1%	5.4%
1949	23.0%	15.3	7.8	3.0	4.8
1959	26.6	17.1	9.5	3.4	6.1
1969	30.1	17.7	12.4	4.5	7.9
1979	30.6	17.6	13.1	5.0	8.1
1985	35.1	22.2	12.9	5.2	7.7

and local government accounted for 75 percent of all government spending. Today total government spending is over 35 percent of the GNP; federal spending is over 60 percent of all government spending (table 2–2).

But the good news is that state and local government in the United States has stopped growing relative to the American economy. Aggregate state and local government spending rose from 7.5 percent of the GNP in 1952, to a peak of 14.4 percent in 1976, and then leveled off at about 13 percent through 1985 (figure 2–1). In contrast, federal spending has continued to rise as a percentage of the GNP through 1985. The relentless rise in federal spending, in both absolute and relative terms, was masked by the conservative rhetoric of the Reagan years. Indeed, it is surprising how many scholars and commentators wrongly believe that the federal government contracted in the 1980s.

Spending by state and local governments includes the spending of federal aid monies, a significant component of the state-local sector that averages between one-fifth and one-sixth of state-local revenues over these years. By

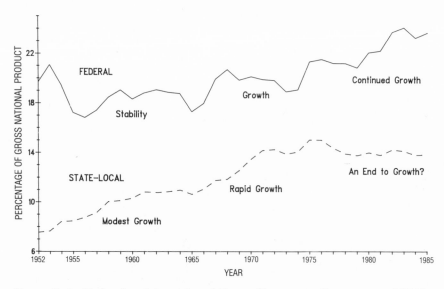

Figure 2–1. Federal and State-Local Expenditures as a Percentage of GNP, 1952–1985

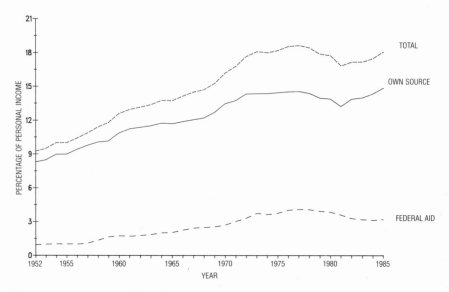

Figure 2–2. State and Local Government Own-Source Revenues and Federal Aid as a Percentage of Personal Income

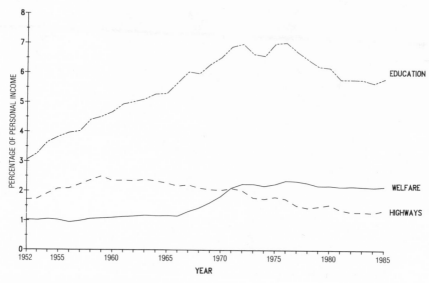

Figure 2–3. **State-Local Expenditures by Function as a Percentage of Personal Income**

disaggregating total state-local revenue from state-local own source revenue, we can distinguish federal transfers from state-local revenues (figure 2–2). It is certainly true that the early expansion and later contraction of the state-local sector is partly attributable to the rapid expansion of federal grant programs in the 1960s and early 1970s, and later reductions in their rate of growth. However, spending by state and local governments from their own sources declined in relative terms after 1976. It has begun to grow again in recent years without the stimulus of federal aid increases.

Now let us observe one more disaggregation—by government function. Education, the largest category of state-local spending, is also the most volatile (figure 2–3). State-local educational spending grew rapidly in the two decades prior to 1976, rising from about 3 percent of personal income in 1952 to about 7 percent. It then declined modestly to about 5.6 percent. Welfare spending, which grew rapidly from 1965 to 1975, has leveled off in recent years. State and local highway spending, and probably spending for infrastructure generally, has steadily declined over the years as a proportion of personal income.

Policy Responsibilities of State and Local Governments

In the broadest sense, public policy is whatever governments choose to do— or not to do. Public policy is actually government activity. From time to time,

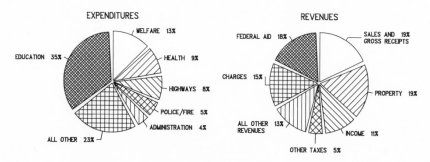

Figure 2–4. All State and Local Governments: Expenditures by Function and Revenues by Source, 1985

respected scholars have attempted to distinguish between public policy and government activity by arguing that "policy" implies continuing, goal-oriented, purposeful activity.[1] Whatever value this distinction may have in theory, it is virtually useless in empirical research. We can never really know whether government activities are goal oriented or purposive, or if so what the goals and purposes are. Indeed, it appears that government activities often have multiple and conflicting goals and purposes. All we can are observe are the government activities themselves.

The nation's eighty-three thousand state and local governments perform many activities; education (elementary and secondary as well as higher education) is the most costly of them, accounting for about 35 percent of all state-local spending (figure 2–4.) The federal government contributes less than 15 percent of the nation's expenditures for education. Welfare activities account for 13 percent of total state-local spending. Most of these funds come from the federal government, but states exercise broad responsibilities in administering public assistance programs. Health care accounts for 9 percent of all state-local spending. Despite federal contributions to state-administered Medicaid programs, state and local governments bear most of the costs of public health and hospital care themselves. Highways account for 8 percent of state-local spending, with state and local governments carrying the major burden in this area. Police and fire protection accounts for 5 percent of state-local spending, with the federal government playing a minor role in police funding and none in fire protection. All other activities of state and local governments combined account for 23 percent of their spending.

To pay for these public goods and services, state and local governments take about 16 percent of nation's total personal income in revenues. These governments raise 82 percent of these revenues themselves and receive the remaining 18 percent from the federal government. Their own revenue sources are divided into sales and gross receipt taxes (19 percent), property taxes (19 percent), income taxes (11 percent), all other taxes (5 percent), charges (15 percent), and other revenues (13 percent) (figure 2–4).

It is true, of course, that state and local governments perform many services that cannot be measured in dollars. These governments have major regulatory responsibilities. Their courts settle by far the greatest number of civil and criminal cases. They regulate the provision of water, gas, electricity, and other services; they share in the regulation of insurance, banking, and commercial enterprise; they regulate the use of land and determine property rights. The importance of these regulatory activities is not reflected in expenditure figures. To the extent that we focus exclusively on taxing and spending patterns, we risk overlooking and underestimating the true impact of state and local government on our lives.

The "Nationalization" of the States

Competitive federalism depends on state and local governments' offering a wide variety of public policies. Individuals and firms must be free to choose from varied packages of public benefits, costs, and burdens. If public policy becomes wholly nationalized, either because the federal government imposes uniformity by law or encourages it through formulas attached to grant programs, then competitive federalism loses its meaning. Its meaning is also diminished if the states themselves move toward uniformity of their own volition.

It is true that differences among the states in their political economies are diminishing over time, a process that has been labeled the "nationalization" of the states. States have become more similar in levels of economic development—urbanization, industrialization, income, and employment. For example, variation in per capita personal income among the states declined markedly from 1952 through 1984 (table 2–3). The coefficient of variation

Table 2–3
Diminishing Economic and Political Variation
Among the States, 1952–1984

	Per Capita Personal Income	Party Competition	Voter Participation
1984	.14	.18	.27
1980	.14	.18	.27
1975	.16	.19	.26
1970	.16	.26	.27
1965	.18	.28	.35
1965	.20	.38	.40
1952	.24	.42	.43

Note: Figures are coefficients of variation: standard deviation divided by the mean.

for the fifty states declined from .24 to .14, a fall of over 40 percent. (A graphic portrayal of diminishing income differences among the states is presented in figure 6–2.) Variation in manufacturing employment as a percentage of total nonagricultural employment also declined. Industry, people, and money are becoming more evenly distributed throughout the states.

The political systems of the states are no longer as distinct as they were historically. Years ago the Democratic party could count on the "Solid South" in national, state, and local elections; the southern states were designated "one-party" states by most political observers (Key 1949; Ranney 1971). The Democrats can still count on winning most state and local offices in southern and border states, but these states are now swing states in presidential elections and occasionally elect Republican governors and U.S. senators. Between 1952 and 1984, the coefficient of variation for party competition in gubernatorial elections declined from 41.6 to 18.4. Historically, voter participation in the South was very low, and it is still lower there than in the rest of the nation. However, one important effect of the civil rights movement was to increase black voter participation in the South. Today voter turnout in the South is higher than in previous decades and closer to the national average. Between 1950 and 1984, the coefficient of variation for voter turnout in congressional elections declined from 42.5 to 27.0.

Continuing Policy Differences Among the States

Despite these trends toward nationalization among the states, policy differences among the states do not appear to be declining. There is no convincing evidence that the policy preferences of the states are becoming homogenized or even that federal intervention is forcing uniform policies on them. For example, the coefficients of variation for per capita state and local tax revenues, total expenditures, and expenditures for education, welfare, health, and highways have remained virtually unchanged over the past three decades (table 2–4). Variation in these and most other measures of public policy show no consistent decrease over time. Kemp (1978) similarly has observed that absolute variance in public spending among the states, as measured in terms of the size of the standard deviations, has actually increased, and relative variance in public spending among the states, as measured by the coefficient of variation, has remained about the same over the last thirty years.

Policy Responsiveness: The Demand-Side Model

An important criterion in evaluating democratic political systems—including American state and local governments—is their responsiveness to citizen pref-

Table 2–4
Continuing Policy Variation Among the States, 1952–1984

| | Per Capita State and Local Government Expenditures | | | | | |
	Total	Education	Highways	Welfare	Health	Total Taxes
1984	.45	.32	.55	.40	.32	.41
1980	.41	.32	.44	.36	.28	.21
1975	.28	.40	.42	.39	.38	.21
1970	.24	.20	.39	.43	.32	.21
1960	.20	.23	.34	.38	.31	.21
1952	.26	.44	.37	.49	.37	.23

Note: Figures are coefficients of variation: standard derivation divided by the mean. $N = 50$, except for 1952, when $N = 48$.

erences. The test of responsiveness is whether public policies reflect the needs, demands, interests, and preferences of voters. The problem arises in specifying a testable theory of responsiveness.

Median voter models have provided economists and political scientists with simplified sets of assumptions about democratic political systems—assumptions that have expressly or implicitly formed the basis of a great deal of empirical research in state and local government (see Bahl 1980, chap. 3). In the basic model, each individual consumer-taxpayer tries to maximize the trade-off between various public goods and services and disposable private income. Each consumer-taxpayer balances the "utilities" obtained from higher levels of public services against the "disutilities" of higher taxes, in order to choose an "optimal" benefit level. After each consumer-taxpayer has made a choice based on his or her own preferences, tastes, needs, and so on, the choice of the median voter in any democratic political system should determine public policy. The "median voter" label is taken from the early work of Duncan Black (1958), who suggested that democratically elected governments would seek to make the median voter's indifference curve the state's indifference curve.

A simple version of the median voter model treats the political system itself as a neutral conversion mechanism, transforming the needs, demands, and preferences of the median voter into public policy. The model is similar to the early systems model in political science literature (Easton 1965; Dye 1966). It was assumed that democratic political processes would produce public policies largely reflective of the preferences of voter-taxpayers. These preferences were usually specified in state policy studies in terms of median or average characteristics of the population—for example, median family income, median school level completed, or percentage of the population aged, young, black, urban, and so on. This required an inferential leap that characteristics of the populations determined median voter preferences and, hence, community preferences. When variations in public policies among the states were shown to correlate with variations in population characteristics, this simple median voter model gained empirical support. The traditional literature on the "determinants" of state and local government taxing and spending policies relied implicitly on this simple median voter model (Sachs and Harris 1964; Fisher 1964; Bahl 1965; Dye 1966; Hofferbert 1966a).

Thus, the median voter model assumes that individual voter preferences in a democracy determine governmental decisions. Elected politicians reflect the preferences of their constituents because they wish to maximize community welfare and to get reelected. Thus politicians seek the package of public services and taxes desired by the median voter; the median voter's indifference curve is considered the state's indifference curve. Public spending will increase as long as the number of votes won by these increases exceeds the number of votes lost by the increasing costs of financing this spending. Politicians must estimate the numbers and preferences of voters in their separate roles as consumers and taxpayers. The point is to balance votes from each expenditure and revenue decision so that the total votes won will exceed the total votes lost.

The median voter model requires us to assume that all individual preferences within a state are singled peaked and that elected officials can maximize those preferences on each public expenditure. Moreover, the median voter model is usually specified in policy studies in terms of median characteristics of the population—for example, the median voter is portrayed as having the median income, the median tax bill, the median preferences for redistribution, and so on. Interestingly although it is unlikely that these assumptions are fully met, empirical studies based on the model still have a great deal of statistical explanatory power.

The problem with the simple median voter model is its failure to specify exactly how the preferences of consumer-voter-taxpayers are translated into public policy. We might say that the simple model is a demand-side model; it assumes that the political system is passive and that elected officials and bureaucrats are motivated to seek to implement the preferences of the median voter. In a critique of early median voter theory, Mitchell (1983) refers to it as a "demand-based framework":

> It was assumed that political processes, although unexamined, would provide right policies that would be implemented effectively by government. The question of just how officials could achieve these ideals was never raised, let alone explored. Apparently some combination of benevolence, political competition, and constitutional constraints were at work in tandem to produce the desired results. (p. 72)

Why should democratic political systems reflect the demands of voters? The answer is usually expressed in terms of competitive participatory elections. Competitive parties and candidates vie for the support of the median voter, trying to offer the package of services and taxes that most closely approximates his or her preferences. Anthony Downs (1957) outlined the basic voter competition model: parties and candidates will offer more public goods and services until the marginal votes gained by these offerings equal the votes lost from additional taxes. Downs's "economic theory" resembles the competitive marketplace, with vote maximizing serving as a motivator of politicians just as profit maximizing motivates firms. Downsian politicians are self-interested, just as competitive firms are self-interested, but the interests of politicians and citizen-voters are reconciled in a competitive democratic political system.

Institutional Forces: The Supply-Side Model

In contrast, supply-side or excessive government explanations frequently portray government itself, or governmental bureaucrats and legislators, as having interests separate from the "public interest." Public choice economists distinguish between the "utility functions" of officials and bureaucrats and those of citizen-taxpayers. The interests of officials and bureaucrats may be to win reelection, garner generous campaign contributions, expand agency budgets, gain greater authority and prestige, or something else. The constitutional rules for governmental decision making may not ensure that the interests of officials and bureaucrats always coincide with those of the median voter. Even a totally selfless, altruistic public official who tries diligently to implement the preferences of his or her constituents—the median voter—may find many obstacles. Government officials do not have continuous information to assess changing preferences of consumer-taxpayers. Unlike marketplace consumers, voter consumers do not engage in continuous voting. When politicians find out what the voters really want, it may be too late, for the election will be won or lost. Even after the contest, elected officials can only guess at what they did right or wrong. Voting outcomes are not always policy informative.

In the absence of good information about citizen preferences, the "natural tendencies" of officials and bureaucrats to expand their power in society are unchecked. They will exaggerate the benefits of government spending programs and understate their costs. Various fiscal illusions—hidden taxes, payroll deductions, and deficit financing—contribute further to the citizens' underestimation of the costs of government. These "political failures" all contribute to government's oversupplying public goods and services and overtaxing its citizens.

Supply-side explanations apply especially well to quasi-public goods—government goods or services that benefit groups in society rather than aid each individual citizen-taxpayer equally. (Indeed, the demand-side median voter model works well only when the percentage share of the total benefits each individual receives is equal to the percentage share of the costs he or she must bear.) It is sensible for individuals and groups to be much more informed, interested, and supportive of government programs that provide them with specific and substantial benefits, while dispersing costs to all taxpayers, none of whom individually bears sufficient costs to justify organizing opposition. An individual's income is derived from a single role as producer or employee, whereas an individual's expenditures are spread over a wide range of goods and services. The individual's consumer-taxpayer role is usually less immediate, visible, and sensitive to action than the income earner role. Income-producing interest groups are easier to form and finance than consumer-taxpayer interest groups. The median voter's income earner role will dominate the consumer-taxpayer role in political decision making. Therefore, political support for concentrated benefits to producers will exceed political opposition to burdens for consumer-taxpayers.

Reconciling Policy Theories

Can demand-side and supply-side theories of public policy be reconciled? Perhaps not. One suspects that ideological commitments play a part in sensitizing scholars to either the responsiveness of governments to citizen demands, or alternatively, to the inefficiencies of governments and inequities of politics. It may be possible, however, to achieve some modest reconciliation of these theories by distinguishing between types of public policies. Some policies may be conceived as pure policy policies: public goods and services for which each consumer-taxpayer receives the same share of societal benefits as he or she pays in societal cost. A quasi public policy may be conceived as one in which some individuals receive more benefits than other, and the costs are also distributed unevenly. It is possible that a simple demand-side model is a better predictor of the level of pure public goods and services than it is of the level of quasi-public policies. Mitchell (1983) writes:

> Many of the theoretical differences between undersupply and oversupply theorists now seem attributable to an understandable failure to conceptualize adequately the nature of the goods involved in public production. Some of these differences can be reconciled by specifying the degree to which the goods are private, public, or some admixture. It is entirely possible that agreement might be forthcoming if one claims that pure public goods are underproduced by markets; that most pure private goods and transfers are

always overproduced by governments; and that public and semipublic goods may or may not be produced in correct amounts by governments depending on the ratio of private and public attributes of the goods and the decision-rules. (pp.78–79)

It is also possible to employ the simple demand-side approach without fully specifying the decision-making process. We know that public policies do get made by governments. We can view public policies as decisions of the political system without direct knowledge of how these decisions were made (e.g., Dye 1966). We can observe what public policies are produced by political systems serving populations with different sets of characteristics. The analogy is research on the relationship between cigarette smoking and the incidence of cancer. We may not be able to specify exactly how smoking affects the functioning of human cells within the body, but it is still important to know about the relationship between smoking and cancer. We may wish to make straightforward atheoretical observations of relationships between public policies and the characteristics of states and communities. Empirical observations may even enrich later theoretical development. Economist Roy Bahl (1980) writes:

[Many] studies are formulated on an *a priori* basis without explicit discussion of a utility function, budget constraint, production functions, or decision-making mechanism. Very often, however, they lead to about the same specifications of the estimating equation as do the studies which build from a theoretical base. (p. 71)

Responsive to What?

What are the needs, tastes, preferences, and demands of citizen-voters to which democratic governments ought to be responsive? Whether inquiries about responsiveness proceed from rigorous, highly specified demand-side or supply-side models or from middle-range hypotheses about the determinants of public policies, it is still necessary to posit specific characteristics of citizen-voters that produce policy demands and specific institutional characteristics of governments that modify these demands. From an almost limitless list of population and institutional characteristics, we are obliged to select some policy-relevant characteristics in order to test for responsiveness.

Resources

Peoples' preferences for public services vary with changes in their income. Income consistently emerges as the most important determinant of variation in levels of public goods and services provided by states and communities. The problem has been in interpreting this result. Does it mean that higher-income residents prefer more public services, that their ability to pay for public services is greater, or that the prices of public services are higher in higher-income states? In other words, do we interpret this relationship as an indication of elasticity of preferences, constraints, or price? There are no statistical procedures that can interpret this relationship for us. It is our subjective judgment that higher-income residents do prefer better public services and that they are willing to sacrifice a larger share of their income for these services.

Earlier in the nation's history, the transition from a rural agricultural society to an urban industrial society brought important changes in demands for public goods. Larger populations and greater housing densities created needs for police and fire protection, street maintenance, sewage and solid waste disposal, parks and recreation, public housing, planning and urban renewal, and others—needs that were far less pressing in rural communities.

Individual states made the rural-to-urban transition at different rates. This meant that cross-sectional studies at any one point in time could distinguish between rural and urban states and observe significant differences in the level of public services associated with urbanization. But today most Americans live an urban life-style and demand urban levels of public service. The relationship between urbanization and public service among the states has diminished over time, although we can still see some differences between predominantly rural and predominantly urban states.

The educational levels of the adult population may come closer to reflecting the true preferences of citizen-taxpayers of a state than measures of income or urbanization. Educational level directly affects taste or preference; it is not a measure of ability to pay. Of course, there is always the problem of multicollinearity among these socioeconomic variables. The significance of any particular indicator depends on what other related variables are included in an estimating equation.

Needs

Redistribution is itself a public good inasmuch as most people do not wish to see the poor, the aged, the young, or minorities live below minimal acceptable standards. People may disagree on what these standards should be, but few would deny the existence of a general interest in eliminating the worst conditions of poverty, or the greatest insecurities and afflictions of old age, or the worst effects of discrimination. And most Americans long ago accepted Jefferson's argument that the education of children was in the interest of everyone, parents or not.

Despite the vitality of voluntary charitable enterprise in the United States, redistribution is a public good. Without the compulsory processes of government, free riders could take satisfaction from the charitable contributions of others without participating themselves. In short, the median voter has a redistributional preference; he or she is willing to sacrifice some income to see that the elemental needs of the poor, aged, young, and minority persons are met.

Admittedly this view of the redistributional preference of the voter contrasts with those set forth by Downs (1957) and Tullock (1971). Downs perceives the redistributional preferences of the median voter arising strictly from the monetary benefits that the voter hopes to receive at the expense of higher-income groups. Because the median voter's income is lower than that of the mean voter (that is, the income distribution is skewed), the benefits received by the median voter will be paid for by taxing the more affluent voter. Tullock predicts that middle-class voters will be the chief beneficiary of redistributional policies and that the compulsory contributors will be both upper- and lower-income groups.

The simple model of a median voter with a preference for some redistributional government activities on behalf of poor, aged, young, and black populations can be developed further by assuming that these groups will contribute independently to the demand for redistribution. Thus, increases in the proportion of the population that is poor, aged, young, or black should result in increases in government spending for education, health, and welfare. Specifically, increases in the youth population should result in increased demands for educational spending, not only because the median voter perceives a need to educate these children but also because their parents make direct demands upon government to do so. Increases in the aged population should result in increased spending for health, not only because the median voter wishes to see that the elderly receive hospital care when needed but also because the elderly themselves make demands on government. And increases in poor populations should result in increased welfare spending through the direct political demands of the poor, as well as the charitable instincts of the median voter.

If it turns out that redistributional spending—spending for education, welfare, and health—is not associated with increases in the young, poor, or aged but is positively associated with income, then we might speculate that it is not the demands of the young, the poor, or the aged that inspire government but rather the demand of the median voter for redistribution.

Bureaucracy and Centralization

Supply-side theories of public spending do not deny the importance of demands by citizen-taxpayers but rather expand their models to include the interests of citizens as consumers, citizens as taxpayers, bureaucrats as suppliers, and politicians as vote maximizers. Government is portrayed as a monopolist and potential exploiter of its monopoly position rather than a neutral mechanism responsive only to the demands of citizen-taxpayers.

Why should public spending increase with increases in bureaucratization and centralization? As Mitchell (1983) explains, "Voters, politicians, and bureaucrats are engaged in spending the money of others. And, since everyone is spending money on others as well as spending the money of others on themselves, a double inefficiency is incurred: spenders have little incentive to economize or to provide the goods most valued by the beneficiary" (p. 89). As economist Milton Friedman (1980) observes: "Nobody spends somebody else's money as carefully as he spends his own" (p. 31).

Bureaucrats overspend in their efforts to maximize agency budgets, add personnel, serve clients, and by so doing increase their own power, pay, and prestige. The power of bureaucrats "to get away with it" flows from their monopoly position relative to the governmental function they perform. They have no competition in determining the price of public goods. There are no market prices for the services of bureaucrats; this is their key to power. Their power is argumented when legislators are faced with take-it-or-leave-it choices. Legislators have no easy way of reducing agency budgets and still maintaining output; that is, they have no way of improving bureaucratic productivity.

Bureaucrats have direct relationships with legislative committees rather than entire legislatures. Committees have a higher demand for the particular public service within their committee jurisdiction than that of the legislature as a whole. The legislative committee also seeks to maximize its own utility by expanding the functions, activities, powers, and budgets of the agencies it oversees. Again the committee can do so because of its monopoly of information on the price of government goods relative to the rest of the legislature. Miller and Moe (1983) enter a partial dissent to the notion of bureaucratic power over the budget, arguing that it does not necessarily apply to government services in high demand. They posit legislative committees as monopoly buyers negotiating with bureaucrats as monopoly sellers. Committees can, if they wish, impose lower prices on bureaucrats.

The legislative budget-making process itself contributes to excessive total spending. Spending decisions are separated from taxing decisions; the budget process is "fragmented" (Wildavsky 1964). It is also "nonprogrammatic"; spending is not directly tied to output of goods and services. Finally it is "political," with bargaining and logrolling expanding overall expenditures.

Centralization of government contributes further to the monopoly power of bureaucrats. It obscures the real price of public goods. If multiple governments in separate jurisdictions provide the same public goods and services, knowledgeable legislators and prudent citizens can compare costs and outputs among jurisdictions. Government bureaucracies operating at high costs and/or producing few benefits can at least be identified. But centralized government prevents these comparisons. No comparative cost or output information is available. This monopoly of information enables bureaucrats to increase expenditures.

Elected politicians may have a better understanding than bureaucrats of the preferences of voter-taxpayers. Bureaucrats face the beneficiaries of government programs in their daily routines; politicians face both beneficiaries and taxpayers. Politicians, then, can be expected to prefer lower spending levels than bureaucrats.

Public choice models of the behavior of elected officials, however, lead to the proposition that they too will overspend relative to the median voter's preference for public goods. In spending money, politicians want to purchase political support—both votes and campaign contributions. Ideally politicians would seek to spend money in such a way that the benefits are highly visible to the beneficiaries but the taxes are hidden from the taxpayers. They also wish to spend in the present (or at least before election time) and defer costs to the future.

Interest Group Activity

Organized interests expand the size of government when they seek concentrated benefits for themselves and dispersed costs for society. It is rational for a small number of individuals seeking specific, limited benefits to organize themselves to pressure government for subsidies, tariffs, privileges, and protection; it is irrational for larger numbers of other individuals, each bearing only a small part of the cost of these benefits, to spend their time, energy, and money in countering the claims of the organized interests. The results is a bias in the pressure group system in favor of the small, homogeneous interests seeking to expand the supply of "impure" public goods and socializing their costs to the larger unorganized segments of society (Olson 1965). Over time, the activities of many special interest groups, each seeking concentrated benefits for themselves and dispersed costs to others, result in an overproduction of government goods and services. Indeed over long periods of time the cumulative effect of such activity is "organizational sclerosis"—a political economy so encrusted with subsidies, protections, and special treatments for organized interest groups that work, productivity, and investment are discouraged (Olson 1982). Later (in chapter 6) we shall examine the evidence regarding the growth-retarding effects of special interest activity. Our initial effort here will be to observe the effect of interest group activity on government spending. There are significant problems in correctly specifying the Olson model and measuring the activity of interest groups (Gray and Lowery 1988). Olson employs time (number of years) since a society has organized or reorganized itself after original settlement or economic upheaval (Olson

1982). In the study of the American states, Olson employs the number of years since a state's admission or readmission to the Union as a surrogate measure for "organizational sclerosis." Other measures might include unionization of the work force and qualitative judgments about the strength of organized interests in state government (Morehouse, 1981).

Federal Interventions

Federal intergovernmental transfers were identified as a major determinant of state and local government spending many years ago (Kurnow 1963; Sachs and Harris 1964; Fisher, 1964). Using federal aid as an independent variable in a regression problem on total state-local spending will produce strong positive coefficients, if for no other reason because the dependent variable, state-local spending, includes the independent variable, federal aid. The real question in fiscal federalism is the stimulative versus substitutive effects of federal aid on state-local own source spending. Do state and local governments simply spend the federal moneys sent to them without altering their own spending patterns? Do they reduce their spending because federal aid can be substituted for their own revenues? Or does federal aid stimulate state and local governments to spend more of their own revenues than they otherwise prefer to do?

The answer depends in large measure on the type of federal aid—whether it is open-ended and unconditional or whether it is conditional and requires state-local matching funds. Gramlich (1977) argues that unconditional federal revenues, like general revenue sharing, are substitutive rather than stimulative. Conditional matching grants are usually found to be stimulative of state-local spending. Overall the aggregate effect of federal aid in the past has been stimulative, since more aid was distributed in conditional project grants than open unconditional grants.

Correlates of Government Spending in the States

Levels of public goods and services provided by state and local governments vary a great deal across the United States. In 1985 per capita state-local spending in New York exceeded $2,100; it was under $900 in Mississippi and Arkansas. Although price differentials may account for a portion of this differential, especially in Alaska, there seems to be little doubt that per capita spending differences in excess of 100 percent connote differing levels of public goods and services. These variations among the states in spending levels have remained constant over many years (table 2–4).

Are spending differences among the states associated with differences in resources and needs, as suggested by demand-oriented median voter models?

Or are they more closely associated with observable differences in government supply-side forces? Again we can begin to sort out these influences by observing cross-sectional relationships at various points in time. Our initial inquiry parallels the early "determinants" studies of state and local government spending (Sachs and Harris 1964; Fisher 1964; Bahl 1965; Dye 1966; Hofferbert 1966a), except that we will make consecutive cross-sectional observations to see how well these relationships hold up over time.

Total Spending

Income remains the principal determinant of levels of public spending in the states. Our results confirm those reported by other researchers over the past several decades regarding the importance of economic resources in determining levels of government activity among the states (table 2–5). However, income levels may have lost some of their explanatory power over the years. There have been modest but consistent declines in the strength of the relationships between per capita personal income and per capita measures of total state-local spending, as well as spending for most functions. The reason behind this decline in the explanatory power of income over time is the increasing importance of federal aid in financing state and local government activity. States are no longer as closely constrained by their own resources in decisions regarding levels of public goods and service because federal aid has partially lifted this constraint. Note that per capita federal aid became the most important determinant of variation among the states in total spending levels in the 1970's. (We shall return to the topic of federal interventions in chapter 4.)

Other demand-oriented measures contribute very little to determining spending levels in the states. The influence of education and urbanization is not independent of the influence of income. (The coefficients reported for education and urbanization collapse in multiple regression problems on spending variables when income is included as an independent variable.)

Overall, our demand-side model succeeds in explaining 57 to 60 percent of variance in total per capita state-local spending in most years. The supply-side model is a little less successful, explaining 42 to 55 percent of this variance. Years—the surrogate measure of institutional sclerosis—appears to have a consistent and independent association with higher spending levels. Public employee unionism—the percentage of state-local employees with union memberships—also appears to have a consistent and independent association with higher spending levels.

Of course, government employment itself—the proportion of the civilian labor force of the state that is employed by government—is strongly associ-

Table 2–5
Total State-Local Government Spending per Capita,
Cross-Sectional Analysis for Selected Years

	1984		1975		1960	
	r	β	r	β	r	β
Resources						
Income	.53*	.71*	.71*	.80*	.61*	.77*
Urbanization	.10	.26	.46*	−.06	.36*	.03
Education	.35*	.02	.55*	.16	.44	.02
Needs						
Poor	−.22	.33*	−.36*	.28	−.50*	.15
Aged	−.42*	−.19	−.58*	−.14	−.10	−.13
Young	.09	.30*	.30*	.08	−.13	.28
Black	−.20	−.26	−.25	−.24	−.49*	−.41*
Total R^2	.57		.60		.57	
Government employment						
State-local employees %	.63*	.63*	.56*	.56*	.55*	.55*
Total R^2	.40		.33		.30	
Federal intervention						
Federal aid	.88*	.88*	.83*	.83*	.54*	.54*
Total R^2	.77		.69		.29	
Bureaucratization and centralization						
Professionalism	−.25	−.12	−.35*	−.10	−.37*	−.18
Public unionism	.33*	.10	.50*	.42*	.39*	.23
State centralization	.35*	.25	.30	.23	.21	.18
Interest group activity						
Years	.32*	.39*	.37*	.34*	.32*	.36*
Unions	.35*	.09	.48*	.30	.34*	.12
Group strength	−.01	−.09	−.13	−.01	−.32	−.31*
Total R^2	.43		.55		.42	

Note: The dependent variable is total state-local government spending per capita. Figures are simple correlation cross-sectional coefficients (r), standardized regression coefficients (β), and total explained variance (R^2) for fifty states, except for "Income," where Alaska is excluded as an external value. An asterisk indicates a statistically significant relationship.

ated with state-local spending levels. But we are reluctant to infer from this that government employees vote themselves more money. A median voter preference for increased government spending would produce higher public employment. It is impossible to sort out the causal sequence—to know whether preference for higher levels of government service creates more government jobs or the votes of larger numbers of government employees inflate government spending.

Spending by Function

Variations in spending levels among the states by function—education, welfare, health, and highways—are examined in table 2–6. For educational spending, income again emerges as a major independent determinant of differences among the states. (Standardized regression coefficients, βs, are not shown in the table to save space. The adjective *independent* in the text indicates that β's values are significant.) The educational level of the adult population is also an important independent determinant of educational spending. Educational spending is lower in states with larger poor, aged, and black populations, but these measures of need are not independently related to lower educational spending. Rather these associations are a product of the effects of lower income and educational levels.

Educational spending does not appear to be strongly influenced by variations in our supply-side measures. Educational spending is somewhat higher in older states, but none of the other supply-side measures is significantly associated with educational spending.

Educational spending is independently associated with federal aid, however. This is true despite the fact that little federal aid goes to education. (The federal aid measure is total federal aid per capita rather than federal aid to each functional area.) We might speculate that federal aid is really fungible; states that are successful in getting federal revenues for any purpose are able to spend more for education.

Welfare spending is also independently associated with income. Higher-income states spend more per capita on welfare than lower-income states. But at least one supply-side variable, unionism—is also an influential independent determinant of variation in welfare spending among the states. Both public employee unionism and the unionized proportion of the total work force are associated with higher welfare spending.

Highway spending is closely associated with the rural-urban dimension of the states. Rural states, not surprisingly, have always spent proportionately more than urban states on highways.

Health spending was once heavily influenced by a state's economic resources. But following the initiation of the Medicaid and Medicare programs by the federal government in 1965, state-local spending for health has been decoupled from economic resources. This is most obvious in consecutive cross-sectional observations that show the gradual disappearance of the relationship between per capita personal income and per capita health spending (.64 in 1960 versus .06 in 1984). (We shall return to this topic in chapter 4.)

The purpose in observing these cross-sectional associations is to suggest that demand-side as well as supply-side measures account for variation among the states in levels of public service. States do offer different packages of public services, and these differences are partly a product of the interplay

Table 2-6
Total State-Local Spending Per Capita by Function, Cross-Sectional Analyses for Selected Years

	Education		Welfare		Health		Highways	
	1984 r	1960 r	1984 r	1960 r	1984 r	1960 r	1984 r	1960 r
Resources								
Income	.44	.49*	.43*	.38*	.06	.64	−.18	−.01
Urbanization	.05	.31*	.29	.36*	.21	.55	−.38*	−.38*
Education	.41*	.51*	.08	.19	−.08	.31	.06	.03
Needs								
Poor	−.22	−.46*	−.24	−.06	.23	−.40	−.05	−.22
Aged	−.30	−.31*	.04	−.16	−.33	−.05	−.04	.22
Young	.14	−.18	−.30	−.31	.06	−.37	.25	.19
Black	−.24	−.45*	−.15	−.11	.38	−.01	−.44	.48
Total R^2	.54	.54	.24	.36	.35	.47	.49	.44
Government employment								
State-local employees	.63*	.33*	.03	.21	.22	.13	.69*	.48*
Federal intervention								
Federal aid	.77*	.55*	.22	.12	.10	.08	.52*	.47*
Bureaucratization								
Professionalism	−.25	−.28	−.46	−.33	−.08	−.38	−.19	.04
Public unionism	.22	.13	.64*	.44	.03	.57	.05	−.06
State centralization	.20	.25	.03	.01	.06	.05	.31	.26
Total R^2	.28	.34	.65	.33	.05	.40	.29	.16

Note: The dependent variables are state-local spending per capita for education, welfare, health, and highways. Figures are simple cross-sectional correlation coefficients for fifty states, except for "Income," where Alaska is excluded as an extreme value. An asterisk indicates a statistically significant relationship.

of economic resources and social needs. But responsiveness cannot be fully assessed in cross-sectional analyses. We also need to know whether changes in economic resources or social conditions in the states bring about observable changes in public policy.

The Demand for Education

It is rare that a major governmental function contracts in size. Yet educational spending by state and local governments has declined modestly over the last decade in relation to the national economy. Educational spending, as a percentage of total personal income in the United States, declined from its peak of 7 percent in 1976 to about 5.6 percent through 1984 (see figure 2–3). This pattern of expansion and later contraction in the burden of educational spending contrasts markedly with the pattern of public spending for other governmental functions, virtually none of which has ever contracted to any significant degree.

The burden of public education is defined as total state and local government spending for education as a percentage of total personal income. We are concerned with levels of educational spending relative to society's ability to sustain government activity. In absolute terms, state and local government spending for education in current dollars in the United States rose from $8.3 billion in 1952 to $174.1 billion in 1984, with increases recorded every year. But as noted in figure 2–3, expressed in relative terms, educational spending has experienced periods of significant contraction as well as expansion. The contraction of educational spending is largely responsible for the contraction of total state and local government spending from its high in 1976.

Our objective is to develop a simple model of the demand for public education and then test this model against aggregate state-local educational spending in the nation over thirty-three years and against educational spending in each of the fifty states over this same time span. How can we explain both the early growth and later contraction in the burden of educational spending in the United States? Is educational spending in the United States responsive to changes in the demand for education over time? Can we identify which states are more or less responsive to the demand for education and which are not?

A simple demand-side model would posit that the principal determinant of educational spending in the states is the number of school-aged children in the population. If we express this demand in relative terms, it would be the percentage of the population aged 5–17. We know that the school-aged population reached its peak of 29.5 percent of the total populations in the late 1960s; it declined significantly in the 1970s to its low of 22.3 percent in 1984.

The principal resource constraint on educational spending is personal income. School budgets may not expand or contract annually in response to changes in personal income, if for no other reason than that officials cannot accurately forecast short-run economic conditions in their jurisdictions. Thus, inelasticity in government spending, combined with contraction in personal income, may cause educational spending to grow as a percentage of personal income when personal income in a state declines.

Federal transfers play a minor role in educational funding. Most federal aid is directed to welfare, health, housing, and community development activities. The federal government provides less than 10 percent of total educational spending in the nation. However, federal aid may be tangible: federal money for other governmental functions may free state and local money to support education.

Our model is deliberately parsimonious, with only three explanatory variables: change in school-aged population, in per capita personal income, and in federal revenues. We view simplicity as a virtue, not only in theory but also in testing, especially when testing it against the experience of fifty separate states, as well as the national aggregate.

Testing a Demand-Side Model for Education

We are concerned with dynamic processes. We are interested in the determinants of change over time. Making inferences about change (a dynamic process) from cross-sectional data (static observations) is risky business. We must therefore test the model in time-series regressions on each of the fifty states. We might initially, however, inquire about the static relationships implied by the model: do states that devote larger shares of personal income to education have larger school-aged populations, or enjoy higher per capita incomes, or receive more federal aid? A simple cross-sectional regression on 1984 data shows that some of the variation among the states in educational burden can be explained by the model:

Educational expenditures as a percentage of personal income	$R^2 = .22\ N = 50, a = .835$
Percent of the total population age 5 through 17	$B = .45, r = .43$
Per capita personal income	$B = .10, r = .12$
Federal aid as a percentage of total revenue	$B = .17, r = .20$

Thus, states with larger educational burdens tend to be the states with larger school-aged populations.

Do changes in school-aged populations result in changes in educational burdens in the states? To test the ability of the simple demand-side model to explain changes over time, time-series regressions were performed on fifty sets of data using both lagged and unlagged procedures. The theoretical justification for lagging some independent variables is that their influence on the dependent variable is not immediate. School-aged population growth requires several years for school administrators to build new classrooms, expand teaching staffs, and incur significantly increased costs. More important, declines in school-aged population will not immediately reduce educational costs, since classrooms and teachers cannot be quickly eliminated. We estimate a four-year time lag for the influence of changes in school-aged population. We estimate a two-year lag for the influence of income changes to be reflected in spending decisions. We left federal aid unlagged on the assumption that it is all spent in a single year and decision makers cannot plan well for annual changes in this aid. Reasonable observers might differ with these assumptions; however, we can report that different assumptions about lagging produce very little change in results.

Fifty separate regression problems were performed on educational spending in each state. The full results for both lagged and unlagged models are presented for New York, by way of example, in table 2–7. The New York example presents R^2s, adjusted R_2, coefficients, and their standard errors, as well as T statistics (coefficients divided by their standard error) for both lagged and unlagged models. Note that in New York, the lagged model explains 93 percent of the variation over time in educational burdens, with

Table 2–7
Simple Demand Model for Education in New York

	Unlagged Model			Lagged Model		
	Coefficient	Standard Error	T Statistic	Coefficient	Standard Error	T Statistic
Const	−.14	.045	−3.1	−.92	.23	−3.9
%POP5–17	.80	.18	4.5	.65	.02	6.6
PCPI	.24	.17	1.4	.06	.13	.5
FEDAID	.25	.14	1.7	.11	.13	.9

$R^2 = .92$ Adjustsed $R^2 = .91$
Durbin Watson 1.92

$R^2 = .94$ Adjusted $R^2 = .93$
Durbin Watson 1.96

Note: Time-series regressions (Cochrane-Orcutt Technique) on educational spending as a percentage of personal income, 1957–1984, with twenty-seven observations for both lagged and unlagged models. %POP5–17 is percent of total population age 5 through 17; PCPI is per capita personal income; FEDAID is percent of total revenue from federal grants. Estimation made with SORETIC from the Sorites Group Inc., Springfield, Virginia.

school-aged population emerging as the only significant component of the model. Inasmuch as the presentation of all of these statistics for each state would use more space than readers would wish, let us instead summarize the results of the fifty separate analyses:

1. School-aged population emerges as the most important determinant of the burden of educational spending over time in thirty-seven states: Alabama, Arizona, Arkansas, California, Colorado, Connecticut, Delaware, Georgia, Hawaii, Illinois, Indiana, Iowa, Kansas, Kentucky, Louisiana, Maine, Maryland, Massachusetts, Michigan, Minnesota, Missouri, Montana, Nebraska, New Hampshire, New Jersey, New York, North Carolina, Ohio, Oregon, Pennsylvania, Rhode Island, South Dakota, Texas, Utah, Virginia, West Virginia, and Wisconsin. In these states educational spending grew as a percentage of total personal income in years in which the school-aged population grew as a percentage of the total population. And in these states, educational spending declined as a proportion of total personal income in later years when the school-aged population declined as a percentage of the total population. In thirteen states (Alaska, Florida, Idaho, Mississippi, Nevada, New Mexico, North Dakota, Oklahoma, South Carolina, Tennessee, Vermont, Washington, and Wyoming) changes in the burden of educational spending are unrelated to changes in school-aged population over the years.

2. Income levels and federal aid are significant determinants of the burden of educational spending in a minority of states. Increases in income are associated with decreases in educational effort in twelve states: Alaska, Illinois, Indiana, Louisiana, Maine, Massachusetts, Missouri, Nevada, North Carolina, North Dakota, South Dakota, and Wisconsin. Increases in federal aid are associated with increases in educational effort in seven states: Arkansas, California, Louisiana, North Carolina, North Dakota, Wisconsin, and Wyoming.

3. If we define responsiveness in educational spending as the ability of the simple demand model to explain at least half of the variation in educational burden over the years ($R^2 . > .50$) and for at least one component of the model to be a significant contributor to R_2, then forty-one states appear to be responsive to the demand for education. In nine states (Florida, Idaho, Mississippi, New Mexico, Oklahoma, South Carolina, Tennessee, Vermont, and Washington) no component of the model proved to be significantly related to educational effort. In these states, educational spending as a proportion of personal income is unrelated or only weakly related to the components of the model.

4. The simple demand-side model succeeds in explaining 92 percent of the variation over the years in aggregate state-local spending for education

as a percentage of personal income in the United States. (This is a marked improvement over the cross-sectional R^2.) The school-aged population contributes significantly to the explanation of aggregate U.S. spending for education.

Plausible Alternative Hypotheses

Supply-side explanations of government spending (or overspending) are currently popular, but they fail to explain contraction in a major governmental function: education in the states. We do not believe that educational bureaucracies have become less expansionist over time, or educational interest groups less active, or school teachers and administrators significantly more productive since 1976. Indeed, supply-side theories do not postulate any conditions under which governments would contract. The earlier cross-sectional literature on state spending (Dye 1966; Hofferbert 1966a) employed urbanization, industrialization, and adult education, as well as income, as explanatory variables. But we know that none of these variables has contracted in recent years.

We cannot dismiss changing political attitudes toward government taxing and spending as a contributing factor to the contraction of education in the state. The "tax revolt" had a profound impact on state and local government revenue growth. We generally think of the tax revolt as beginning with California's Proposition 13 in 1978 (Sears and Citrin 1982). But total state and local tax revenues as a percentage of personal income actually peaked in 1976, the same year in which educational spending peaked. And, of course, any cross-sectional or time-series analyses that posit revenues as determinants of expenditures produce very high coefficients, so it is virtually impossible to disentangle the effects of the revenue constraints from the effects of school-aged population on educational spending. (We will return to a discussion of the tax revolt in chapter 3.)

We can only speculate that the decline in school-aged population facilitated cutbacks in both taxation and educational spending in the states. It is difficult to imagine large state and local revenue rollbacks occurring in the face of expanding school enrollments. We suspect that the tax revolt was made easier by reduced demand for state and local government's largest public service, education.

State and local educational spending has been responsive to both the early expansion and later contraction of the school-aged population. There appears to be a modest lag (about four years) between the beginning of a contraction in demand and the beginning of declines in educational spending burdens, suggesting some short-term inelasticity in state spending. A decline in a demand for education takes several years to work its effect on educational bureaucrats and budget makers, some of whom may not wish to acknowledge a reduction in demand for their services.

Competitive Federalism and Policy Responsiveness

Competitive federalism requires that states offer differing levels of public services. Competitive federalism means policy diversity. And indeed, despite "nationalization" of the states in economic resources and political systems, we do find continuing, significant policy variations among the states. Interstate variations in per capita spending for public services—education, welfare, health, highways—are not diminishing.

It is difficult to make an overall judgment about the responsiveness of state and local governments to citizen preferences. The traditional determinants literature in economics and political science revealed close associations between spending policies and characteristics of the populations of states and municipalities. The implicit assumption in these studies was the median voter model—a demand-side theory that postulates that the median voter's indifference curve would be the indifference curve of the political system.

Over the years, the simple median voter model has come under increasingly critical scrutiny. It has become clear that the model assumes single-peaked preference curves, as well as proportional allocation of both benefits and costs among all voters, conditions seldom met in the real world of politics. Moreover, simplified versions of the model fail to specify why elected officials or bureaucrats would be bound by the preferences of the median voter. Yet despite these theoretical problems, empirical work has continued to produce highly predictive models of state and local government taxing and spending based on the characteristics of median voters.

Certainly the most interesting theoretical work in politics and economics in recent years has centered on "political failures"—the discontinuities between the rational motives of decision makers in a democracy and the preferences of citizens. Public choice theory has provided fresh insights into the oversupply of government goods and services. Unquestionably state and local governments are affected by bureaucratization, centralization, public employee activity, and interest group pressures. Even rough surrogate measures of these supply-side forces correlate independently with increased public spending.

We cannot argue that competition among governments will ensure that citizens' preferences prevail over bureaucratic interests or group pressures. Indeed, our own calculations suggest that both demand-side and supply-side variables correlate with spending differences among the states.

But the largest functional category of state-local spending, education, appears to expand and contract in relation to the school-aged population. On the whole, state and local governments are responsive to the demand for education. Some states are more responsive than others, but in very few states is there no association between spending on education and numbers of school-aged children.

In summary, we have evidence that some of the minimal conditions for competitive federalism are being met. States do offer different levels of public services, and these levels appear to be determined partly by changes in citizen demands.

Note

1. See, for example, Lasswell and Kaplan (1970, p. 71); Friedreich (1963, p. 70); Eulau and Prewitt (1973, p. 465). For an elaboration of the view that policy is government activity, see Dye (1987, chap. 1).

3
Raising Revenue in the States

No doubt the raising of a very exorbitant tax, as the raising as much
in peace as in war, or the half of even the fifth of the wealth of the
nation, would as well as any gross abuse of power, justify resistance
in the people.
—Adam Smith, *Lectures in Jurisprudence*

There is no part of the administration of government that requires
extensive information and a thorough knowledge of the principles
of political economy so much as the business of taxation.
——Alexander Hamilton, *Federalist*, Number 35.

Competitive federalism envisions constrained decision making by
states and communities. The provision of public services must be accompanied by costs—reductions in disposable personal income. In
the marketplace the benefits derived from goods and services are considered
simultaneously with their costs. Unfortunately, this is not true in government
decision making, where costs are usually separate from benefits. This separation of taxing and spending decisions in government reduces constraints on
spending, a problem accentuated in centralized monopoly government. At
least under competitive federalism, individuals and firms can compare revenue burdens among states and communities. These comparisons can provide
rough informational guides about the costs of public services. Consumer-
taxpayers—individuals, families, small businesses, large corporations—can
register their preferences by moving or threatening to move to other jurisdictions or by staying put. Perhaps more important, public officials, in antici-
pation of these responses, can make better estimates of the preferred balance
between services and costs.

Bearing the Burdens of Government

How burdensome is government? The calculation of the true burden of government activity must include all government revenues, the indirect costs of
regulation, and the secondary effects of both revenues and regulations on
economic growth. The true costs of government are not just the taxes we pay
but also the expenditures we must make to comply with government regu-

lations and, most important, the income we forgo because taxes and regulations reduce our incentive to work, save, and invest. Later we assess these secondary effects of state and local government activity (chapter 7), but for now let us examine the direct costs of these governments.

We can view the direct burdens of government on society by examining governmental revenues in relation to personal income. The assumption is that all government revenues derive from personal income. It is not only the personal income tax that must be paid from personal income but sales and excise taxes, property taxes, user charges, and lottery revenues as well. And we can assume that corporate income taxes, severance taxes, and other nonpersonal levies also come out of someone's personal income.

All government revenues in the United States captured 44 percent of personal income in 1985. This contrasts with an estimated 8 percent of personal income in 1902 (table 3–1). Clearly the burdens of government have grown much faster than the nation's income.

The burden of state and local government almost doubled in the twenty-year period from 1952 to 1972 (figure 3.1). The peak of state-local revenue burdens was in 1976. These burdens moderated somewhat through 1982, but they then started upward again. Diminished federal aid (relative to income) has been replaced by state-local own source revenues, which are now reaching toward previous high levels of burden on personal income.

State government revenues, considered separately from combined state and local government revenues, reflect these same trends (figure 3–2). State government total revenues and tax revenues reached their high in relation to personal income in 1976, retreated somewhat through 1982, and then began

Table 3–1
Total Government Revenues, 1902–1985

	Amounts ($ billions)	Federal Percentage	State-Local Percentage	Percentage of National Income
1902	1.7	38.5	61.5	8.2
1913	3.0	32.3	67.7	8.6
1922	9.3	45.7	54.3	14.7
1932	10.3	21.6	78.4	24.2
1940	17.8	39.3	60.7	21.8
1950	66.7	80.3	19.7	27.6
1960	153.1	65.2	34.8	36.7
1965	202.9	62.0	38.0	39.4
1970	342.6	61.6	38.4	40.6
1980	932.0	60.5	39.5	43.1
1985	1,418.4	56.2	43.1	44.0

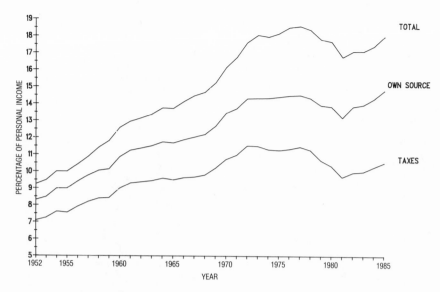

Figure 3–1. State-Local Government Revenues as a Percentage of Personal Income

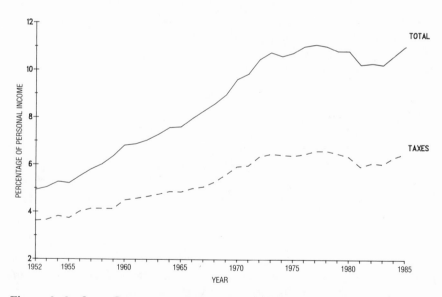

Figure 3–2. State Government Revenues as a Percentage of Personal Income

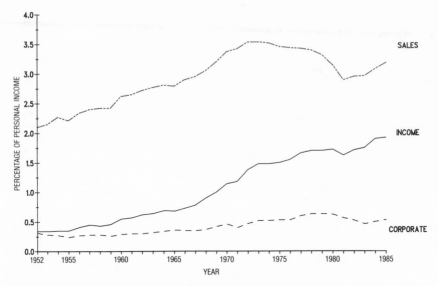

Figure 3–3. Types of State Taxes as a Percentage of Personal Income

to surge upward again. State sales taxes were the most volatile of state revenue sources (figure 3–3). State income taxes have creeped steadily upward as a burden on personal income. State corporate taxes have remained below 1 percent of personal income over the years.

Explaining Revenue Choices

In politics, the taxing game is played separately from the spending game. In the marketplace, we consider the costs of goods and services at the time of purchase and weigh this cost against anticipated benefits. In other words, costs and benefits are considered in a simultaneous and coordinated fashion. This is not true in government.

Segmented Decisions

Government decisions about revenue raising are distinct from those about spending. This separation occurs not only within the governmental process but also at the individual level. Consumer-taxpayers generally separate their dual roles as beneficiaries of government services and as taxpayers. Individual evaluations of tax burdens are only loosely tied to evaluations of the level or quality of public service. This separation of roles enables individuals to demand more governmental services and lower taxes simultaneously. This is not necessarily contradictory; rather it reflects the separation of taxing and spending decisions.

Voters as taxpayers have a general interest in reduced government spending, lower taxes, and increased economic growth. This interest focuses on the overall size of government spending. But voters as consumers have an interest in increased spending for particular government services that benefit them directly. This interest focuses on a particular segment of government spending. The voter as a consumer can call for increased spending for a particular service, and the same voter as a taxpayer can call for reductions in overall taxing and spending. The market offers very few opportunities to escape the task of weighing costs against benefits, but government offers many such opportunities.

Rational Voter Model

The simple rational voter model envisions a constrained choice. Elected officials will expand public services until the marginal vote gained by the benefits is offset by the marginal vote lost by the increased costs. This rational model resembles a market; citizens will "buy" public goods with their taxes according to the benefits received. The problem with the model is that the separation of taxing decisions from spending decisions leaves spending relatively unconstrained, while placing downward pressure on taxes. Indeed, Anthony Downs once predicted that governmental budgets in democracies will be smaller than true citizen preferences because support for spending is intense and directed to particular services, while opposition to taxing is passive and generalized (Downs 1960, pp. 545ff.). If we carry the logic of the rational self-interested voter-taxpayer to its extreme, we would be forced to conclude that democratic governments can never raise taxes (see Hansen 1983, chap. 2). Economist Lester Thurow contends that democracies cannot make difficult "zero-sum" decisions: "We have a government process that goes to great lengths to avoid having to overtly lower someone's income. Such decisions are always being made of course, but they are made implicitly, under the guise of accomplishing other objectives" (Thurow 1980, p. 17).

Clearly this formulation of the rational voter model fails to explain the massive increases in tax burdens imposed by governments in the United States over the past fifty years. Not only has the federal government vastly reduced the share of personal income taxpayers are permitted to keep but state and local governments have also done so (see figure 3–1). It may be true that few politicians build successful campaigns around promises to raise taxes, but taxes do get raised.

The rational voter model may be appropriate for selected types of revenue-raising efforts. For example, referendum voting on tax increases earmarked for specific benefits may indeed encourage simultaneous and coordinated decision making in the public arena analogous to market decision making. Social security may also represent a fairly close approximation of the constrained preferences of rational consumer-taxpayers. This is because the social security tax is earmarked, the tax itself is proportional for most Americans, and the benefits are distributed fairly equally to beneficiaries. This may help explain the political popularity of social security—the fact that few Americans object to the tax though it now exceeds the burden of federal income taxes for more than half of the nation's taxpayers.

In summary the rational median voter model is appropriate for analyzing revenue-raising decisions under very limited assumptions. If (a) taxes are earmarked, (b) they are decided by referendum, (c) their burdens are shared equally among all taxpayers, and (d) their benefits are shared equally, then consumer-taxpayers can make a rational decision that resembles a market choice.

The reason that taxes do in fact get raised—the reason that democratic governments can coerce their citizens into giving up substantial portions of their personal income—is that the institutional structures of government protects officials from the full wrath of rational citizen-taxpayers. Government provides multiple opportunities to escape the need to balance costs against benefits. Indeed, the effect of governmental institutions is to produce higher taxes than the true preferences of citizens.

Public Choice Theory

Modern public choice theory has provided many insights into the effects of institutional structures and rules of decision making on budgets. We know that a variety of institutional forces are at work exaggerating the benefits of public services and underestimating their costs to citizen-taxpayers. Among the reasons offered by public choice theory are the following:

Election period discounts: The length of time between elections allows officials to discount citizen preferences. Taxes can be raised at the beginning of a term. Benefits can be dispersed just before elections.

Limited electoral agendas: Parties and candidates limit the choices at election time to two packages of taxing and spending policies, neither of which maximizes the preferences of any citizen (Breton 1974). Both options have higher overall taxing and spending levels than preferred by most citizens; citizens can choose only the option that provides them more direct benefits.

Rational ignorance: The rational ignorance of voter-taxpayers prevents them from knowing about, or effectively organizing themselves against, generalized tax increases. In contrast, groups directly benefiting from concentrated spending have incentives to work for higher budgets.

Monopoly government:. Governments themselves, as well as elected officials and bureaucrats, may be viewed as self-interested, rational monopolists. They seek to maximize their revenue, particularly their discretionary revenues, to add to their own power, pay, and prestige.

Fiscal illusion: Numerous fiscal illusions are available to allow governments and politicians to raise revenues without arousing the opposition of taxpayers. Even the liberal economist Lester Thurow admits that taxes are usually raised "under the guise of accomplishing other objectives." Since increasing taxes raises the opposition of voter-taxpayers, governments and politicians resort to a wide array of devices to conceal, obfuscate, and disguise taxes.

Whatever the theoretical merits of these public choice explanations of taxation, empirical research by political scientists confirms "the monumental ignorance of the U.S. public concerning not only the basic structure and economics of taxes, but the amounts they themselves pay and the government services that they receive" (Hansen 1983, p. 257). Whether as a result of fiscal illusion practiced by governments and politicians or not, voter-taxpayers are ignorant not only of general questions of redistribution and equity but also of specific knowledge of how a particular tax proposal will personally affect them. Popular attitudes toward taxation are "confused, multi-dimensional, and fluctuate considerably over time" (ibid., p. 256). Media coverage of taxation and economic issues generally is very poor. Public opinion studies frequently structure choices for respondents on tax questions and thereby largely create "opinion." But in fact tax attitudes are better described as "non-opinions." Few Americans have strong, well-defined, consistent attitudes on tax issues.

Responsiveness of State-Local Taxation

The political test of tax policy is its relationship to citizen preferences—its responsiveness to public beliefs and attitudes. It is our argument that multiple competitive governments are more constrained in fiscal policy than monopoly government Specifically we shall argue that state and local tax policies are more responsive than federal tax policy to citizen preferences. Certainly all of the institutional forces driving up tax burdens are present in state capitols and city halls. But there are other institutional forces at work in states and communities that tend to ensure that their tax policies will be more efficient and responsive than those of the national government. What theoretical justification can we offer for this optimism?

Limits on Fiscal Illusion

The two principal sources of fiscal illusion—inflation and deficit spending—are largely unavailable to state and local government officials. The states do not have the options of monetary or fiscal policy manipulation. First, all states have constitutional or statutory balanced budget requirements for their operating budgets, and all states require local government budgets to be balanced. It is true that state and local capital budgets are financed through debt, but this debt is constrained by the private bond market, which must consider the risk of default by these governments. While market oversight of municipal debt has occasionally failed, as in the case of New York City in the 1970s, the overall record of state and local fiscal responsibility is good. Second, inflation can be neither created nor relied upon by state and local governments. State income taxes are not steeply progressive, and "bracket creep" provides no great windfall. The overall incidence of state and local taxes is usually estimated to be mildly regressive and somewhat inelastic. The result of these restraints is that state and local governments must collect the great bulk of their own revenues from taxes. State and local officials must confront, more directly than federal officials, the opposition of citizen-taxpayers to higher tax burdens.

Prevalence of Earmarking

A substantial fraction of state and local revenues is earmarked for specific purposes. Traditionally gasoline tax revenues in the states have been earmarked for highway purposes. Most states continue to earmark these funds today, though the trend has been to broaden the purposes for which transportation funds may be spent. Earmarking is often accompanied by the establishment of separate trust accounts and prohibitions on the use of these trust funds for anything other than specified purposes.

Earmarking is not limited to highway revenues. Other revenue sources—for example, lottery revenues—are often dedicated, by constitutional or statutory provision, to education. State unemployment insurance and workman's compensation taxes are earmarked, and separate trust funds are maintained in all of the states to receive these revenues and disperse them only for insurance purposes. Occasionally, broad-based taxes—income or sales taxes—are officially pledged to education or public welfare. But the link between taxes and benefits in these broad pledges is very obscure.

Earmarking establishes a direct link between the benefits of a government service and the taxes collected to pay for it. It allows citizen-taxpayers to see the cost of a specific public service, in contrast to the lump or package of services that they would otherwise confront. This brings public choice closer to the constrained preference-maximizing model of the marketplace. By linking benefits received to taxes collected, a form of indirect pricing is achieved; people can see what they are getting for their money. The fact that elected officials frequently resort to some earmarking in order to get new and otherwise unpopular taxes accepted testifies to the public's appreciation of the linkage mechanism. People are more willing to approve of taxation when they know what the money will be used for.

Earmarked trust funds also contribute to informed public choice. If a separate trust fund is employed, governments are discouraged from collecting any less than the full cost of the service; to do so will create a politically embarrassing deficit in the trust fund and inform citizen-taxpayers of the actual cost of the service. Similarly governments are discouraged from collecting more in taxes than the full cost of the service; to do so will create a politically embarrassing surplus and inform the citizen-taxpayer that taxes are too high. Another advantage of earmarking is that it frequently permits costs to be directed to users, as in the case of highway spending from gasoline taxes. But even when an earmarked tax is not exclusively directed toward users, it still provides pricing information for a particular public service.

The often-encountered complaint that earmarking removes specified revenues and expenditures from direct annual legislative control is actually an added advantage of the practice. The pricing effect of earmarking is protected from legislative interference. Citizen-taxpayers are given direct information on benefits and costs of a particular governmental service. As political scientist Susan Hansen explains:

> With earmarked, lump-sum, or head taxes, individuals' tax decisions are roughly analogous to market decisions where the connection between price paid and quantity received is readily apparent. But indirect, progressive, or proportional taxes make it harder for individuals to predict their personal tax liability or the amount of revenue to be raised. Politicians can resort to various fiscal illusion to disguise the true size or incidence of the tax burden. (Hansen 1983, p. 39)

Growth of User Charges

A large and growing proportion of state and local government revenue comes from user charges, which, even more than earmarked revenue, directly link the benefits and costs of public goods in the fashion of the marketplace. Wherever it is possible to keep nonpayers from enjoying the benefits of a particular service, then the values of equity and efficiency are better served by providing the service on a user fee basis rather than financing it from general taxation. By charging prices that reflect the costs of the service and by exacting these fees from the actual users of the service, the efficiency purpose of the market can be achieved. Government will be restrained from overproducing the service. If the government service is provided at no charge to users, we would expect more of the service to be consumed than is socially optimal. And citizen-taxpayers generally appear to favor the equity aspects of user fees. Public opinion polls regularly report that voters prefer user charges to any other form of government revenue raising; the idea of "paying for what you get" is considered fair (ACIR 1987).

User charges are the fastest growing source of state-local government revenue. Today user charges and miscellaneous revenues constitute about 15 percent of state-local revenue. (This figure is actually the combination of user charges, utility and liquor store revenues, lottery, and miscellaneous revenues.) A more rigorous accounting definition of user charges produces a figure of about 7 percent. The growth of user charges, in both absolute and relative terms, has been rapid and steady over the past three decades. In 1952, user charges and miscellaneous revenues of state and local governments captured a little more than 1 percent of personal income.

The limits of user charge revenue growth, however, may be reached fairly soon. Equitable and efficient user charges can be employed only where the benefits of a service accrue solely to the payers. If benefits spill out to the general public, user charges will fail on both equity and efficiency grounds. Often the administrative costs of collecting the fee and ensuring that only payers benefit from it is too high; we could hardly place toll booths on every street. And there are always arguments about externalities in any public service, or else it would not be considered public. That is, it is always arguable that the general public, as well as the direct beneficiaries, benefit from a particular service. For example, when all children are educated, the general public benefits, not just the children or their parents; when the poor are protected against hunger or remedial illness, the general public benefits, not just the poor themselves. Most cities have even decided that mass transit facilities are beneficial by relieving congestion to the general public, not just the riders; riders pay only a small proportion of the costs of their transportation in most cities. In short, most government services are public goods or at least quasi-public goods, which involve recognized externalities. This limits the extent to which user charges can ever replace taxation.

Initiative and Referendum Voting

State and local governments make frequent use of citizen initiative and direct referendum voting in decisions regarding public spending and tax burdens. The rise of the initiative and referendum in state and local government is attributed to the progressive reform movement of the early twentieth century.

The progressives viewed "bosses," parties, and even "politics" as corrupt and distasteful. They sought to bypass politics and political institutions with a variety of structural reforms, including primary elections to replace party caucuses and direct election of U.S. senators to replace selection by state legislatures (the Seventeenth Amendment to the U.S. Constitution). The progressives were also responsible for the widespread adoption in the states of the initiative and referendum, devices they believed would link citizens directly to public policy choices.

All states require referendums on amendments to their state constitutions. (Only in Delaware can the legislature amend the state constitution without a popular referendum.) Most state constitutional amendments are initiated by state legislatures, state constitutional conventions, or constitutional revision commissions before submission to the voters (Dye 1987, pp. 36–45). Most states also require that municipal indebtedness be undertaken only with the approval of the voters. Tax increases tied to debt service usually require a referendum.

Voter initiatives bypass the legislature and allow citizens directly to propose and adopt constitutional amendments or statutory laws. The popular initiative for constitutional revision was introduced in Oregon (1902), and today seventeen states allow it (table 3–2). We shall argue that popular initiatives can have a direct effect on tax burdens. Not all tax-limiting initiatives and referendums are successful, and not all that win voter approval succeed in actually lowering tax burdens. But the overall effect of the initiative and referendums, including indirect effects on the behavior of politicians anticipating their use, is to make tax policy more responsive to citizen preferences than it otherwise would be.

Intergovernmental Competition

State and local governments must consider competition with other jurisdictions when deciding about taxes. Aside from whatever responsiveness effects that might be generated by widespread informed voter participation in competitive elections, responsiveness occurs when citizen-taxpayers—either individuals or firms—have the ability to exit. Moreover, governments must also compete among themselves for new citizen-taxpayers—individuals or firms who are relocating and offering to bring additional resources to the state or community.

Tests of Revenue Responsiveness

Our initial tests of the responsiveness of tax policy focus on cross-sectional relationships among the fifty states between tax levels and burdens and var-

Table 3–2
Initiative and Referendums in the States

Initiative for Constitutional Amendment (Signatures Required to Get on Ballot)[a]	Initiative for State Legislation (Signatures Required to Get on Ballot)[a]	Referendum on State Legislation
Arizona (15%)	Alaska (10%)	Alaska
Arkansas (10%)	Arizona (10%)	Arizona
California (8%)	Arkansas (8%)	Arkansas
Colorado (5%)	California (5%)	California
Florida (8%)	Colorado (5% secretary of state election)	Colorado
Illinois (8%)		Connecticut
Massachusetts (10%)	Idaho	Florida
Michigan (10%)	Maine (10%)	Georgia
Missouri (8%)	Massachusetts (3%)	Idaho
Montana (10%)	Michigan (8%)	Iowa
Nebraska (10%)	Missouri (5%)	Kansas
Nevada (10%)	Montana (5% total qualified elections)	Kentucky
North Dakota (4% of state population)	Nebraska (7%)	Maine
Ohio (10%)	Nevada (10%)	Maryland
Oklahoma (15%)	North Dakota (2% of state population)	Massachusetts
Oregon (8%)	Ohio (3% electors)	Michigan
South Dakota (10%)	Oklahoma (8%)	Missouri
	South Dakota (5%)	Montana
	Utah (10%)	Nebaraska
	Washington (8%)	Nevada
	Wyoming (15%, general election)	New Jersey
		New Mexico
		New York
		North Dakota
		Ohio
		Oklahoma
		Oregon
		Pennsylvania
		Rhode Island
		South Dakota
		Utah
		Virginia
		Washington
		Wisconsin
		Wyoming

Source: Council of State Governments, *The Book of the States, 1986–87.*

[a]Figures expressed as percentage of the vote in last governor's election unless otherwise specified. Some states also require distribution of votes across counties and districts.

ious indicators of demand and supply for government services. Tax levels are simply per capita tax measures, and tax burdens are taxes expressed as a percentage of personal income. The rationale behind the selection of various indicators of demand and supply was developed in the discussion regarding the responsiveness of public policy. These indicators tap economic resources, social needs, bureaucratization, government employment, federal intervention, and interest group activity (see chapter 2, pp. 46–51).

Tax Levels in the States

Citizen-taxpayers in the states are taxed at very different levels. The range of variation in taxes collected by state and local government per person in 1985 extended from highs of $2,334 in New York and $2,580 in Wyoming (and Alaska's high of $4,585) to lows of under $1,000 in Tennessee, Alabama, Mississippi, and Arkansas. In other words, some states collected over twice as much in taxes from each citizen as other states, a range of variation that has persisted over the decades.

A generation of studies in economics and political science has shown that the most important statistical determinant of variation among the states in levels of taxation is income (Fisher 1964; Dye 1966; Aronson and Hilley 1986). Taxes are higher in "rich" states than in "poor" states. This relationship has been persistently strong over the decades, with correlation coefficients ranging from .68 to .88 in various years. Income is more influential in determining interstate differences in tax levels than any other measure of economic resources or social needs, or any measure of bureaucracy or interest group activity.

It is not surprising that tax revenues are a function of economic development. And the ability to raise revenue is the most important determinant of overall spending levels. In summarizing several decades of empirical research on this topic, economists J. Richard Aronson and John L. Hilley observe:

> Efforts have been made to discover and measure the significant variables (other than population) that explain the diversity among the states. The most important other variable or "cause" is income. In general more will be spent by state and local government in a "rich" state—one with a high per capita income—than in a "poor" state. (p. 33)

Tax levels are so closely related to income that inverse relationships with indicators of social need—poor, aged, and black populations—are created among the states (table 3–3). In contrast, measures of interest group strength—public employee organizations, the size of the state-local employee

Table 3–3
Tax Levels in the American States, Cross-Sectional Analysis for Selected Years

	1984		1975		1960	
	r	β	r	β	r	β
Resources						
Income	.68*	.99*	.75*	.53*	.72*	.54*
Urbanization	.23	−.22	.51*	.16	.51*	.15
Education	.41*	.03	.54*	.13	.44*	.05
Demand for redistribution						
Poor	−.23	.28	−.55*	.03	−.61*	.31*
Aged	−.44*	−.11	−.26	−.03	−.10	.09
Young	−.04	.26	−.05	.13	−.12	.02
Black	−.21	−.19	−.31*	−.14	−.49	−.29
Total R^2	.63		.63		.61	
Government employment						
State-local employees (%)	.50*	.50*	.10	.10	.31*	.31*
Total R^2	.25		.01		.10	
Federal intervention						
Federal aid	.78*	.78*	.34*	.34*	.11	.11
Total R^2	.61		.12		.01	
Bureaucratization and centralization						
Professionalism	−.33*	−.08	−.47*	−.19	−.48	−.22
Public unionism	.46*	.34*	.65*	.35*	.53*	.31*
State centralization	.21	.16	.06	.11	.12	−.07
Interest group activity						
Years	.17	.27	−.15	.04	−.09	.16
Unions	.46*	.30*	.61*	.31*	−.43*	.14
Group strength	−.07	.05	−.52*	−.27	−.52*	−.34
Total R^2	.41		.65		.52	

Note: The dependent variable is state-local tax revenues per capita. Figures are simple correlation coefficients (r), standardized regression coefficients (β), and total explained variance (R^2), for fifty states, except for "Income" where Alaska is excluded as an extreme value. An asterisk indicates a statistically significant relationship.

work force, and unionization of the general work force—are all positively related to higher tax levels.

For every 10 percent increase in a state's per capita income, state-local tax revenues increase, on the average, by approximately 7 percent. This relationship has many exceptions, however. Some states tax themselves more heavily than we would expect based on their incomes; Minnesota, Wisconsin, and New York are in this category. Some states with relative low per capita incomes tax themselves fairly heavily; Montana is an example. Other states

Table 3–4
Tax Burdens in the States, Cross-Sectional Analysis for Selected Years

	1984		1975		1960	
	r	β	r	β	r	β
Resources						
Income	.12	−.03	.31*	.43*	−.12	−.22
Urbanization	.15	.09	.22	.00	−.07	.05
Education	.28	.26	.34	.23	.08	.08
Demand for redistribution						
Poor	−.24	−.01	−.22	.24	.03	.21
Aged	−.02	.13	−.15	.10	−.12	−.36
Young	.02	.13	.09	.27	.05	−.29
Black	−.29	−.26	−.22	−.20	−.29	−.56
Total *R²*	.16		.21		.25	
Government employment						
State-local employees (%)	.50*	.50*	−.12	−.12	.11	.11
Total *R²*	.25		.01		.01	
Federal intervention						
Federal aid	.36*	.36*	.05	.05	.17	.17
Total *R²*	.13		.00		.03	
Bureaucratization and centralization						
Professionalism	−.31	−.08	−.25	−.10	−.05	.01
Public unionism	.39*	.30*	.48*	.27	.01	.09
State centralization	.32	.25	.05	.10	.01	−.10
Interest group activity						
Years	.29	.34*	−.24	−.09	.32*	.48*
Unions	.46*	.35*	.34*	.10	−.19	−.24
Group strength	−.07	.00	−.46*	−.27	−.11	−.34*
Total *R²*	.47		.55		.24	

Note: The dependent variabale is state-local tax revenues as a percentage of personal income. Figures are simple correlation coefficients (*r*), standardized regression coefficients (β), and total explained variance (*R²*), for fifty states, except for "Income," where Alaska is excluded as an extreme. An asterisk indicates a statistically significant relationship.

tax themselves less than one would expect based on their income levels, as do Texas, Florida, and New Hampshire. In short, although income is the principal determinant of tax levels among the states, it is clear that some states carry greater tax burdens than others.

Tax Burdens in the States

We must also be concerned with the burden of taxation on citizen-taxpayers. A variety of measures of tax burden have been devised. The Advising Commission on Intergovernmental Relations (ACIR) has sought to measure the tax capacity of governments by estimating the yield of the average tax rates applied to personal income, retail sales, and value of property (ACIR, *Tax Capacity of the Fifty States*, annual). But we are concerned not so much with the capacity of governmental units to raise revenue as with the tax burdens of citizen-taxpayers. And all major sources of state and local revenue—income, sales, and property taxes—are paid from personal income. Hence our measure of tax burden is simply tax revenues as a percentage of personal income.

Variations in tax burdens among the states are only slightly less in magnitude than variations in tax levels. For example, in 1985, the percentage of personal income devoted to state-local taxes varied from a low of 7.6 percent in New Hampshire to a high of 14.6 percent in New York.

Tax burdens in the states are unrelated to economic resources. In cross-sectional comparisons among the states over three decades, there is no significant or consistent tendency for wealthy, urban, industrial states to impose greater burdens on their citizens than poor, rural, agricultural states. States with larger proportions of dependent populations impose no greater burdens on taxpayers than states with smaller proportions of the needy. Table 3–4 is noteworthy only for the absence of significant relationships.

Bureaucratic, supply-side influences have only a modest relationship with tax burdens in cross-sectional observations. There is a modest tendency for states with centralized bureaucracies, public employee organizations, and large state-local employee work forces to impose heavier tax burdens on their citizens, and there is a slight tendency for older states with strong union movements to do so.

Dynamics of Tax Burdens

In developing a model to explain change over time in state-local tax burdens, we are confronted again with the need to explain contraction as well as growth. As we have already observed, the state-local tax burden in the United States rose to a peak of over 10 percent of personal income during the mid-1970s, retreated to about 8 percent in 1980, and then moved upward again (figure 3–1).

No doubt institutional, supply-side forces contribute to tax burdens. Our cross-sectional analysis lends some support to this notion. But we really want to know whether changes in tax burdens have any relationship to changes in demands confronting state and local government. We want to test the demand-side model against changing tax burdens just as we tested it against changing spending levels. Are state and local government tax burdens responsive to demands for public goods? Can a simple dynamic model—focus-

Table 3–5
Explaining Growth and Contraction in Aggregate
State-Local Tax Burden

	State-Local Tax Revenue As a Percentage of Personal Income	
	Unlagged	*Lagged*
Adjusted R^2	96.7	96.8
T statistics		
% POP 5–17	2.7*	2.7*
% POP 65	0.3	0.3
% Poor	−0.4	−0.4
PCPI	−2.8*	−3.0*
Federal aid	0.2	0.3
Durbin-Watson	1.6	1.6

Note: Time-series regression (Cochrane-Orcutt), annual observations, 1952–1984.

ing on the changes in youth, aged, and poor populations as well as income and federal aid—explain changes in state-local tax burdens?

Tax burdens appear to respond to changes in income. If personal income declines or fails to rise significantly in any year, state-local tax burdens grow heavier. This is the meaning of the negative coefficients reported in table 3–5. This suggests that state-local taxes are inelastic, at least in the short run. Taxes increase steadily from year to year; if rises in income do not match these increases, the tax burden will rise. Conversely, if income growth spurts, state-local tax burdens will moderate. The lesson for citizens and policymakers alike is that economic growth reduces tax burdens.

There is some evidence that at least one demand variable—school-aged population—also affects state-local tax burdens. It has a direct impact on educational spending. Its effect on tax burdens is not quite so strong, yet it is clearly evident. However, changes in other demand variables—the poor and aged populations—have no significant effects on state-local tax burdens. But the influence of the youth variable, representing the demand for education, is noticeable in state-local tax burdens. Tax burdens do reflect over time the need to educate children.

Types of Taxes and Tax Incidence

Overall state and local government revenue sources are very diversified. It is true that some states rely more heavily on income or sales taxes and local governments nearly everywhere rely heavily on property taxes, but in the

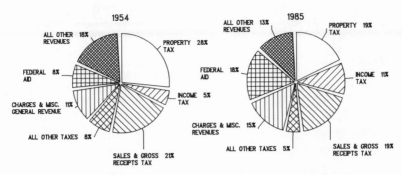

Figure 3–4. Sources of State-Local Government Revenue, 1954 and 1985

aggregate, state-local revenues in the United States are more diversified than those of the federal government. And state-local revenue sources appear to be growing more diversified (figure 3–4).

Property Tax

At the turn of the century, the general property tax reigned as the only important source of state and local revenue. Today property taxes are the major source of revenue for local governments. Real estate is easy to find, and it cannot be easily moved about. A local sales tax can result in merchants and their customers moving beyond city boundaries, and a city income tax can speed the population exodus to suburbia. Because of the dependence of local governments on property taxation, the role of this tax in the total state-local revenue system in the United States remains significant.

Sales Tax

While the property tax is the most important source of revenue for local communities, the general sales tax is the most important source of tax revenue for state governments. Consumers are a notoriously weak pressure group, and opposition by retailers can usually be squelched by state kick-backs of a certain percentage of a tax for the retailers' efforts in collecting it. It is difficult for taxpayers to count pennies dribbled away four or five at a time. The tax is not paid through obvious payroll deductions, as in income taxation, or year-end tax bills, as in property taxation, so its burden is not as visible as that of those other taxes. Even when large items are purchased, the purchaser usually considers the tax as part of the item's cost. In 1985 only five states did not impose a general sales tax (table 3–6).

Table 3–6
States Without Sales and Income Taxes, 1985

States Without General Sales or Gross Receipts Taxes	States Without Individual Income Taxes	States Without Corporate Income Taxes
Alaska	Alaska	Nevada
Delaware	Connecticut[a]	Texas
Montana	Florida	Washington
New Hampshire	Nevada	Wyoming
Oregon	New Hampshire[a]	
	South Dakota	
	Tennessee[a]	
	Texas	
	Washington	
	Wyoming	

[a]These states tax income from interest, dividends, or capital gains but not wages income.

Income Tax

In 1911, Wisconsin passed the first modern, enforceable state income tax. Many other states fell in line after the national government began to tax income in 1913. Like the general sales tax, the income tax can produce a great deal of revenue. In 1985, forty-one states taxed all sources of individual income, and three additional states taxed nonwage income. Some state income taxes have flat rates of 2 percent or 5 percent of taxable income, but most are graduated and progressive like the federal individual income tax. Rates of progressive state income taxes may run from a modest 0.5 percent to 3.5 percent (Ohio) to a steep 2 percent to 16 percent (Minnesota). The corporate income tax is even more popular than the individual income tax; all except four states taxed corporate income in 1985.

Distributional Effects

The state-local tax burden in the United States is estimated to be only mildly regressive. Actually, federal, state, and local tax systems have little distributional effect (see Pechman 1985). Whatever distributional effects government activity produces, these effects are accomplished through government spending, notably transfer payments, rather than through taxing. Nonetheless, it is possible to show that the overall effective rates of state-local taxes "are regressive at the low end of the income distribution, roughly proportional between the second and ninth decile, and progressive at the top decile if the corporate income tax and the property tax are regarded as taxes on capital, or regressive if they are partly a tax on consumption" (ibid., pp. 6–7). However, variations in the estimated effective rates across income classes are so minor (according to Pechman, the lowest income decile pays an effective tax rate of 9.0 percent, while the top decile pays 7.9 percent) that the overall state-local tax incidence is very close to proportional.

While the overall incidence of state-local taxes is close to proportional, some states are more progressive than others in their tax structures. The problem is to measure this variation and then seek to determine what might account for it. There have been relatively few scholarly efforts to measure tax incidence in each of the fifty states. This failure is largely a product of the exceedingly complex calculations about tax incidence across all income categories that must be applied to a wide range of different taxes in the states and then combined according to each state's reliance on separate types of taxes into a single index.[1]

It is likely that the incidence of a state's tax system is closely related to its reliance on income taxes rather than sales or property taxes. The view that property taxes are regressive depends on two assumptions: that renters actually pay these taxes through increased rentals levied by landlords and that high-income individuals have greater proportions of their wealth in untaxed forms of property than middle-income individuals. Since the property tax is the foundation of local government revenue in every state, it is reasonable to conclude that states that rely largely on local governments for the financing of public services—the decentralized states—are relying on more regressive tax systems than states that centralize financing and rely upon state income taxes.

The view that sales taxes are regressive depends on the assumption that low-income groups must devote most, if not all, of their income to purchases, while high-income groups devote larger shares of their income to savings. Many states, however, exclude some of the necessities of life from sales taxation, such as food, housing, and drugs, in order to reduce the burden of sales taxation on the poor. These exemptions make estimates of the incidence of sales taxation very risky. Most state sales taxes are progressive at the lowest income deciles, proportional through the middle deciles, and regressive only at the highest deciles.

State income taxes are frequently recommended on the ability-to-pay principle. This is the theory that the marginal dollar of personal income decreases in value to recipients, and therefore a larger share of it can be taken in taxes at no more of a personal sacrifice than smaller shares of earlier dollars. Most, but not all, state individual income taxes are progressive in their rates (table 3–7). Five states (Illinois, Indiana, Massachusetts, Michigan, Pennsylvania) impose flat rate taxes. A few states have steeply progressive rates, rising from 2 or 3 percent of taxable income to 8 or 10 percent or even 14 percent (New York) and 16 percent (Minnesota).

Table 3–7
State Individual Income Tax Rates

State	Rate Range (Percent)	State	Rate Range (Percent)
Alabama	2.0–5.0 (3)	Mississippi	3.0–5.0 (3)
Arizona	2.0–8.0 (7)	Missouri	3.0–5.0 (3)
Arkansas	1.0–7.0 (6)	Montana	2.0–11.0 (10)
California	1.0–11.0 (11)	Nebraska	20% U.S. tax
Colorado	3.0–8.0 (11)	New Jersey	2.0–3.5
Delaware	1.4–13.5 (15)	New Mexico	0.7–7.8 (19)
Georgia	1.0–6.0 (6)	New York	2.0–14.0 (13)
Hawaii	2.25–11–0 (11)	North Carolina	3.0–7.0 (5)
Idaho	2.0–7.5 (6)	North Dakota	2.0–9.0 (8)
Illinois	3.0	Ohio	0.95–9.5 (8)
Indiana	3.0	Oklahoma	0.5–6.0 (7)
Iowa	0.5–13.0 (13)	Oregon	4.2–10.7 (7)
Kansas	2.0–9.9 (8)	Pennsylvania	2.45
Kentucky	2.0–6.0 (5)	Rhode Island	26% of U.S. tax
Louisiana	2.0–6.0 (3)	South Carolina	2.0–7.0 (6)
Maine	1.0–10.0 (8)	Utah	2.75–7.75 (6)
Maryland	2.0–5.0 (4)	Vermont	26% of U.S. tax
Massachusetts	5.375 (r)	Virginia	2.0–5.75 (4)
Michigan	6.1 (t)	West Virginia	2.1–13.0 (24)
Minnesota	1.6–16.0 (13)	Wisconsin	3.4–10.0 (8)
District of Columbia	2.0–11.0 (10)		

Source: Council on State Governments (1984).
Note: The table excludes the following state taxes: Connecticut taxes interest and dividends at 6 to 13 percent and capital gains at 7 percent. New Hampshire taxes interest and dividends at 5 percent. Tennessee taxes dividends and interest at 6 percent; it imposes a 4 percent tax on dividends from corporations with property at least 75 percent of which is assessable for property tax in Tennessee.
Figures in parentheses are the number of steps in the range.

In addition to property taxes paid to local governments, corporations in forty-six states pay a corporate income tax, ranging from 4 percent of net profits to 12 percent (Minnesota). Raising corporate taxes is popular with voters because individuals do not pay corporate taxes directly. But these taxes may be passed along to consumers in higher prices. Pechman (1985) makes alternative estimates of the incidence of corporate tax: progressive in the top decile if they are regarded as taxes on capital but regressive if they are regarded as taxes on consumption.

Variations in Tax Incidence

We have some limited empirical support for the idea that tax incidence in the states varies with reliance on these different types of taxes. Political scientist David Lowery reports that at least one independent measure of incidence—the Phares measure of combined state and local government tax incidence for each of the fifty states in 1975–1976 (Phares 1980)—is closely related to the early adoption and continued reliance on income taxation (Lowery 1987): "Early adoption of broad-based taxes, especially individual income taxes, is associated with more progressive taxation" (p. 155). Lowery also reports that progressivity is related to larger manufacturing sectors, growing levels of personal income, and competitive political party systems.

In the absence of direct measures of tax incidence in each of the states and with the assumption that progressivity is related to reliance on income taxes, we can examine income tax burdens in the states as a surrogate for tax incidence. Variation among the states in the burdens of income taxation in 1984 ranges from highs of 4.1 and 4.2 percent of personal income in Delaware and Minnesota to a low of 0.1 percent in Tennessee, and, of course, zero in the states without any income tax. We can also examine top marginal tax rates on personal incomes as a measure of tax incidence. It has been argued that by targeting the highest-income persons in the states, high top marginal rates have significant growth-retarding effects on a state's economy. Top marginal income tax rates vary from zero in states without a personal income tax to highs of 14 and 16 percent (table 3–7).

Income tax burdens and top marginal rates are closely related—the simple correlation coefficient for these two measures for 1984 was .79—suggesting a general dimension of progressivity in state tax systems.

Explaining Progressivity

Why have some states developed more progressive tax systems than other states? More specifically, why do some states rely more heavily on income taxation and adopt high top marginal rates than other states? A demand-side explanation might begin by citing the propensity of wealthy, educated, urban populations to enact more progressive taxes in recognition of the ability-to-pay principle. These populations might be hypothesized not only to tax themselves more heavily for more public services but also to be more willing to redistribute some income through progressive taxation: "Simply put, it should be easier to redistribute income from the wealthy to the poor when the wealthy are truly wealthy in an absolute sense" (Lowery 1987, p. 141). Alternatively, we might consider direct demands for redistribution by poor, aged, or black populations. Increases in the proportion of these populations in the electorate might be hypothesized to lead to more progressive tax systems in the states.

A supply-side explanation might begin by focusing on the successful efforts of experienced, professional bureaucrats to enact an income tax with its greater elasticity and potential for revenue. We know that public employee unions in the states, and labor organizations generally, support progressive income taxation over sales and property taxation. Centralization of state government would also be expected to lead to greater reliance on progressive income taxes inasmuch as local governments have greater difficulty in capturing potentially mobile personal income. Over the years, interest group demands may require progressive income taxation to finance accumulated benefits. While income taxation may not be the direct object of interest group activity, an extensive array of government benefits, subsidies, and supports can best be financed by progressive income taxes.

Despite the intuitive appeal of these explanations, there is little evidence from the experience of the states to support either demand-side or supply-side explanations of tax incidence. Progressivity does not appear to be related to income. Wealthier states are no more likely to rely on income taxes or impose higher top marginal rates than poorer states (table 3–8). Nor is progressivity related to demands for redistribution as estimated by the proportion of poor, aged, or black in a state's population. Even more surprising, progressivity in state tax systems is not related to public employee unionism, interest group activity, or even state centralization.

How do we explain the failure of both demand-side and supply-side models to determine variation among the states in our measures of tax incidence? First, these findings are limited to the particular measures employed—income tax burdens and top marginal rates. We believe these are important characteristics of tax system, whether or not they are valid surrogates for tax incidence. But it is possible that some other measure of incidence would better fit our demand or supply model. For example, Lowery (1987) used an updated estimate of Phares's highly complex measure of state-local tax incidence in the fifty states. Lowery produced significant positive coefficients between the Phares measure and per capita personal income; however, his analysis concludes that "the most important finding concerns the importance of past decisions"; by that, he means that the best predictor of progressivity is the early adoption of the income tax. States that first adopted it historically are the states today with the most progressive tax systems. But this historical pattern does not advance our theoretical understanding of the forces contributing to progressivity.

The failure to find support for a demand-oriented explanation for progressivity is not difficult to understand if we consider the "monumental ignorance" (Hansen 1983) of the general public regarding taxation. A median

Table 3–8
Income Taxes in the American States, Cross-Sectional Analysis, 1984

	Income Tax Burden		Top Marginal Rate	
	r	β	r	β
Resources				
Income	−.03	−.34*	−.10	−.16
Urbanization	.06	.02	−.11	−.12
Education	.11	.19	.16	.37*
Demands for redistribution				
Poor	−.14	−.44*	−.05	−.2
Aged	.06	.09	.11	.24
Young	−.03	−.02	.08	.09
Black	.04	.29	−.17	−.11
Total R^2		.11		.14
Government employment				
State-local employees (%)	−.13	−.13	.16	.16
Total R^2		.03		.03
Federal intervention				
Federal aid	.02	.02	.23	.23
Total R^2		.00		.05
Bureaucratization and centralization				
Professionalism	−.08	.08	−.12	−.02
Public unionism	.24	.03	.19	.12
State centralization	−.04	−.01	.11	.11
Interest group activity				
Years	−.29	−.14	.03	.12
Unions	.31	.26	.20	.15
Group strength	−.33	−.21	−.15	−.09
Total R^2		.18		.09

Note: The dependent variables are state personal income taxes as precentage of personal income and top marginal income tax rate. Figures are simple correlation coefficients (r), standardized regression coefficients (β), and total explained variance (R^2), for fifty states, except for "Income," where Alaska is excluded as an extreme value. An asterisk indicates a statistically significant relationship.

voter model cannot be expected to function well where voters lack basic in-formation about taxes and even knowledge of their own tax liabilities. And, of course, equity considerations are only one criterion by which taxes are evaluated. Voters may also consider revenue elasticity, tax simplicity, and ease of collection. To the extent that these other criteria impinge on the selection of tax sources by the states, we would not be able to predict tax reliance by theories explaining only incidence.

The failure to find support for a supply-side explanation—an explana-tion centering on the self-interest of politicians, bureaucrats, or interest groups—is more puzzling. Presumably their information levels and knowledge of the effects of various tax systems are very high. The income tax provides the revenue-generating capability, the elasticity, and even the potential for fiscal illusion through bracket creep, which we would expect to appeal to these groups.

Revolting Against Taxes

Nothing inspires fear in politicians and bureaucrats more than the prospect of a genuine popular revolt against taxation. The American tradition of tax revolts is long-standing. The Boston Tea Party in 1773 was a leading event in the movement toward independence, Shay's Rebellion in 1786 was an important stimulant to the writing of the Constitution and the Whiskey Rebellion in 1794 attracted the personal reprisal of the commander in chief, George Washington.

Today the threat of a tax revolt is a major influence in state and local politics. This is true despite the fact that popular grievances against taxes are directed (accurately) at federal taxation. The federal income tax is most often mentioned as "the worst tax. . . the least fair" (table 3–9). But there is no constitutional mechanism for a national initiative or referendum on taxation. Popular opposition to taxation is institutionally deflected toward state and local taxation. Citizen tax grievances can be expressed directly in statewide initiative and referendums in many states and in referendum voting on taxes and debt in many local governments.

The "tax revolt" is often associated with a 1978 California referendum known as Proposition 13. California citizens were sufficiently aroused to ignore the pleas and warnings of business, labor, and government leaders and pass a property-tax-cutting citizens' referendum by a two-to-one margin. In

Table 3–9
Tax Attitudes

"Which Do You Think is the Worst Tax—that is, the least fair?"				
	1987	1985	1982	1975	1972
Federal income tax	30	36	36	28	19
State income tax	12	10	11	11	13
State sales tax	21	15	14	17	13
Local property tax	24	29	30	33	45
Don't know	13	10	9	11	11

Source: ACIR, *Changing Public Attitudes on Governments and Taxes*, various annual editions.

that same year, ten other state referendums were approved by voter-taxpayers in the states (table 3–10). The tax revolt generated a great deal of commentary by scholars as well as politicians (Citrin 1979; Levy 1979; Field 1978; Sears and Citrin 1982). But in terms of referendum voting, the tax revolt was short-lived. More tax-limiting referendum propositions were defeated than passed in subsequent years through 1986. Some states defeated proposals identical to those passed by other states. Indeed California voters in 1980 rejected Proposition 9, a constitutional amendment to limit state income taxes (Lewis 1980).

Tax limitation proposals fall into several general categories.

Property-Tax Limits

The Proposition 13 type of limitation directed at property taxes usually limits allowable tax rates to 1.0 or 1.5 percent of the full value of property, limits annual assessment increases, and allows reassessments only when the property is sold. This form of limitation applies mainly to local governments and

Table 3–10
Tax Limitation Referendum in the States, 1978–1986

State	Referendum	Yes	No
1978			
Alabama	Restricting property tax increases	60.4%	39.6%
Arizona	State spending limited to 7% of total personal income	78.2	21.8
California	Jarvis Gann Proposition 13 limits on property taxes		
Colorado	Spending increases by state and local governments limited to increases in price index and population	41.5	58.5
Hawaii	State spending can increase only at rate of state economy	66.8	33.2
Idaho	Limit property taxes to 1% of market value	58.4	41.6
Michigan	Tisch amendment to limit annual property tax increases to 2.5%	37.3	62.7
Michigan	Headlee amendment to limit taxes to 9.5% of state personal income	52.5	47.5
Nevada	Limit property taxes to 1% of market value	77.8	22.2
North Dakota	New tax rates require two-thirds vote of legislature	65.1	34.9
Oregon	Limiting property taxes to 1.5% of market value	48.3	51.7
South Dakota	Increases on sales or property tax requires two-thirds vote of legislature	52.9	47.1
Texas	Homestead exemptions and reductions for elderly	84.1	15.9
1980			
Arizona	Tax increase only by two-thirds vote of legislature or voter approval	30.1	19.9

Table 3–10 continued

State	Referendum	Yes	No
California	Proposition 9 limiting state income taxes		
Massachusetts	Proposition 2, limiting local taxes	*59.6*	40.4
Michigan	Tisch amendment, lowering property taxes, requiring 60% voter approval to raise state taxes	44.2	*55.8*
Missouri	General limit on taxes	*55.4*	44.6
Montana	Index state taxes to inflation rate	*69.4*	30.6
Nevada	Limit property taxes	42.4	*57.6*
Oregon	Limit property taxes	34.8	*65.2*
South Dakota	Limit property taxes	37.2	*54.8*
Utah	Limit property taxes	45.2	*54.8*
	Abolish state sales tax	44.1	*55.9*
1982			
Alaska	Limit increases in state appropriations	*60.8*	39.2
Colorado	Limit rate of increase in property taxes	*65.6*	34.4
Maine	Index income taxes to inflation rate	*56.7*	43.3
Oregon	Limit property taxes to 1.5% of the true value	49.2	*50.8*
West Virginia	Property tax limitation and homestead exemption	*80.0*	20.0
1984			
Arizona	Lower limit on state spending	45.3	*54.7*
California	Jarvis amendment to plug looopholes in Proposition 13	45.3	*54.7*
Louisiana	Limit appropriations to growth in personal income	39.4	60.6
Michigan	Require voter approval for all new taxes	40.3	59.7
Nevada	Require new state and local taxes to be proposed by two-thirds vote of legislative body and approved by majority of voters	48.09	*52.0*
Oregon	Limit real property tax rate; require elections for new taxes	49.1	*50.9*
1986			
Alaska	Limit increases in state appropriations	*71.0*	29.0
California	Limit salaries of state officials	34.1	*65.9*
Colorado	Require voter approval of tax increases	37.6	*62.4*
Massachusetts	Limit growth of state revenue	*54.7*	45.3
Montana	Abolish property taxes	44.2	*55.8*
	Limit property taxes; require voter approval for substituting sales or other taxes	*54.9*	45.1
Oregon	Limit property tax rates and assessed value increases	43.1	*56.9*

Sources: *Public Opinion* (November–December 1978; February–March 1981; December–January 1983; December–January 1955; January–February 1987). Winning percentage in italics.

school districts. It may actually increase state taxes if state governments take over local services.

Personal Income Limits

A somewhat more complex scheme, yet one that promises to limit all forms of state and local taxes, is to hold state taxes to a certain percentage of the state's personal income. For example, if state taxes currently amount to 7 percent of a state's total personal income, a constitutional amendment could be offered to voters that limits all future state taxes to a total of no more than 7 percent of personal income. This prevents state government from growing at a faster rate than personal income, but it does allow tax revenues to rise. Such a limit can be effectively administered for state budgets; it is difficult to administer for local governments.

Expenditure Limits

Similar restrictions can be placed on state expenditures. Spending can be limited to a certain percentage of a state's total person income. Presumably expenditure limits would hold down taxes over the long run, and therefore expenditure ceilings can be considered an indirect form of tax limitation.

Public Employment Limits

Another indirect method of containing taxation is to limit state government employment. A state could fix the maximum public employment percentage of the state's population by law or by constitutional amendment and thereby prohibit state and local government employment from growing at a faster rate than the state population. Presumably such a limit would hold down taxes over the long run.

Prohibitions on Specific Taxes

State constitutions can be written or amended to prohibit certain types of taxes or require specific types of exemptions. For example, the state constitution might bar an income tax, a very effective tax limitation.

The homestead exemption is a popular method of excluding some part of the value of owner-occupied homes from property taxes. Homestead exemptions go only to home owners, not to business. These exemptions may be expressed in dollar amounts of assessed value (where the first $5,000 or $10,000 of assessed value of a home is nontaxable) or in terms of percentages of assessed value (where the first 25 percent or 50 percent of assessed value of a home is nontaxable). Personal property tax exemptions are common—exemptions of automobiles, boats, furniture, stocks and bonds, and the like—in part because of the difficulty in identifying and assessing the true value of these types of property. Some states have adopted circuit-breaker programs that exempt property from taxation for individuals who are poor, aged, disabled, and so forth.

Explaining Tax Revolts

Why do people support tax limitation measures? A variety of explanations have been offered and tested in opinion polls, but no single explanation seems to explain why people vote for or against tax limitations.[2]

Self-interest explanation: People who benefit most from government spending should oppose tax limitation measures, while people whose tax burdens are heaviest should support these measures. Despite the popularity of rational theory, this explanation finds only limited support in opinion surveys. High-income home owners are only slightly more supportive of tax limits than beneficiaries of government services.

High-tax explanation: People who pay high taxes should support tax limitations, while people who pay modest taxes should show little interest in the tax revolt. Again, there is little solid evidence to support this theory. Although people who say taxes are high tend to vote in favor of tax limitations, the states that have passed limitations are not necessarily the high-tax-burden states.

"Waste-in-government" explanation: People who think government wastes a lot of money should support tax limitation proposals. Opinion polls do show a relationship between perceived waste and support for tax limits. This implies that tax limitation referendums can be defeated if people can be convinced that tax dollars are not wasted.

Ideological explanation: According to this explanation, conservatives should support tax limits, and liberals should oppose them. According to this rationale, the tax revolt itself is a product of the increasing conservatism of the electorate in the late 1970s and early 1980s. There is some support for this explanation in opinion polls. Conservatives and Republicans tend to support tax limitation measures more than liberals or Democrats do.

Fairness explanation: People who perceive the tax system as unfair should be more likely to vote for tax limitations than people who do not. Some limited evidence in opinion polls supports this explanation.

Alienation explanation: This explanation views the tax revolt as a reflection of declining confidence in government. Negative feelings about government go beyond perceptions of waste, fairness, burdensome taxation and tap deeply felt resentment and alienation from the political system. There is some limited support for this explanation in opinion polls.

It is not surprising that no single explanation of the tax revolt can be offered. Even a combination of the preceding explanations does not fully explain voting on tax proposals. Other explanations may be derived from the specific characteristic of politics in the states in which tax limitation referendums have been voted on. Still other explanations may focus on the specific provisions of the tax limitation amendments being voted upon.

Why do states enact tax limitation measures? The results of opinion polls can tell why individuals support or oppose tax limits, but we would like to inquire whether characteristics of states' political systems are associated with successful tax revolts. It turns out that there were no significant tax policy differences between states that adopted tax limits and those that did not between 1978 and 1982. Political scientist Susan Hansen (1983) found no significant differences between adopters and nonadopters with regard to taxes per capita, taxes as a percentage of personal income, tax progressivity, or reliance on income tax and sales taxation. What she found, however, was that the constitutional availability of direct voting on initiatives and referendums was the most important distinguishing characteristic between states that adopted tax limits and those that did not. She concludes that "the combination of high taxes, progressive taxes, and opportunities for direct legislation has resulted in efforts by citizens in the states to change their tax burdens" (p. 234). In other words, the preferences of individual citizen-taxpayers for lower tax burdens, fairer tax systems, and less waste in government are best reflected in states with constitutional provisions for direct voting on initiatives and referendums.

The Effectiveness of Tax Revolts

Do tax revolts reduce tax burdens? The evidence on this crucial point is difficult to derive. We can observe whether the adoption of tax limitation proposals in specific states was followed by a significant reduction in tax burdens. That may seem like a straightforward test of the effectiveness of tax revolts, but it can always be argued, in "what-might-have-been" fashion, that tax burdens would have come down even without the adoption of a tax limitation initiative. Or, alternatively, it can be argued that tax burdens, in cases where they continue to rise after the adoption of a tax limit initiative, would have risen even faster if the tax limit had not passed.

It is also quite possible that the anticipatory actions of government officials may obscure the direct effect of tax initiatives. Officials may hope to head off more drastic citizen initiatives by reducing taxes. Or passage of a citizen initiative may be taken as a signal to politicians to lower taxes even beyond that required by the initiative itself.

Tax limitation initiatives come in various shapes and sizes. There are many ways for governments to sidestep their intent. For example, restrictions on property taxes may simply result in heavier burdens of income, sales, or corporate taxes. Restrictions on local governments may result in heavier state-level taxation. Certain moneys may be exempted from restrictions (for example, unemployment insurance, workman compensation, and other earmarked funds); expenditures can then be shuffled between restricted and unrestricted uses. If restrictions apply to some governmental units and not others, taxes and expenditures can be shifted from restricted to unrestricted units. The ceilings on some restrictions are quite generous, permitting increases for population growth and inflation in addition to personal income. Most states also exempt user charges and utility revenues from limitations. Finally, administration of the limits may not be effective.

In short, there are many reasons for questioning the effectiveness of tax limitation initiatives. Indeed, Aronson and Hilley (1986) conclude that "fiscal limitations have not always been completely effective" (p. 224). Hansen (1983) concludes: "But what about ordinary taxpayers? Have their taxes been reduced? The answer to that seemingly straight forward question is mostly 'no'" (p. 234).

Our concern here with the effect of tax limitations on total state and local tax burdens. Our measure—total state and local government (combined) tax revenues as a percentage of personal income—should capture any shifting of tax burdens from one unit of government to another or from one tax source to another. It should also capture any anticipatory behavior of government officials.

Let us observe trends in total state and local tax burdens in the three states in which tax revolts captured nationwide attention: California, Massachusetts, and Michigan. California's Proposition 13 affected local governments by rolling back property tax assessments and placing a ceiling on property tax rates. Massachusetts's Proposition 2½ in 1980 was also aimed at local property taxes. Both initiatives left open the possibility of shifting tax burdens from local to state government. Michigan's Headlee amendment in 1978 was more complex. It was essentially a limit on state government, holding own-source state revenues to a constant share of state personal income while prohibiting state government from mandating expenditures to local governments without paying for them. It also constrained local property taxes on existing property not to grow at a rate faster than the consumer price index, although larger increases could be voted in local referendums.

These provisions would seem to prevent shifting of taxes among levels of government. To observe whether the burdens on citizen-taxpayer in these states were actually affected by these initiatives, we should look at combined state and local taxes.

The effect of Proposition 13 on tax burdens in California appears dramatic (figure 3–5). Total state and local tax burdens, which had risen somewhat bumpily in that state from 9½ percent of personal income in 1957 to 13½ percent in 1978, dropped to 10½ percent in the year the proposition took effect—a 22 percent drop in tax burden in a single year. It would be difficult to attribute such a dramatic drop to anything other than the state's tax revolt.

It is more difficult to attribute reductions in tax burdens in Massachusetts directly to Proposition 2½ (figure 3–6). Personal income began to grow rapidly in that state after 1978. Taxes have not risen at the same rate as personal income in recent years; hence tax burdens have declined steadily. The Massachusetts tax burden reached its peak years in 1977 and 1978. The decline in burdens began before Proposition 2½, which passed in 1980 and took effect in 1981. It certainly can be argued that this tax initiative was consistent with the continued downward trend in tax burdens, but the evidence is weak that Proposition 2½ caused a reduction in tax burdens. Massachusetts's good fortune must be attributed mostly to its economic recovery.

The effect of the Headlee amendment in Michigan is virtually imperceptible (figure 3–7). Tax burdens in that state were not noticeably reduced by

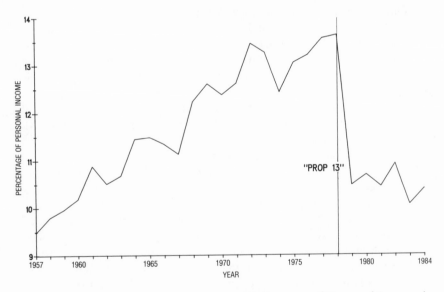

Figure 3–5. State-Local Tax Revenue as a Percentage of Personal Income in California, 1957–1984

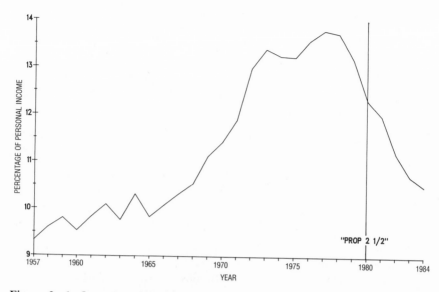

Figure 3–6. State-Local Tax Revenue as a Percentage of Personal Income in Massachusetts, 1957–1984

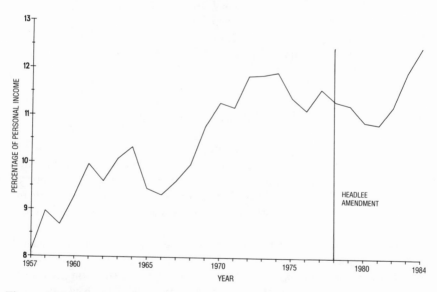

Figure 3–7. State-Local Tax Revenue as a Percentage of Personal Income in Michigan, 1957–1984

Table 3–11
The Impact of Tax Limitation Initiatives on Tax Burdens

State	Year Adopted	Limit	Tax Limit as Dummy Variable	
			Coefficient	T statistic
California	1978	Proposition 13	− .04	− 15.21*
Massachusetts	1980	Proposition 2½	− .03	− 6.87*
Michigan	1978	Headlee	− .004	− 0.98

Note: Time series (Cochrane Orcutt), total state and local government tax revenues as a percentage of personal income, 1952–1984. An asterisk indicates a statistically significant relationship.

the amendment, though it would seem to be the most strongly worded constitutional restraint.

Formal modeling of these tax limitations in California, Massachusetts, and Michigan confirms the judgments derived from figures 3–5, 3–6, and 3–7. In table 3–11 each tax initiative is treated as a dummy variable in a time-series regression on total state-local tax revenues as a percentage of personal income. The results confirm that California's Proposition 13 was very influential in reducing tax burdens; Proposition 2 ½ in Massachusetts is also influential in lowering tax burdens although less so than Proposition 13; and Michigan's Headlee amendment failed to have a significant impact on tax burdens in that state.

Competitive Federalism and Constrained Choice

The separation of taxing from spending decisions generally confounds rational voter-taxpayers, lessens constraints on government activities, and leads to an oversupply of government goods and services. But multiple competitive governments are more constrained than centralized monopoly government. Competition better informs both decision makers and taxpayers of the costs of public services.

State and local government is generally more responsive than the federal government to the fiscal preferences of taxpayers. This greater responsiveness is not only a product of competition but also a result of institutional arrangements in these governments that link taxing and spending decisions. Earmarked revenues, user charges, initiative and referendum voting, and requirements for balanced budgets all function to constrain state and local spending decisions.

Bureaucratic supply-side forces are evident in state and local government, but so also are demand-side forces, notably school-aged population. The state-local tax burden contracts when demand contracts. Economic growth—growth in per capita personal income—lowers state-local tax burdens even as it increases levels of tax revenues.

The overall incidence of state-local taxation in the United States is close to proportional. It is true that some states appear to have more progressive tax structures than other states, as well as higher top marginal income tax rates. This variation appears to be more a product of historical experience than any identifiable demand for redistribution or even any identifiable bureaucratic influence.

Tax revolts, defined as popular initiatives and referendums to limit state or local taxes, are probably more important for the fear they inspire in politicians than their actual success in reducing tax burdens. More tax-limiting referendums have been defeated at the polls than have been approved. And it is sometimes difficult to identify significant effects of those that passed. But state-local tax burdens can be lowered by direct citizen action, as the California experience demonstrates.

In summary, government whose tax incidence tends toward proportionality, whose tax burdens tend to reflect legitimate demands for public services, whose institutional arrangements tend to link taxing and spending decisions, and whose tax burdens can be reduced by direct citizen action are preferable to centralized monopoly government that lacks these features.

Notes

1. Pechman (1985) performed these kinds of calculations to estimate the overall incidence of state-local taxes in the nation; this task would be multiplied by fifty for anyone wishing to make estimates of tax incidence for each state. Scholars have experienced only limited success in this task (Fry and Winters 1970; Phares 1980).

2. The following discussion relies on the theoretical concepts and reports of opinion surveys in Lowery and Sigelman (1981); Buchanan (1979); Beck and Dye (1982); Ladd (1979); and Hansen (1983).

4

Federal Interventions

> When all government . . . shall be drawn to Washington as the center of all power, it will become as venal and oppressive as the government from which we separated.
> —Thomas Jefferson, 1805

> By divorcing expenditure from revenue, what people want is separated from what they are willing to give. Revenue sharing distorts state citizenship and state responsibility.
> ——Aaron Wildavsky, "Birthday Cake Federalism," 1982

To what extent do federal interventions distort the taxing and spending decision of states and communities and lessen the responsiveness of public policies to the preferences of consumer-taxpayers? One of the assumptions of our competitive federalism model is that the federal government refrains from activities that distort the calculation of benefits and burdens by consumer-taxpayers in states and communities. Let us turn to an assessment of the extent to which federal interventions degrade the model.

Money, Power, and Federalism

The date 1913 marked the beginning of the end of traditional federalism in the United States. The states, by ratifying the Sixteenth Amendment to the Constitution and granting the national government the power to tax incomes directly, unwittingly set in motion the institutional forces that would shift the balance of power from the states to Washington. The income tax gave the federal government the power to raise large sums of money, which it proceeded to spend for the general welfare as well as for defense. Congress did not restrict its spending to its enumerated functions in Article I, section 8 of the Constitution. Instead it chose to spend money for functions previously thought to be reserved to the states. It is no coincidence that the first major cash grant-in-aid programs (agricultural extension in 1914, highways in 1916, vocational education in 1917, and public health in 1918) came shortly after the inauguration of the federal income tax.

At the beginning of the twentieth century, most government activity in the United States was carried on at the local level. Table 4–1 shows that local

Table 4–1

**A Comparison of the Expenditures of Federal, State, and Local
Governments over Eight Decades**
(percentages of total general expenditures of governments)

	Federal[a]	State[b]	Local[b]
1902	35	6	59
1927	31	13	56
1936	50	14	36
1944	91	3	7
1950	60	16	24
1960	60	15	25
1970	62	10	28
1980	64	9	27
1985	65	10	25

Source: U.S. Department of Commerce *Statistical Abstract of the United States 1988*, p. 257.
[a]Figures include social security and trust fund expenditures.
[b]State payments to local governments are shown as local government expenditures; federal
grants-in-aid are shown as federal expenditures.

governments once made about 59 percent of all government expenditures in
the United States, compared to 35 percent for the federal government and 6
percent for state governments. But the Great Depression of the 1930s and
World War II in the 1940s helped bring about centralization in the federal
system. In recent decades, federal spending has amounted to 55 to 60 percent
of all government spending in the United States.

The extent of centralization of government activity in the American federal system varies widely according to policy area (table 4–2). In the fields of
national defense, space research, and postal service, the federal government
assumes almost exclusive responsibility. In all other fields, state and local
governments share responsibility and costs with the federal government. State
and local governments assume the major share of the costs of education,
highways, health and hospitals, sanitation, and fire and police protection.
Welfare costs have gradually shifted to the federal government, and the federal government assumes the major share of the costs of natural resource
development and housing and urban renewal.

The federal grant-in-aid has been the principal instrument for the expansion of national power. Federal land grants are as old as the nation itself. The
First Congress of the United States, in the famous Northwest Ordinance, providing for the governance of the territories to the west of the Appalachian
Mountains, authorized grants of federal land to the states for the establishment of public schools and in the process showed a concern for an area "re-

Table 4–2
Federal and State-Local Shares of Expenditures by Policy Area, 1927–1985

	1927		1938		1970		1985	
	Federal	*State and Local*	*Federal*	*State and Local*	*Federal*	*State and Local*	*Federal*	*State and Local*
National defense	100%	0%	100%	0%	100%	0%	100%	0%
Education	1	99	6	94	15	85	14	86
Highways	1	99	23	77	23	77	27	73
Welfare	6	94	13	87	41	59	72	28
Health and hospitals	18	82	19	81	34	66	29	71
Police and fire	7	93	5	95	8	92	14	86
Natural resources	31	69	81	19	77	23	85	15
Housing and urban renewal	—	—	—	—	56	44	65	35

Source: U.S. Bureau of the Census *Government Finances 1984–85*.
Note: Federal grants-in-aids are shown as federal expenditures.

served" to the states by the Constitution's Tenth Amendment. In 1863 in the Morrill Act, Congress provided grants of land to the states to promote higher education. The first cash grant has been traced to an 1887 federal law financing state-operated agricultural experiment stations. But the real impetus for intergovernmental cash transfers came in the period 1914–1921, immediately following the adoption of the Sixteenth Amendment. In 1936 the Supreme Court agreed to a broad interpretation of the power of the national government to spend money for the general welfare (*United States* v. *Butler*). According to the Court, Congress's power to spend money was not limited in purpose to its other enumerated powers.

As late as 1952, federal intergovernmental transfers amounted to about 10 percent of all state and local government revenue (figure 4–1). Federal transfers creeped up slowly for a few years, leaped ahead after 1957, with the National Defense (Interstate) Highway Program and a series of post-Sputnik educational programs, and then surged in the welfare, health, housing, and community development fields during the Great Society period (1965–1975). President Richard Nixon not only expanded these Great Society transfers but added his own general revenue-sharing program. Federal financial interventions continue to grow despite occasional rhetoric in Washington about state and local responsibility. By 1980, over 20 percent of all state-local revenue came from the federal government. So dependent had state and local governments become on federal largess, that the most frequently voiced rationale for continuing federal grant programs was that states and commu-

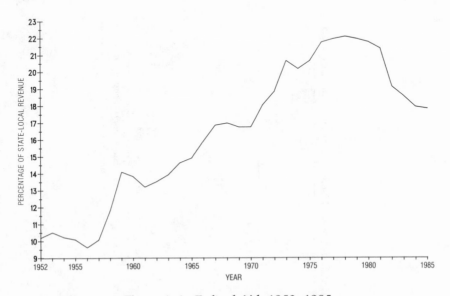

Figure 4–1. Federal Aid, 1952–1985

nities had became accustomed to federal money and could not survive without it.

Ronald Reagan challenged the nation's movement toward centralized government:

> Our citizens feel they have lost control of even the most basic decisions made about the essential services of government, such as schools, welfare, roads, and even garbage collection. They are right. A maze of interlocking jurisdictions and levels of government confronts the average citizen in trying to solve even the simplest of problems. They do not know where to turn to for answers, who to hold accountable, who to praise, who to blame, who to vote for or against. The main reason for this is the overpowering growth of federal grants-in-aid programs during the past few decades. (State of the Union Address, January 1982).

Washington had heard that kind of rhetoric from Republican presidents before, but Reagan actually proceeded to reverse the growing dependency of state and local governments on federal money. Federal intergovernmental transfers fell from a high of about 22 percent of total state-local revenue to a more modest 18 percent by 1985 (figure 4–1). Most of what Reagan accomplished in this area occurred in the first years of his presidency.

The Reagan administration failed in its more ambitious efforts to restructure American federalism, however. Reagan proposed to turn back a variety of policy responsibilities to the states, including welfare and social services, food stamps, mass transit, adult education, health services, housing, and community development, in exchange for federal assumption of Medicaid costs and a turnback of federal excise taxes to the states. But this major effort at "devolution of responsibilities to governments that are closer to the people" met with widespread political opposition. State and local officials wanted relief from federal guidelines, regulations, and conditions attached to federal funds, but they feared the financial burdens of independent responsibility for major welfare, food stamp, transportation, and housing programs. Welfare lobbyists predicted that transferring these responsibilities to the states would result in lower benefit levels than they could elicit from the federal government. And although public opinion surveys regularly reported that voters believed welfare was too expensive and too many people got on welfare rolls who were not "truly deserving," no widespread popular support emerged for Reagan's version of "New Federalism." Most voters—despite their preference for lower welfare spending—believed it was a federal responsibility.

The Reagan administration did succeed in its efforts to eliminate general revenue sharing (GRS), to consolidate many categorical grant programs in larger block grants with greater local control over revenue allocation, and to

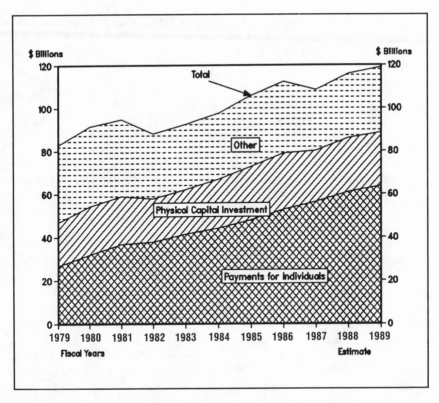

$ Billions $ Billions
120 ──────────────── Total ────────────────── 120
                                                              100
100 ─
                              Other   80
 80 ─
                    Physical Capital Investment   60
 60 ─
 40 ─   40
                         Payments for Individuals   20
 20 ─
  0 ┴── 0
    1979 1980 1981 1982 1983 1984 1985 1986 1987 1988 1989
    Fiscal Years   Estimate

Figure 4–2. Federal Grants to State and Local Governments, 1979–1989

reduce the rate of growth in federal intergovernmental transfer payments. Regarding GRS, the president argued that it was unreasonable to expect the federal government, which was running deep deficits, to turn over revenues to state and local governments, which had no deficits. Most GRS funds went for traditional services (police, fire, streets, sanitation, sewage, parks and recreation, etc.) that local taxpayers should fund themselves. For several years, state and local government officials successfully lobbied Congress to restore GRS funds cut from the president's budget, but deficit pressures finally ended GRS in 1986.

The Reagan administration also succeeded in consolidating many categorical grant programs into fewer large block grant programs. A block grant is a payment to a state or local government for a general function, such as community development or education. State and local officials may use such funds for their stated purpose without seeking the approval of federal agencies for specific projects. Many categorical grant programs were merged, but many others remained independent.

Table 4–3
Trends in Federal Grants-in-Aid

| | | Federal Grants as a Percentage of: | | |
	Total ($ billions)	Total Federal Spending	State and Local Expenditures	Gross National Product
1950	2.3	5.3	10.4	0.8
1960	7.0	7.6	14.6	1.4
1970	24.1	12.3	19.2	2.4
1975	49.8	15.0	22.7	3.3
1980	91.5	15.5	25.8	3.4
1985	105.9	11.2	21.1	2.7
1988 (est.)	106.3	10.4	20.6	2.2

Source: U.S. Office of Management and Budget, *Special Analysis of the Budget 1988*, p. H-22.

Total federal aid dollars to state and local government continued to rise during the Reagan administration but not at the same rate of increase as in previous years. Some dips occurred in 1982 and 1987 (figure 4–2), yet overall grant-in-aid expenditures rose from $79 billion in 1978 to $106 billion in 1988. Nonetheless, many state and local officials sought to blame "cutbacks in federal aid" for any troubles they encountered. It is true, of course, that federal aid declined somewhat in relative terms: as a percentage of GNP, as a percentage of total federal outlays, and, most important, as a percentage of state-local revenue (Table 4–3). But this occurred because grants did not rise as fast as these denominators, not because of any overall cutbacks.

A critical summary of the Reagan accomplishments in federalism concludes:

> In sum, the administration has reversed the trend of growing financial dependence of lower levels of government on the national government, put in place a grant structure that is less restrictive and provides less encouragement to local spending, challenged the assumption that there should be uniform national standards for public services, and more fully engaged the states as partners in the effort to contain domestic program costs. (Palmer and Sawhill 1984, p. 18)

A Rent-Seeking Theory of Government Centralization

Debates about federalism are seldom constitutional debates; rather, they are debates about policy. People decide which level of government—national, state, or local—is most likely to enact the policy they prefer. Then they argue that that level of government should have the responsibility for enacting the policy. Political scientist David Nice (1987) explains "the art of intergovernmental politics": "trying to reduce, maintain, or increase the scope of conflict in order to produce the policy decisions you want" (p. 24).

Arguments for federal intervention are seldom made on efficiency grounds. A concern for externalities in state government policies—costs or benefits that may spill over state boundaries and policy effects that are truly national in scope—is never seriously debated in the political arena. Although economists in the fiscal federalism tradition are concerned with economies of scale and spillovers, political scientists have rarely been concerned with efficiency. Indeed, the scholarly work of Paul Peterson (1981, 1986, 1988) on American federalism is exceptional in its serious consideration of the externalities of state policy, especially welfare policy.

Rather, the case for federal intervention is almost always one of substituting the policy preferences of national elites for those of state and local officials. It is not seriously argued on constitutional grounds that national elites better reflect the policy preferences of the American people. Federal intervention is defended on policy grounds—the assertion that the goals and priorities that prevail in Washington should prevail throughout the nation.

The national government is more likely to reflect the policy preferences of the nation's strongest and best organized interest groups than eighty-three thousand state and local governments. This is true, first, because the costs of "rent seeking"—lobbying government for special subsidies, privileges, and protections—are less in Washington in relation to the benefits available from national legislation than the combined costs of rent seeking at eighty-three thousand subnational centers. Organized interests, seeking concentrated benefits for themselves and dispersed costs to the rest of society, can concentrate their own resources in Washington. Even if state and local governments individually are more vulnerable to the lobbying efforts of wealthy, well-organized special interests, the prospect of influencing all fifty separate state governments, or worse, eighty-three thousand local governments, is discouraging to them. The costs of rent seeking at fifty state capitols, three thousand county court houses, and tens of thousands of city halls, while not multiplicative by these numbers, are certainly greater than the costs of rent seeking in a single national capitol.

Moreover, the benefits of national legislation are comprehensive. A single act of Congress, or a federal executive regulation, or a federal appellate court ruling can achieve what would require the combined and coordinated action by hundreds, if not thousands, of state and local government agencies. Thus, the benefits of rent seeking in Washington are larger in relation to the costs. Lobbying in Washington is efficient.

Finally, and perhaps most important, the size of the national constituency permits interest groups to disperse the costs of specialized, concentrated benefits over a very broad constituency. Cost dispersal is the key to interest group success. If costs are widely dispersed, it is irrational for individuals, each of whom bears only a tiny fraction of these costs, to expend time, energy, and money to counter the claims of the special interests. Dispersal of costs over the entire nation better accommodates the strategies of special interest groups than the smaller constituencies of state and local government.

In contrast, state and local government narrows the constituencies over which costs must be spread, thus increasing the burdens to individual taxpayers and increasing the likelihood that they will take notice of these burdens and resist their imposition. Economist Randall G. Holcombe (1986) explains:

> One way to counteract this [interest group] effect is to provide public goods and services at the smallest level of government possible. This concentrates the cost on the smallest group of taxpayers possible and thus provides more concentrated costs to accompany the concentrated benefits. (p. 174)

He goes on to speculate whether the tobacco subsidies granted by Washington to North Carolina farmers would be voted by the residents of that state if they had to pay the full costs of these subsidies. Lobbying in Washington disperses costs.

The rent-seeking efficiencies of lobbying in Washington are well known to the organized interests. As a result, the policies of the national government are more likely to reflect the preferences of the nation's strongest and best-organized interests. This is not to say that state and local governments are immune to the entreaties of organized interests; on the contrary, individually they are probably more vulnerable than the national government. It is widely reported that lobbying in state capitols is less restrained and more coercive than lobbying in Washington (Zeigler 1983). But collectively state policies reflect a greater diversity in interests. Interests that are strong in some state are not necessarily strong in other states (see Morehouse 1981). Indeed, the diversity of interests represented in fifty state capitols helps to explain the variation in public policy among the states.

The Baneful Effects of Federal Grants

Federal interventions are designed to substitute the policy preferences of a national elite for the preferences of multiple state and local elites. The effect of federal intervention is to reduce the responsiveness of state policies to the preferences of state citizen-taxpayers.

Federal grants to state and local governments distort the relationship between benefits and burdens of public services. Even if the federal grant is unconditional (that is, it requires no matching local funds), it nonetheless causes local governments to provide a level of public service that is greater than the willingness of consumer-taxpayers to pay for these services. In other words, it creates an oversupply of public goods. If it is a conditional or matching grant, requiring some local outlays to receive federal funds, it creates two distortions: it causes governments to provide an oversupply of public goods, and it results in an increase in the burdens of local government. In other words, a matching grant not only affects the expenditures of local governments but also stimulates local revenue raising. Consumer-taxpayers are bribed into providing far more public goods than they would otherwise choose for themselves. And they are blackmailed into doing so by the realization that if they do not provide these federally favored services, their own federal tax dollars will flow to other jurisdictions, which are more willing to accept these dollars.

To the extent that the judgments of consumer-taxpayers are distorted by federal grants, the efficiency effects of competitive federalism are diluted. Consumer-taxpayers are given the wrong information about the true costs of public services. They are informed that these public services cost less than they actually do. This misinformation results in higher levels of public service, and in the case of matching grants, higher local tax levels, than consumer-taxpayers would otherwise purchase for themselves.

Economists have theorized that federal aid would have different distorting effects on the public-private trade-off depending on the form of the grant: whether it was a required matching grant or an unrestricted grant (see Hirsch 1970). Unrestricted grants encourage higher levels of government spending, but part of the federal aid will be used to decrease local contributions to government activity and allow some money to be retained for private purposes. In other words, unrestricted federal aid may be substitutive of local effort. But most federal aid is provided on a matching basis in order to avoid substitution. When aid is provided on a matching basis, it is stimulative of local effort. Federal aid also distorts spending among different government services. Unrestricted grants to a federally favored government activity may be substitutive, but matching federal grants to a favored activity will reduce resources to all other state and local government activities.

Recently political scientist John E. Chubb (1985) wrote that these economic models "overlook the influence of political and administrative hierarchy" in directing state and local government activity. He argues that various forms of federal coercion—"for example financial audits, field inspections, reporting requirements, and the cultivation of professional allegiances [among state and local bureaucrats]"—can "encourage state and local governments to use federal grants appropriately" (p. 1005). Coercive tactics can be used to make all forms of federal grants stimulative; without coercion, matching grants can become substitutive. Federal bureaucrats "can audit, investigate, threaten, encourage, and most important, cultivate professional support among state and local governments to bring about the desired level of compliance" (p. 1011). This "good news" may relieve the doubts of Washington lobbyists regarding the power of federal money, but if anything, its adds to our contention that federal aid distorts the relationships between policies and preferences in states and localities.

Federal Aid and Decreased Responsiveness

Empirical research on the distorting effects of federal grants grew out of the early economic research on the determinants of state and local government expenditures. In one of the earliest empirical studies of state and local spending, using data for 1942, economist Solomon Fabricant found that variations among the states in economic resources (per capita income, population density, and urbanization) accounted for 72 percent of the variation (cross-sectional) among the states in total state-local spending (Fabricant 1952). Because so much policy variation was shown to be related to these social and economic characteristics of state populations, it was easy to infer that state-local policies were highly responsive to economic conditions in the states. By 1960, however, it appeared that economic resources were losing some of their explanatory power in relation to state-local spending, especially spending for welfare and health. Economists Seymour Sachs and Robert Harris (1964) observed that the ability of income, density, and urbanization to explain interstate variation in total state-local spending declined from 72 percent in 1942 to 53 percent in 1960 (table 4–4). They particularly noted the decline in the explanatory power of these resources in the area of welfare spending (from 45 percent of explained variation in 1942 to 11 percent in 1960) and health (from 72 percent of explained variance in 1942 to 44 percent in 1960).

The decline in the explanatory power of economics resources was largely attributable to the intervening effect of federal grants-in-aid. Federal grants were outside money, freeing state and local officials from the constraints of their own economic resources—hence the decline in the closeness of the relationship between state resources and state spending.

Simple replication and updating, by means of consecutive cross-sectional analyses, of the Sachs and Harris study reveals the continuing decline in constraints placed upon the states by their own resources. (See the "Economic Development" columns for 1970 and 1980 in table 4–4.) The explanatory power of economic resources on state-local spending has continued to decline through the 1970s and early 1980s.

More important, we can estimate the growing importance of federal aid in determining levels of state and local government spending. Table 4–4

Table 4–4
State Economic Resources, Federal Aid, and State-Local Spending

| | Economic Development | | | State-Local Spending, Percentage Determined by: | | | | | |
	1942	1957	1960	Plus Federal Aid, 1960	Economic Development, 1970[b]	Plus Federal Aid, 1970	Economic Development, 1980[b]	Plus Federal Aid, 1980
Total	.72	.53	.53	.81	.47	.89	.37	.88
Education	.59	.62	.60	.81	.36	.55	.37	.68
Welfare	.45	.14	.11	.83	.18	.20	.09	.12
Health	.72	.46	.44	.47	.28	.31	.03	.08
Highways	.29	.34	.37	.83	.36	.81	.22	.65

Source: Early figures from Sachs and Harris (1964). Figures for 1970 and 1980 from $TATE$ (see Appendix).

Note: Figures are R^2s, explained variance, among forty-eight states for 1942, 1957, and 1960 and among fifty states for 1970 and 1980.

[a]Economic development for 1942, 1957, and 1960 defined by Sachs and Harris as per capita personal income, population density, and urbanization.

[b]Economic development for 1970 and 1980 defined as per capita personal income, education, and urbanization.

shows what happens when per capita federal aid is included in the explanation of state-local spending. The original Sachs and Harris study showed an increase in explained variance for total state-local spending for 1960 from 53 percent to 81 percent and an equally dramatic increase in explained variance for spending in each functional area. We have replicated the Sachs and Harris analyses for 1970 and 1980 (and other years not shown). Note that federal aid increases the explained variance in total state-local spending in 1970 from 47 to 89 percent and in 1980 from 37 to 88 percent. In summary, although it is true that income remains an important "determinant" of levels of public spending among the states, the explanatory power of income has decreased over time, and that of federal aid has grown. This suggests that levels of public spending are now less constrained by resources and more dependent on federal money.

Reducing the constraints on state-local officials and citizen-taxpayers in the states results in larger expenditures for public purposes than they otherwise would choose. The cross-sectional evidence indicates that federal aid closely correlates with both levels of spending in the states and burdens imposed by this spending (table 4–5). This cross-sectional association has become stronger over the years as the states have became more dependent on federal aid. In recent years, state-local taxation has also been closely correlated with federal aid, suggesting a federal stimulative effect.

Do changes in federal aid help explain expansion and contraction in state-local spending? The cross-sectional evidence (table 4–5) shows that states with higher levels of per capita federal aid spend more and tax more than states with lower levels of federal aid. But we also want to know whether changes in state-local taxing and spending levels and burdens over time are related to changing levels of federal aid. The time-series results are presented in table 4–6. Note that changes in federal aid also have a strong positive effect on changes in spending—both levels and burdens. Changes in federal aid do not have a similarly strong effect on tax levels or burdens.

Table 4–5
Federal Aid and State-Local Taxing and Spending, Cross-Sectional Analyses for Selected Years

	1984	1975	1970	1960
Total state-local spending				
Levels: Spending per capita	.88	.83	.74	.54
Burdens: Spending as a percentage of income	.93	.79	.89	.54
Total state-local taxing				
Levels: Taxes per capita	.71	.34	.15	.11
Burdens: Taxes as a percentage of income	.89	.35	.21	.17

Note: The independent variable is per capita federal intergovernmental revenue. Figures are simple cross-sectional correlation coefficients.

Table 4–6
Federal Aid and Changes in State-Local Taxing and Spending, Time-Series Analyses, 1952–1984

Dependent Variables	T Statistics			
	Per Capita Personal Income	Per Capita Federal Aid	R_2	D-W
State-local spending				
Levels: Spending per capita	8.4*	3.7*	99.8	1.7
Burdens: Spending as a percentage of income	−2.8*	2.6*	97.2	1.7
State-local taxing				
Levels: Taxes per capita	7.8*	1.8	99.8	1.7
Burdens: Taxes as a percentage of income	−2.2*	0.1	96.3	1.4

Note: Time-series regressions (Cochrane-Orcutt), annual observations, 1952–1984. An asterisk indicates a statistically significant relationship.

The Nontargeting of Federal Aid

A principal rationale for federal aid over the years has been its assumed equalizing effect across jurisdictions. Poorer state and local governments, serving larger proportions of needy persons—the aged, poor, and minorities—were assumed to benefit the most from the redistributional effects of federal grants. By compensating for the lack of local resources and by directing federal aid to those jurisdictions confronting the most pressing demands, the federal grant-in-aid system was seen as a major equalizing mechanism and a guarantee of minimum nationwide levels of public service. The federal government was supposed to rectify the mismatch of demands and resources across states and communities and offset fiscal disparities among subnational governments. Indeed, allocation formulas in some federal aid programs included income and poverty measures, indicating congressional interest in directing funds to governments with greater social needs and fewer resources.

It turns out, however, that most federal aid is not targeted to governments with the greatest needs or fewest resources. The thrust of empirical research on this important question in recent years has been to demonstrate that federal intergovernmental transfers are not targeted toward governments with larger proportions of needy persons or toward governments with fewer resources of their own. On the contrary, total federal aid allocations are only weakly related to measures of social need and fiscal capacity. Moreover, it turns out that state governments on the whole have demonstrated a much greater ability than the federal government to target their intergovernmental transfers to needy cities.

Comparative analysis of federal and state aid allocations to cities found a significant but modest targeting effort only for state aid allocations. Federal aid allocations were not significantly related to any measure of fiscal capacity or effort (Dye and Hurley 1978). In contrast, state aid allocations were closely tied to measures of community need, fiscal capacity, and effort. Separate studies (Pelissero 1984, 1985; Pelissero and Morgan 1987) of state aid allocations to large cities and school districts confirmed these early findings. Stein's (1981b, 1982) analyses of interstate variation in state aid allocations provided an important qualification to this body of research. The targeting capacity exhibited by all states in a pooled analysis was actually a function of the targeting efforts of only a handful of states ($N = 16$), with the majority of states exhibiting no significant targeting capacity.

Studies of federal aid allocations have shown only modest evidence of significant targeting on fiscal capacity or effort. Copeland and Meier (1984) failed to detect any evidence of a disproportionate allocation of federal aid monies to high-effort and low-capacity states. Saltzstein (1977) also found no evidence of significant federal aid targeting to Texas cities, and Cuccitti's (1978) analysis of federal aid allocations to the forty-five largest cities found only modest evidence of preferential treatment for distressed and low-capacity communities. Finally, the distributional impact of federal project grants—those allocated on the basis of competitive applications—has shown similarly modest and inconsistent targeting efforts on dimensions of fiscal capacity and effort (Gist and Hill 1981; Stein 1981a).

To end all doubts about the generalizability of these findings to all local governmental units, Stein and Hamm (1987) examined the universe of over 35,000 municipal governments in 1977 and 1982. Their results must be considered the most authoritative in the field: "The absence of a strong or even modest federal effort to redistribute aid monies to the modest and lowest capability communities confirms . . . findings for an earlier period and generalizes these findings to the universe of general purpose municipal governments" (p. 463). In short, the cumulative evidence does not support the argument that state or local fiscal disparities are best redressed by a federal aid system. Moreover, the data suggest that states are more effective than the federal government in their own efforts to redress the disparities in fiscal capacity and need that exist among their substate governments.

Federal intergovernmental aid is distributed very unequally among the states. For example, in 1986 per capita federal aid allocations to Florida were only $278, compared to per capita federal aid allocations of $697 and $1,244 to, respectively, New York and Alaska. These large variations in total per capita federal aid among the states have continued over the years. Political complaints about these differences have been surprisingly muted, perhaps under the mistaken assumption that federal aid has been directed to jurisdictions with the greatest need and fewest resources.

Table 4–7
Federal Aid in the American States, Cross-Sectional Analysis for Selected Years

	1984	*1970*	*1960*
Economic resources			
Income	−.10	−.06	−.13
Urbanization	−.15	−.22	−.19
Density	−.00	−.22	−.20
Education	.04	.24	.08
Demand for redistribution			
Poor	−.01	−.05	−.07
Aged	−.24	−.55*	−.43*
Young	.19	−.33*	−.30*
Black	−.20	−.26	−.33*
Government bureaucracy			
State centralization	.36*	.56*	.63*
Government employment	.35*	.33*	.65*
Professionalism	.24	.11	.14
Public unionism	.39*	.25	.13
Interest group activity			
Years	.31*	.47*	.61*
Unions	.38*	.24	−.02
Group strength	−.06	.16	.23

Note: The dependent variable is per capita federal intergovernmental revenue. Figures are simple cross-sectional correlation coefficients. An asterisk indicates a statistically significant relationship.

Yet confirmation of the non-targeting of federal aid at the state level can be found in table 4–7. Federal aid has not compensated for differences among the states in economic resources; there have been no significant relationships between per capita aid and various measures of economic resources in the states. Nor has federal aid been targeted to the states with the largest proportions of poor, aged, young, or black populations. Indeed, in the past, federal aid allocations have occasionally appeared to be negatively associated with these indicators of need.

Variations in per capita federal aid allocations are more closely associated with measures of bureaucracy than measures of need or resources. Federal aid has long been associated with the centralization of state bureaucracies and the size of the governmental work force. We are tempted to speculate that large and centralized state bureaucracies, not the presence of social needs or the absence of economic resources, are the key to getting federal money.

Federal Aid and the Erosion of Federalism

Federal interventions dilute the benefits of competitive federalism. Competitive federalism requires that states and communities have significant and autonomous responsibility for the welfare of people living in their jurisdictions. It requires that these governments be free to pursue a wide range of public policies. Most important, competitive federalism requires that the costs of state and local government goods and services be fully reflected in the revenues collected by these governments. Federal grants-in-aid create distortions in the relationships between the preferences of citizen-taxpayers in the states and the policies of state and local governments.

The argument that the federal agencies administering grants-in-aids can avoid substitutive effects by stronger hierarchical controls (Chubb 1985) is no doubt true. But the implementation of this principal-agent model would only make things worse in terms of the overall satisfaction of citizen preferences in a federal system.

State and local officials view federal aid as outside money. The net effect of this aid is to cause state and local governments to spend more money than they otherwise would, to tax their own citizens more than they otherwise would, and to devote more government money to federally favored activities than they otherwise would.

5
Politics and Public Policy in the States

A dependence on the people is, no doubt, the primary control on the government; but experience has taught mankind the necessity of auxiliary precautions.

———James Madison, *Federalist*, Number 51

C ompetitive federalism would be unnecessary if democratic political processes were sufficient to guarantee policy responsiveness. Creating opposite and rival interests among state governments is unnecessary if rivalry within state political systems fully protected the interests of citizen-voters. Why should we worry about "voting with our feet" if voting in competitive elections did the job?

But there are many unresolved questions about the policy relevance of parties and elections in American state politics. How important are the parties in shaping public policy in the states? Is public policy responsive to shifts in party control of state government? Can voter-taxpayers raise or lower state taxes or expenditures by electing Democrats or Republicans to the governor's office or the state legislature?

Parties and Public Policy

Political scientists have long placed great faith in party government. E.E. Schattschneider expressed this faith when he wrote: "The rise of political parties is undoubtedly one of the principal distinguishing marks of modern government. . . . Political parties created modern democracy and modern democracy is unthinkable save in terms of parties" (1942, p. 1). Sarah McCally Morehouse reaffirmed faith in the centrality of political parties in the states: "The single most important factor in state politics is the political party. It is not possible to understand the differences in the way sovereign states carry out the process of government without understanding the type of party whose representatives are making decisions that affect the health, education, and welfare of its citizens" (1981, p. 29).

In contrast, rational theories of parties suggest that parties have little policy relevance given a unimodal distribution of opinion on most policy questions. Anthony Downs explained: "In the middle of the scale where most voters are massed, each party scatters its policies on both sides of the mid point. It attempts to make each voter in this area feel that it is centered right at his position. Naturally this causes an enormous overlapping of moderate positions" (1957, p. 135). Downs acknowledged that a left or right party may "sprinkle these moderate policies with a few extreme stands in order to please its far-out voters," but overall "both parties are trying to be as ambiguous as possible" about policy positions. "Political rationality leads parties in a two-party system to becloud their policies in a fog of ambiguity" (p. 136).

Certainly the parties are central to the selection process for public office in the states. But are they relevant to the policymaking process? If there is a unimodal distribution of voters' preferences in a state and if the state parties are devoid of strong organizations and ideologically motivated activists, then the parties will converge to the center of the policy spectrum, and the party system will have little meaning for public policy (figure 5–1). The party system can be policy relevant if there is a bimodal distribution of voters' preferences in a state and if the parties have strong organizations and ideologically motivated activists.

The problem is that we do not know the distribution of voter opinion in each state. We do not know whether these distributions are unimodal in some states and bimodal in others, whether the shape of these distributions changes from one issue to another, or whether the shape of these distributions changes over time even within the same state.

Conflicting notions of the policy relevance of the Democratic and Republican parties in the states pose important questions for research. Richard Winters explained the "substantial normative issue" at stake: "American politics is preeminently party politics. We define our candidates in party terms and our issues in party terms; in fact, we define ourselves politically in terms of the political party. Yet the consequences of these definitions have not systematically been appraised. Does it mean anything to have one political party control the government as opposed to another?" (1976, p. 629). Winters's own research suggested that party control of state government makes "little or no difference" in the distribution of tax burdens and spending benefits. In explaining his findings, he reflected on "technical considerations," federal involvement, and the possibility that "standard spatial models of the electorate" (that is, models such as Downs's) may be correct.

Party Competition

The preeminent American party theorist, V.O. Key, Jr., focused more on the policy consequences of party competition than on the policy consequences of Democratic or Republican control of state government. Key believed that

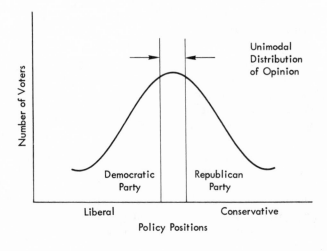

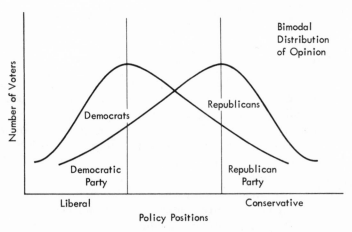

Figure 5–1. Party Positions and Public Opinion

"political parties perform functions essential to the operation of a democratic order" (1958, p. 311). Yet he did not confuse normative propositions with his empirical observations of state politics:

> The institutions developed to perform these functions in each state differ markedly in form from the national parties. It is an error to assume that the political parties of each state are but miniatures of the national party system. In a few states that condition is approached, but . . . each state has its own pattern of action and often it deviates markedly from the forms of organization commonly thought of as constituting party systems. (p. 312)

Key's theorizing about the impact of competition was very persuasive: competition served the interests of have-nots by organizing them into the political system; competition for their votes led politicians to provide increased levels of public services; have-nots clearly preferred increased public spending from which they benefited directly. The assumptions were that public services were undersupplied in relation to true citizen demands and that these demands were repressed by noncompetitive politics; therefore, an increase in competition should result in increased levels of public spending. Key wrote:

> In the two-party states the anxiety over the next election pushes political leaders into serving the interests of the have-less elements of society, therefore putting the party into the countervailing power operation.
> . . . In the one-party states it is easier for a few powerful interests to manage the government of the state without party interference since the parties are not representative of the particular elements that might pose opposition to the dominant group.
> . . . Over the long run the have-nots lose in a disorganized politics. (Key 1949, p. 307)

Economic Models

When these assertions were tested, however, it turned out that there were few significant independent relationships between party competition and levels of public taxing and spending in the states. Once the effects of income, urbanization, and education were controlled, the initial relationships among competition, participation, and public policy largely disappeared (Dye 1966; Dawson and Robinson 1963; Hofferbert 1966a; Fry and Winters 1970; Winters 1976). Competition and participation were dependent on levels of economic development, and so were levels of public taxing and spending. The associations between competitive politics and public policies turned out to be largely spurious (for exceptions and qualifications, see Sharkansky and Hofferbert 1969 and Cnudde and McCrone 1969). Or as Dye explains:

> Economic development shapes both political systems and policy outcomes, and most of the association that occurs between system characteristics and policy outcomes can be attributed to the influence of economic development. Differences in the policy choices of states with different types of political systems turn out to be largely a product of differing socioeconomic levels rather than a direct product of political variables. (1966 p. 293).

Facilitative Effects

These comparative state policy studies revealed the importance of economic development in shaping public policy, but they were criticized for their failure to test for the facilitative effects of political competition. These studies treated competition as a direct determinant of public policy. Measures of party competition were included as independent variables in regression equations, implying an additive function. Findings of no significant independent effect of competition on public policy tell us that characteristics of political systems do not cause variations in public policy. But these tests employing additive models do not tell us how political system characteristics might facilitate relationships between citizens' demands and public policies. This theoretical shift—treating political systems as conversion mechanisms rather than causal variables—is explained by Goodwin and Shepard:

> Previous studies have placed both socioeconomic variables and political process variables in a single regression equation which is used to predict the level (or distribution) of expenditures in a given state or municipality. While the use of socioeconomic indices as surrogate measures of collective demand is justified, such a treatment is inappropriate for *political process* variables. Using political variables in this manner is inconsistent with those models of representative government which view representation as a process through which the demands of citizens are linked to policy outputs. Political process attributes should be viewed not as *determinants* of the shape or location of the demand curves of citizens, but as *modifying variables* which either facilitate or inhibit the accurate translation of demands into outputs, i.e., mediatorial. (1976, pp. 1128–1129)

Conditions for Policy-Relevant Parties

A careful specification of the conditions under which party competition and Democratic or Republican control of state government would directly affect public policy was provided by Edward T. Jennings (1979). He correctly observed that the early assumption that party competition will always assist the have-nots is not theoretically valid. He reasoned that party competition will increase policy benefits to have-nots only when parties in the state reflect class divisions and the party associated with the lower or working class gains control of government. His theory explains why previous empirical studies (Dye 1966; Dawson and Robinson 1963; Hofferbert 1966a; Fry and Winters 1970; Winters 1976) found that party competition was not independently related to welfare benefits. According to Jennings:

> Such findings are not surprising. Party labels have been used as policy relevant variables; however, the important thing is not the label, but the extent to which parties vary in policy-relevant attributes. . . . Party constituency is one policy-relevant attribute of party systems. Other relevant dimensions might be the political values and ideologies of the leaders of competing parties and the degree of party cohesion. Only if parties vary in these types of

characteristics would we expect policy outputs to vary with differences in control of government. *Party labels as such are theoretically meaningless.* (1979, p. 429; italics added)

The theoretical elaborations and empirical findings reported in this literature on party and policy in the states challenge us to identify those competitive states in which party politics are relevant to public policy and distinguish them from both competitive and noncompetitive states in which party has little or no relevance. To do this, we must examine each state over time and try to determine whether shifts in public policy are associated with changes in Democratic and Republican control of the governor's office and the state legislature.

Political Competition in the States

Over the past several decades, party competition has risen dramatically in the southern states. Historically the Democratic party held a near monopoly in states and local politics in the South. Even today, despite occasional Republican successes, the GOP fails to run candidates for many state and local offices in the South. Nonetheless, the growth of party competition in the South has narrowed the variation among the fifty states in the character of their political systems. To illustrate, the coefficient of variation among the fifty states for a standard indicator of state party competition—one minus the winning percentage in gubernatorial elections—declined from 41.6 percent in 1950 to 18.0 percent in 1984.

Voter participation in the southern states has also increased dramatically over the past several decades. From an estimated 5 percent of voting-age blacks registered in the South in the 1940s, black registration rose to 25 percent in 1956 and 37 percent in 1964. As a direct product of the Civil Rights Act of 1964 and the Voting Rights Act of 1965, black voter registration grew to 56 percent in 1980 and 61 percent in 1986. This figure remains slightly lower than the comparable figure for white registration in the South (70 percent) because white registration also increased in these years.

Voter participation in the South remains slightly lower than in the rest of the nation. In the 1984 presidential election, 48.6 percent of the voting-age population of the South cast votes, compared to 54.6 percent for the Northeast, 58.9 percent for the Midwest, and 51.9 percent for the West. Despite these remaining regional differences, overall variation among the states in voter participation has declined dramatically. The coefficient of variation for a standard measure of state voter participation—the percentage of voting-age population casting votes in congressional elections—fell from 42.5 percent in 1950 to 26.1 percent in 1984.

Although differences among state political systems in competition and participation are declining, it is still possible to classify the states as competitive or noncompetitive based on variation in measures of interparty competition and voter turnout in state elections. The states' relative positions on these measures remain stable over time. The correlation between competition in 1984 and competition in 1950 is $r = .81$; the correlation between voter turnout in 1984 and voter turnout in 1950 is $r = .77$. We can group the states into competitive and noncompetitive sets and use these same sets over time without worrying too much about states' changing categories.

Different grouping schemes might accomplish this objective. We have chosen to identify twenty competitive and twenty noncompetitive states. Competitive states are those that ranked in the upper half of the fifty states on measures of interparty competition and voter participation for at least twenty-five of thirty years. Noncompetitive states are those that ranked in the lower half of the fifty states on these same measures for at least twenty-five of thirty years. Ten states did not meet either of these criteria; they are not consistently competitive or noncompetitive and hence are labeled mixed.

The groupings illustrated in figure 5–2 are similar to previous classifications (Ranney 1971; Tucker 1982a). Massachusetts and Rhode Island are excluded from the competitive group because of their heavily Democratic

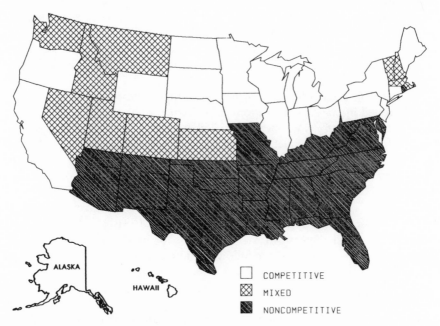

Figure 5–2. Party Competition in the States

voting; New Hampshire and Vermont are excluded from the competitive group because of their heavily Republican voting. These determinations are based on voting in gubernatorial elections.

These groupings by competition reflect regional patterns. The exceptions to traditional regional groupings are the states already noted: Vermont, New Hampshire, Massachusetts, and Rhode Island. These exceptions are important because they allow us to separate the effects of regionalism from the effects of competition.

Testing for Party-Policy Linkages

Is public policy responsive to shifts in party control of state government? The policy-relevant hypothesis is that public policy will change with changes in party control of state government. The competing hypothesis is that changes in public policy occur only with changes in economic resources (income) and that changes in party control of state government have little or no policy consequences.

Designing a Test

Party politics is relevant at the margins of government policy if it is relevant at all. We cannot expect absolute levels of government taxing, spending, or regulation to be determined by party politics. These absolute levels of public goods and services are largely determined by social and economic forces over which parties and policymakers have little control (Dye 1966). Instead, our focus is on different rates of change under Democratic and Republican administrations. According to Downs, "Both the government and the voters are interested in marginal alterations in the structure of government activity. By marginal alterations we mean partial changes in the structure of government behavior patterns which each administration inherits from its predecessor" (1957, p. 54). Cross-sectional analysis of levels of public taxing or spending cannot adequately test for the effects of a discontinuous or episodic independent variable such as party control of state government: "Only if one measures the impact of *change* in partisan control and *change* in expenditures will the real relationship be revealed" (Hofferbert 1981, p. 724; italics in original). The policy measures we used to test for party-policy linkages are expressed as measures of change following state elections.

Examining Tax Increases

Can electing Republicans to governorships and state legislatures hold down taxes? Do Democratic governors and legislators raise taxes more than Republican governors and legislators? Certainly the rhetoric of the national Republican party with its frequent references to tax reductions and "getting government off our backs and out of our pocketbooks" suggests that electing Republicans is a way in which voter-taxpayers can indicate their preference for lower taxes. If state taxes are responsive to these preferences as they are expressed in the electoral process, then we would expect taxes to be lowered in Republican administrations or at least the rate of increase to be moderated. To test for these party-policy linkages, we must examine whether expected changes in taxing occur with the changes in party control of governorship and state legislatures.

We test for the effect of party governance in two ways. First, we observe whether a Democratic or a Republican governor is associated with a positive or negative change in tax burdens or welfare spending. Second, we observe whether a Democratic- or Republican-controlled upper or lower house together with a Democratic governor is associated with positive or negative changes in these policy variables. We have coded party controls as:

Democratic governor:
  1 = Democratic governor
  0 = Republican governor

Democratic governor or legislature:
  3 = Democratic control of governorship and both houses of legislature
  2 = Democratic control of governorship and one house of legislature
  1 = Democratic control of governorship
  0 = Republican control of all bodies

This coding is in the direction of Democratic control of state government, so a positive sign indicates that taxing and spending increases with Democratic party control.

Income is a strong determinant of tax revenues as well as government expenditures. In any states the happenstance of Democratic or Republican control during four, six, or eight years of relative prosperity (two, three, or four of sixteen observations) can confound attempts at identifying the impact of party on policy change, so we examine party-policy relationships in each of the states over time, controlling for changes in income. With such a small number of observations, the introduction of controls requires extensive caution in the interpretation of the resulting coefficients.

We show results for each of the fifty states, though theoretically our focus is on party-policy linkages in the competitive states. Nonetheless, minority party governors and even minority party legislative houses have occasionally been elected in noncompetitive states over the thirty-year period under study, so we present findings for all of the states. In Alabama, Georgia, and Missis-

Table 5–1
Party and Tax Policy in the States

	T Statistics for Change in:					
	Total Taxes with Democratic		Income Taxes with Democratic		Corporate Taxes with Democratic	
	Governor	Governor and Legislature	Governor	Governor and Legislature	Governor	Governor and Legislature
Competitive states						
Alaska	-1.14	-.42	-.69	-.33	-.02	-.17
California	2.42*	1.68	1.64	1.25	1.60	.15
Connecticut	1.02	1.37	.80	.54	.44	.51
Hawaii	-.94	-.94	-.35	-.35	-.44	-.44
Illinois	.67	.57	.25	.31	.13	.14
Indiana	.09	.15	.05	.62	.02	1.41
Iowa	-1.10	-1.78	-.59	-.90	-1.31	-1.87
Maine	-.43	.24	.49	.63	.18	.25
Michigan	.01	.32	.50	.59	.06	.65
Minnesota	.26	.50	.94	1.13	1.99*	2.90*
Nebraska	.85	NA	.34	NA	.22	NA
New Jersey	.75	.27	.39	.10	1.28	1.11
New York	.55	.09	.31	.04	.74	.37
North Dakota	-.78	-1.89	-.71	-.67	-.60	-1.46
Ohio	.08	.09	1.46	1.30	1.89	1.29
Oregon	-.59	-.50	.02	.05	-.68	-.61
Pennsylvania	.26	.17	.19	.86	1.37	.69
South Dakota	.24	.20	—	—	.50	.50
Wisconsin	.14	.14	.59	.32	.92	1.15
Wyoming	.07	.07	—	—	—	—
Mixed						
Colorado	.19	.27	.59	.70	-.27	.19
Idaho	.53	.45	1.23	1.06	.40	.28

Kansas	.15	.12	.36	.25	.01	.37
Massachusetts	-.39	-.39	-.31	-.26	-.54	-.63
Montana	.40	.71	.53	.54	.03	1.10
Nevada	.80	.93	—	—	—	—
New Hampshire	.29	.28	—	—	2.33*	—
Utah	-.13	-.04	-.59	-.17	-.21	2.25*
Vermont	-.51	-.66	-.79	-1.12	-1.41	-.25
Washington	1.22	2.14*	—	—	—	-.68
Noncompetitive states						
Alabama	—	—	—	—	—	—
Arizona	.15	.80	.17	-.09	.15	.49
Arkansas	.41	—	.87	—	.68	—
Delaware	.65	.48	.42	-.34	.93	1.07
Florida	.26	—	—	—	.01	—
Georgia	—	—	—	—	—	—
Kentucky	.53	—	.57	—	1.41	—
Louisiana	.37	—	.41	—	.35	—
Maryland	.03	—	.51	—	.13	—
Missouri	.23	.18	-.84	-.92	1.96*	1.98*
Mississippi	.09	—	—	—	—	—
New Mexico	.70	.33	.47	.72	-.81	-.53
North Carolina	.04	—	2.00*	—	1.46	—
Oklahoma	—	—	.37	.00	.60	—
Rhode Island	.51	.63	.02	.04	.21	.29
South Carolina	1.59	—	1.96*	—	.81	—
Tennessee	.40	—	.91	—	.38	—
Texas	.80	—	—	—	—	—
Virginia	.73	—	1.02	—	.75	—
West Virginia	.07	—	.41	—	.37	—

Time-series regressions, 1954–1984, (Cochrane-Orcutt technique) controlling for effects of income.

Figures are t statistics (coefficients divided by their standard errors) for the effects of party, while controlling for income, in time-series regressions for each state. Most state series have thirty annual change observations for each dependent variable. A dash indicates that a state did not elect a Republican governor or legislature during this time period, or it has no income or corporate tax. An asterisk indicates a statistically significant relationship.

sippi, no Republican governor or legislature has served since Reconstruction, so no analysis of party differences is possible. The Republican party has never controlled either house of the state legislature in a number of other noncompetitive southern and border states (Alabama, Arizona, Florida, Georgia, Kentucky, Louisiana, Maryland, Mississippi, North Carolina, Oklahoma, South Carolina, Tennessee, Texas, Virginia, and West Virginia), so we cannot test for the effect of changing legislative control in these states.

Parties and Tax Policy

Party control of state government appears to have little relevance to tax policy. Table 5–1 shows time-series regressions for each of the fifty states for changes in total tax revenues, income tax revenues, and corporate tax revenues, with party control of the governorship and with party control of the governorship and the legislature combined. If tax policy responded to changes in party control of state government, we would expect to see significant T statistics under each of the three tax variables for the election of Democratic governors and legislatures, but we do not. Table 5–1 is notable only for the absence of any significant relationships in any of the states between changes in tax revenues and changes in party control of state government.

Democratic and Republican governors are equally likely to raise taxes—total taxes as well as income and corporate taxes. We expected party changes to produce some consistent changes in tax policy at least in the competitive states, but party control of state government was no more relevant to tax policy in these states than in noncompetitive states.

We can confirm this assessment by examining some of the competitive states more closely. Figure 5–3 shows annual tax increases in California under Democratic and Republican governors from 1952 through 1984. Note that the largest annual tax revenue increase in California occurred in 1968, the second year of the administration of Republican governor Ronald Reagan. Total tax revenues for the state leaped from $3,485 million to $4,664 million, an increase of 33.8 percent. Tax hikes were more modest in Reagan's second term. Annual tax hikes were consistently high in Democratic governor Jerry Brown's first term but much lower in his second term. Thus, over the years, California taxpayers have not had any consistent tax policies based on party control of state government.

The taxpayers of New York did not experience any lower taxes by electing Republicans either. Republican governor Nelson Rockefeller served four four-year terms in Albany. Tax revenues increased an average of 11.5 percent annually during the Rockefeller years (figure 5–4). Annual tax increases under Democratic governor Hugh Carey were much more modest (7.5 percent).

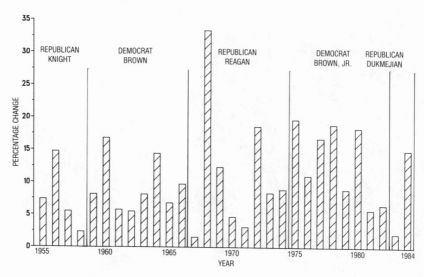

Figure 5–3. Annual Change in Total State Revenues, California

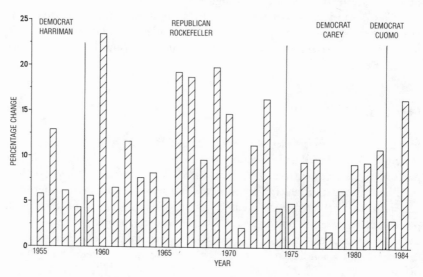

Figure 5–4. Annual Change in Total State Revenues, New York

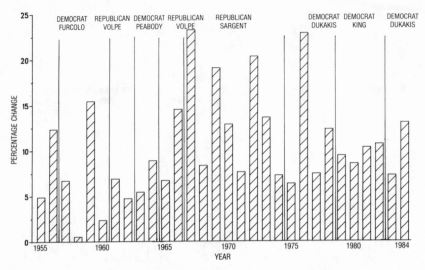

Figure 5–5. **Annual Change in Total State Revenues, Massachusetts**

No consistent tax policies have attached to Republican or Democratic administrations in Massachusetts (figure 5–5). Democratic governor Michael Dukakis raised state tax revenues significantly in his first term; Democratic governor Edward J. King kept tax increases modest. The largest tax increases in the state occurred in the late 1960s and early 1970s under the administration of Republican Francis Sargent.

Parties and Welfare Policy

Can electing Democrats to governorships and state legislatures increase state expenditures for welfare? Certainly the rhetoric of the national Democratic party with its frequent references to "care," "compassion," "the poor," and the like suggests that electing Democrats is a way in which consumer-voters can indicate a preference for greater welfare spending and expect to see this preference reflected in public policy. If state welfare spending is responsive to these preferences as they are expressed in the electoral process, then we would expect welfare spending to increase with the election of Democrats to state office.

Party control of state government, however, appears to have welfare policy relevance in fewer than half of the states. This question has been investi- gated a study using the same statistical tests described above identifying party-policy linkages in tax policy (Dye 1984). The results suggested a somewhat stronger role for parties in welfare spending. In twenty of the fifty states, per capita state welfare spending increases with Democratic control of the governorship and with Democratic control of the governorship and one or both houses of the state legislature. But in thirty of the fifty states, Democratic party control fails to increase welfare spending significantly, and in a few cases—Alaska, North Carolina, and Virginia—Democratic control is associated with lower welfare spending.

Party-policy linkages in welfare are evident in fourteen of twenty competitive states: California, Hawaii, Iowa, Maine, Michigan, Minnesota, Nebraska, New Jersey, North Dakota, Ohio, Oregon, Pennsylvania, Wisconsin, and Wyoming. In three states—New Jersey, Ohio, and Pennsylvania—electing Democratic governors failed to increase welfare spending. Only when Democrats controlled the governorship and both houses of the legislature was welfare spending positively affected.

In five competitive states—Connecticut, Illinois, Indiana, New York, and South Dakota—Democratic party control has not increased welfare spending significantly over the increases occurring under Republican control. Evidently the Republican parties in these five states, or the Republican governors and legislators elected to office, did not differ significantly in their decisions on welfare spending from their democratic adversaries.

Among the mixed states, Democratic control of state governments appears to influence welfare spending in five additional states: Idaho, Massachusetts, Montana, Nevada, and Utah. Or stated inversely, Republican control of state government in these states is associated with significantly lower welfare spending.

Generally an absence of competition means an absence of policy-relevant parties. Among the twenty noncompetitive states, only Rhode Island displays an association between Democratic control of state government and increased welfare spending.

The Need for Auxiliary Precautions

Federalism was recommended by the nation's founders as an "auxiliary precaution" for the control of government. While the founders were true republicans, they were not content to rely exclusively on electoral processes to ensure responsible government. Contemporary research on state politics confirms their wisdom.

Generalizing about state politics is a difficult task. V.O. Key, Jr., wrote modestly:

> What are the consequences of these variations among the states in the organization of political activity? The question cannot be answered with much

confidence; the estimation of the effects of institutional arrangements belongs in the realm of art rather than precise measurement. Generalization is most difficult. Yet a few more or less educated guesses may be made. (1958, p. 327)

Key then approaches the task by classifying states on the basis of party competition. We have approached the same task by trying to classify states on the basis of both party competition and the policy relevance of their party system. And we have examined policy relevance in terms of both tax revenues and welfare spending.

Competitive policy-relevant party systems are found in only a minority of states. The ideal "responsible party" model—competitive parties that offer clear policy alternatives to the voters and ensure that elected officials enact their party's policy positions after the election—does not really describe politics in the states. Party competition is absent in many states, and even in the competitive states, the parties do not necessarily offer clear policy alternatives.

The distinction between competitive parties and policy-relevant parties is an important one. John H. Fenton recognized this distinction in his now-classic study of six midwestern states (1966). All of these states were competitive, but according to Fenton, three of them (Michigan, Wisconsin, Minnesota) had "programmatic, issue-oriented parties," and three (Ohio, Indiana, and Illinois) had "traditional job-oriented parties." Our investigation of party-policy linkages in all fifty states confirms Fenton's idea that "the theoretical benefits of two-party competition are realized in issue-oriented as opposed to job-oriented political systems" (p. 219).

There are neither good theoretical reasons nor clear empirical evidence to support the notion that competitive parties will necessary offer the voters significantly different policy positions. Indeed, if Downs is correct and if many state electorates cluster at the midpoints of their respective opinion distributions on policy issues, then competitive parties have no incentive to offer clear policy alternatives. Certainly in tax policy there is no empirical evidence to support the view that Democratic or Republican state administrations cause significantly different policies to emerge. And earlier research demonstrated that in welfare spending policy, Democratic or Republican state administrations make a significant difference in only a minority of states (Dye 1984). Of course, we might continue to search for other policy areas or different dimensions of taxation and welfare policies in which changing party control of state government makes a difference.

In summary, the weakness of the responsible party model in the states, the absence of competitive parties in many states, and the irrelevance of party control of state government to many important policy decisions confirm the wisdom of auxiliary precautions in the pursuit of responsible government.

6
The Wealth of the States

> The natural effort of every individual to better his own condition, when suffered to exert itself with freedom and security, is so powerful a principle, that it is alone and without any assistance, not only capable of carrying on the society to wealth and prosperity, but of surmounting a hundred impertinent obstructions with which the folly of human laws too often encumbers its operations.
> —Adam Smith, *The Wealth of Nations*, 1776

> It cannot be very difficult to determine who have been the contrivers of this whole mercantile system; not the consumers, we may believe, whose interest has been entirely neglected; but the producers, whose interest has been so carefully attended to; and among this latter class our merchants and manufacturers have been by far the principal architects.
> ——Adam Smith, *The Wealth of Nations*, 1776

The American states are "political economies" insofar as they strive, in Adam Smith's words, "to enrich both the people and the sovereign." State governments and their local subdivisions produce and distribute tangible goods and services; they raise revenues and distribute costs; they establish rules by which individuals, households, and firms must operate; and they even try to encourage research and innovation and attract industry to their jurisdictions. All of these activities affect the economic well-being of their citizens.

It is true that these government activities are usually felt at the margins of economic activity and that many other factors affect the economic fortunes of citizens in the states. But the "wealth of states," like the "wealth of nations," is affected by what governments do. It should be possible to compare the performances of state political economies, across jurisdictions and over time, and to observe the economic consequences of variation in state government policies.

We shall postpone the discussion of the economic impact of state and local taxing and spending to the next chapter. Let us first turn to some general theories of economic growth, then observe differences among the states in economic development and rates of growth, and explore some popular explanations of differing growth rates among the states. We shall then be in a better position to understand the problems we shall confront in testing for the effects of governmental taxing and spending policies on the wealth of the states.

Theories of Economic Growth

Classical economists attributed economic growth to increases in the quality or quantity of the factors of production: land, labor, and capital. Today the classical model is still viable, with some modifications: economic growth is attributable to the accumulation of productive capital goods; to growth in the size and skills of the labor force; to improved use of natural resources (land); and to research, innovation, and technological advances, which permit greater productivity with any given amount of land, labor, and capital (see Dennison 1962). All of these factors are affected in turn by the social and political environment: cultural mores, attitudes toward work, propensities to save, receptivity to technological change, barriers to competition, and the like. Finally, of course, growth is affected by governmental policies that encourage or discourage hard work, capital accumulation, training and education of the labor force, utilization of natural resources, and technological innovation.

The literature on differentials in growth rates among nations is fairly well developed. Beginning with Simon Kuznets's landmark work (1955, 1957, 1966), economists have developed models to predict growth in output in nations based on both cross-sectional and time-series data (Temin 1967; Adelman and Morris 1973; Cherney 1975). Later political scientists investigated the political preconditions for national economic development (Holt and Turner 1966; Cutright 1967) and the effect of governmental policies on national economic growth (Jackman 1975; Wilensky 1975; Ward, 1978).

Determinants of Regional Growth

There is no comparable body of literature explaining the economic and political determinants of growth rates among the American states, but we can turn to locational theory and regional science for some initial guidance in thinking about state growth rates (for a classic, and readable, introduction, see North 1955). Frequently cited as major determinants of regional growth or decline are the following:

1. Changes in demand outside a region for the region's existing exportable commodities.
2. Discovery of new natural resources or exhaustion of existing natural resources.
3. Increasing or decreasing costs of land or labor in relation to competing regions.
4. Developments in transport that alter a region's transfer costs and change its competitive position relative to other regions.

5. Changes in technology that increase demand or improve processing of the region's exportable commodities.

6. The development of new exportable commodities for a region.

These factors are exogenous to a state and, more important for our purposes, not easily manipulated by state governments.

Policy Impact

Nonetheless, state and local government policies can be hypothesized to affect economic growth in several ways. Consider, for example, an economic growth model for the states that includes (1) accessibility to markets and raw materials, (2) the costs and availability of the factors of production—capital, labor, energy, land, and materials, (3) climatic and natural environmental factors, and (4) state and local taxing and spending policies (see, for example, Plaut and Pluta 1983). State and local government may affect accessibility to markets through investment in transportation (Dye 1980a). Today capital appears to flow freely across states, as evidenced by almost equal interest rates across regions. But the availability, productivity, and costs of labor vary significantly across states. We can hypothesize that some of this variation is a product of educational and welfare policies of states that affect the supply of "human capital." Energy costs and availability differ across the states, but it is not clear what, if any, impact government policies have on energy (Dye 1980b). The costs and availability of land and raw materials may be only minimally affected by state and local government regulatory policies. A warm and sunny climate is usually thought to be more important to families than to business firms in deciding where to live. But it may be increasingly important to management-controlled light industries. Climate attracts managers as householders, and managers then rationalize locational decisions for their firms.

Governments have not yet discovered a way to affect warmth and sunshine; however, they can affect the business climate in many ways. In addition to regulatory policies, state and local government taxing and spending policy may directly influence economic growth. On the spending side:

1. Government spending on transportation may improve accessibility to markets.

2. Government spending for education—public schools and higher education—may improve the supply of quality labor and increase the likelihood of innovation and technological advance.

3. Government spending for welfare may reduce the availability of labor and increase production costs.

4. All government spending may increase the burdens of government and slow economic growth.

On the revenue side:

5. The total revenue burdens of government may reduce resources available to the private sector and slow economic growth.

6. Income taxation, especially top marginal rates, may provide disincentives for individuals to work, save, risk, and invest.

7. Corporate taxes may raise costs of production or reduce after-tax profits to investors and therefore slow corporate expansion.

These general propositions will be developed and tested in the next chapter, but it is important to note here that a considerable body of empirical literature on the states challenges these propositions.

It has proved very difficult to show that state and local government policies, especially tax policies, have any significant effect on the location of firms and, hence, on economic growth rates in the states. Tax burdens vary, of course, among the states, but it is frequently argued that variations in tax burdens are not enough to overcome other differences among states—for example, in labor costs or energy costs or access to markets. A very small differential in wage rates can outweigh a very large differential in taxes. Many other locational advantages may outweigh whatever benefits accrue to business from government spending for transportation or education. In short, we must be aware that many factors other than government policy are important in determining state economic growth rates.

Finally, competition among states and the mobility of capital and labor may ensure that state taxing and spending policies do not have major long-term effects on economic growth. This is not to say that taxes do not matter or that public spending is irrelevant to growth. Rather, it is to recognize that over the long term, no state can pursue taxing or spending policies that adversely affect investment and disadvantage the state relative to neighboring states. Interstate competition and the mobility of capital and labor prevent any state from getting too far out of line. In other words, even if there is little statistical or survey evidence linking state and local government taxing or spending policies to economic growth rates, the conclusion that these policies do not matter may be inappropriate. Interstate competition itself may ensure that no state pursues antigrowth policies for very long.

Variations in Wealth Among the States

The wealth of the states varies a great deal. Let us focus initially on levels of individual economic well-being, as measured by per capita personal income.

Later we will examine change over time in both total and per capita personal income in the states. We will observe that wide variations in individual economic well-being among the states persist, even though variation among the states has diminished over time and relative rankings of the states have been very stable over the decades.

While it is true that economic life throughout the nation is interdependent, the continuing variations among the states in levels of individual well-being are striking. In 1985, per capita income in Alaska ($18,187) and Connecticut ($18,089) was twice that of Mississippi ($9,187) (figure 6–1). Variation among the states in income levels is closely related to other measures of development—for example, urbanization and education—and it is inversely related to most measures of social need—poverty, aged, and youth populations (table 6–1). These relationships have continued over the years. Income differences among the states today are less of a regional phenomenon than they once were. Regional relationships (South and Sunbelt states treated as dummy variables) have diminished over time.

The relative positions of the states on measures of economic resources have remained surprisingly stable over a century. The Spearman rank-order correlation between the states' per capita personal income in 1952 and 1985 is .77. Earlier research traced this stability back to 1890 (see Hofferbert

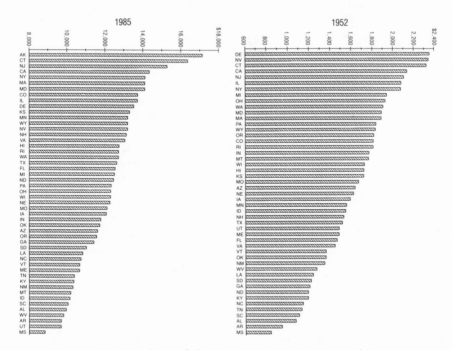

Figure 6–1. Ranking of the States' Per Capita Personal Income

Table 6–1
Correlates of Per Capita Personal Income among
the States

	Per Capita Personal Income	
	1985	1952
Economic resources		
Urbanization	.65*	.70*
Education	.50*	.52*
Social needs		
Poverty	−.63*	−.72*
Aged	−.28*	−.44*
Youth	−.46*	−.53*
Black	−.19	−.35*
Region		
South	−.38*	−.62*
Sunbelt	.37*	.45*

Note: Figures are simple correlation coefficients. An asterisk
indicates a statistically significant relationship.

1966b). Mississippi has been the nation's poorest state for at least a century. Nonetheless, some states have made noteworthy economic progress relative to other states. Texas and Florida have moved from thirtieth and thirty-third, respectively, in 1952 in per capita personal income to twentieth and twenty-first, respectively, in 1985. Pennsylvania fell from thirteenth to twenty-fourth, Ohio fell from ninth to twenty-fifth, and Michigan dropped from eighth to twenty-second.

Overall variation among the states in economic well-being is diminishing over time. A graphic portrayal of diminishing income differences over the century among regions is presented in figure 6–2.

This "nationalization" of the economies of the states suggests that the poorer states have enjoyed a higher average growth rate over the years than the wealthier states. We want to examine change over time and suggest some explanations for varying rates of change.

Economic Growth in the States

Economic development is a dynamic process. We are concerned with why some states' economies grow more rapidly than others. We are not asking why some states have higher levels of income than other states. Rather the question is, Why do some state economics grow faster than others? Thus, our dependent variables must be expressed as rates of change.

What indicators of change should we examine? If we are concerned with

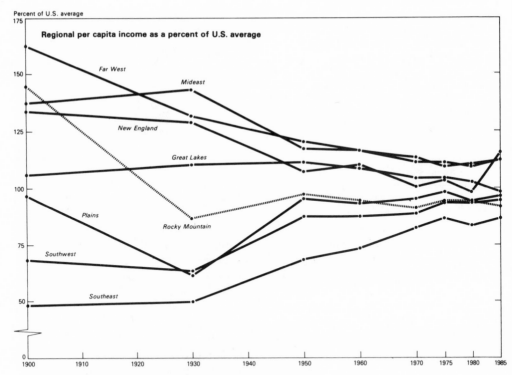

Percent of U.S. average

Regional per capita income as a percent of U.S. average

Far West

Mideast

New England

Great Lakes

Plains

Rocky Mountain

Southwest

Southeast

175 · 150 · 125 · 100 · 75 · 50 · 0

1900 1910 1920 1930 1940 1950 1960 1970 1975 1980 1985

Source: *Public Opinion* (May–June 1986).

Note: Bureau of Economic Analysis regional groupings: *New England* = Maine, New Hampshire, Vermont, Massachusetts, Connecticut, Rhode Island. *Mideast* = New York, Pennsylvania, New Jersey, Delaware, Maryland, District of Columbia. *Southeast* = Virginia, West Virginia, North Carolina, South Carolina, Georgia, Florida, Kentucky, Tennessee, Alabama, Mississippi, Arkansas, Louisiana. *Southwest* = Oklahoma, Texas, Arizona, New Mexico. *Rocky Mountain* = Colorado, Wyoming, Montana, Idaho, Utah. *Far West* = Nevada, California, Oregon, Washington. *Plains* = Minnesota, Iowa, Missouri, North Dakota, South Dakota, Nebraska, Kansas. *Great Lakes* = Ohio, Michigan, Indiana, Wisconsin, Illinois. Not classified, Alaska, Hawaii.

Figure 6–2. Regional Economic Convergence

the political economy of state—its ability to increase wealth—we may wish to measure growth in aggregate income and employment. We could then assess the impact of government policies on attracting and creating income and jobs in the state. Of course, measures of change in aggregate income and employment are affected by population growth. A state may increase its own wealth simply by attracting people. But we also want to observe change in individual well-being within the states. Hence we must also examine change in per capita personal income over time.

Observing change requires the designation of some time period. As simple as this sounds, it poses one of the most critical problems confronting scholars concerned with economic development. Very different results can be

Table 6–2
Income Growth in the States: Correlations among Various Time Periods

	Growth in Per Capita Personal Income				
	1980–1984	*1975–1980*	*1970–1975*	*1960–1970*	*1952–1960*
Long-term growth					
1952–1984	.57*	−.08	.40*	.74*	.79*
Short-term growth					
1980–1984		−.07	.06	.36*	.48*
1975–1980			.50*	−.07	−.17
1970–1975				−.03	.27
1960–1970					.45*

Note: Figures are simple correlation coefficients for fifty states. An asterisk indicates a statistically significant relationship.

produced by studying change over different time periods in the states. Indeed, it is likely that differences in reported research results on the determinants of economic development are frequently a product of the selection of different time periods for the observation of change (see Pryor 1983).

To demonstrate the importance of the time period selected, we can observe relationships between growth rates in the states over the fairly long time period 1952–1984 and shorter time periods within that span. The purpose is to show that economic growth in most states occurs in spurts and lags.

There is very little correlation between state economic growth rates in various time periods (table 6–2). States in which total income grew most rapidly between 1980 and 1984 are not the same states in which income grew most rapidly between 1975–1980 or 1970–1975. Obviously this complicates the search for general explanations of growth.

Long-term economic growth rates—1952–1984— are shown for each state in figure 6–3. Two separate measures are shown: growth in per capita personal income and growth in total personal income. The growth indexes are simply $[[t_2 - t_1] \div t_1] \div 32$. Note that growth in per capita personal income among the states is unrelated to growth in total income. (The simple correlation between growth in per capita personal income and total income is .08.) Individual economic well-being grew least in Nevada even as that state grew rapidly in total income and employment.

Explaining Growth Rates

The Convergence Theory

The convergence theory of economic growth asserts that latecomers to industrialization will grow more rapidly than more advanced economies. Econ-

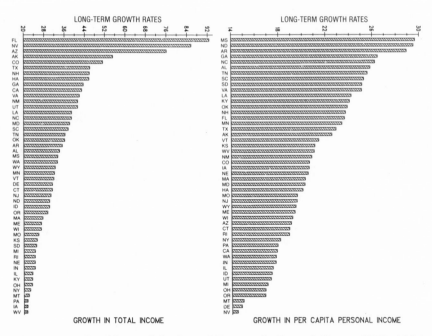

Figure 6–3. Rankings of the States' Economic Growth Rates, 1952–1984

omies at the beginning of the process of industrialization—in the take off period (Rostow 1961)—will grow more rapidly than economies in later stages of development. One reason is the different relationships that emerging and advanced economies have toward the most important factor of production: technology. It is easier for emerging economies to transfer, borrow, and adapt existing technology than it is to invent new technology. Hence, economies that are behind can grow faster through the diffusion of existing technology than advanced economies, which find themselves at the technological frontier and must generate new technology to advance further.

The convergence theory is also supported by the diffusion of labor and capital. When productivity growth in an older industry falls below average for the economy, wages will rise more rapidly than output per worker, driving firms in that industry to seek locations with lower wages. Firms will relocate to where returns are maximized. The net result will be more rapid growth in less developed recipient locations (Norton 1986).

Empirical support for the convergence theory is offered by Baumol (1986), who shows that growth in gross domestic product among industrialized nations from 1870 to 1979 is negatively correlated with an initial (1890) level of output. He describes convergence as a "pervasive" phenomenon. It is true, of course, that nonindustrial societies frequently remain nonindustrial; hence there is no worldwide convergence between industrial and nonindustrial nations. The convergence theory applies only to developing, industrializing nations.

The convergence theory can be supported by reference to the experience of the American states. Even a cursory examination of state rankings in figure 6–3 suggests that growth is inversely related to the level of development at the beginning of the period. Mississippi, renowned for occupying the last place among the states in most measures of individual well-being, has experienced the most rapid increase in per capita personal income since 1952. Simple cross-sectional correlation analysis between per capita personal income in 1982 and growth in this same variable from 1952 to 1984 produces a very strong coefficient: −.84 (table 6–3). Growth in total income and employment is also negatively related to earlier levels of income and employment, although the relationships are not strong. The relatively rapid economic growth of some states appears to be a result of catching up by the latecomers.

It is not surprising that the convergence theory applies to the American states. There are no strong barriers to free mobility of capital, labor, and technology. Catching up is much easier among states than among nations. Convergence of regional and state income was fairly rapid from 1930 to 1950 and continued to 1970 (figure 6–2).

Convergence among the states, however, has slowed to a virtual standstill since 1970. And tests of the convergence theory based on data after 1970 are less impressive. For example, growth in per capita personal income from 1970 to 1980 correlates with per capita personal income in 1970 at −.34, and growth in per capita personal income from 1980 to 1984 correlates with per capita personal income in 1980 at only −.12. So we might expect that

Table 6–3
Relationship between Long-Term Growth Rates and Levels of Development at Beginning of Period

	Long-Term Growth Rates, 1952–1984		
	Per Capita Personal Income	*Total Personal Income*	*Nonagricultural Work Force*
1952 levels			
Per capita personal income	−.84*		
Total personal income		−.28*	
Nonagricultural work force			−.30*

Note: Figures are simple correlation coefficients for fifty states. An asterisk indicates a statistically significant relationship.

in the future, lagging states cannot expect to close the gap between themselves and more advanced states simply by waiting for the diffusion of capital, labor, and technology.

The Sclerosis Theory

The rise and decline of nations and empires has long fascinated scholars. Historians in the fashion of Spengler and Toynbee claim to see common patterns in the early rise and later decline of civilizations. It is easy to observe that "older" civilizations appear to decay and eventually succumb to newer, more vigorous societies. But generalized explanations of this pattern—explanations that go beyond ad hoc references to unique events or trends in a particular society—are rare.

The sclerosis theory of economic growth asserts that the age of society itself is a determinant of growth rates; growth is inversely associated with the length of time that a society has been organized under a continuing economic and political regime. Mancur Olson sets forth a generalized explanation of the sclerosis theory in his *The Rise and Decline of Nations* (1982). He argues convincingly that institutional sclerosis develops in mature stable societies as they accumulate a variety of organizational retardants to economic growth. Special interest organizations—governmental, corporate, professional, labor, environmental, and others—tend to slow innovation, limit entry, and reduce productivity. The older a society is the longer these organizations have been in existence and the larger is the accumulation of retardants to growth. Special interest organizations shift the focus of societal activity away from growth-stimulating policies and toward redistributional policies. Special interests seek a larger share of society's output rather than an increase in total societal output. These special interest redistributional gains come at the expense of everyone else and eventually at the overall expense of society's growth rate. Like wrestlers struggling over the contents of a China shop, the special interests eventually destroy the economic growth on which the welfare of society depends.

This sclerosis theory developed out of Olson's earlier work, on *The Logic of Collective Action* (1965). Small groups with narrow concentrated interests are more likely to organize themselves to make claims upon society than larger groups with broader goals. The start-up costs of collusive organizations are high. Initially only very narrow, producer organizations will emerge. The concentration of benefits and the diffusion of costs encourage special interests to overcome the barriers to organization. Large numbers of organizations will undertake to provide privatized benefits to members at socialized costs to everyone else. Coalitions of organizations will form, and logrolling will proliferate. Government will enact more and more special privileges and protections, loopholes and preferences, subsidies and tariffs.

War or revolution upsets the political order required for the development of effective special interest organizations. These upheavals force would-be collusive organizations to begin anew to organize themselves and reestablish their special privileges, preferences, and protections. Thus, long-run political stability (such as Great Britain has experienced) tends to reduce the rate of economic growth.

How can the sclerosis theory be tested? Testing Olson's theory has become a modest growth industry itself in academic circles. Provocative theories produce prodigious testing (Choi 1983; Dye 1980a; Pryor 1983; Maitland 1985; Vedder and Galloway 1986; Nardinelli, Wallace, and Warner 1987; Gray and Lowery 1988; Mueller 1983). Some of these tests involve nations; others involve the American states. Although no consensus has been reached regarding the empirical validity of the theory, it is fair to say that the theory remains influential in the social sciences.

The first tests on the American states employed an acknowledged imperfect proxy for institutional sclerosis: the length of time a state has been settled and politically organized, as represented by its date of admission to the Union or its date of readmission for states whose social and economic organizations were restructured by the Civil War. Olson defends this simple test: "The logic of the argument implies that countries [or states] that have had democratic freedom of organization without upheaval or invasion the longest will suffer the most from growth-repressing organizations and combinations" (Olson 1982, p. 77).

Using the date of readmission for eleven southern states depends on an arguable assumption: that the social and economic organizations of these states were in fact altered by their defeat in the Civil War. The analogy would be the defeat of Germany and Japan in World War II. Some scholars might argue that the Civil War did not change life in the southern states much. Our argument would be that the Civil War marked the beginning of the end of the plantation system and that the date of readmission is a closer approximation of the end of that socioeconomic system than the original date of admission. Readmission was a political event signifying that the military governments of the U.S. Army were to be replaced by governments whose constitutions were approved by Congress and whose legislatures had approved the Thirteenth, Fourteenth, and Fifteenth Amendments to the U.S. Constitution.

By the simple test of time and economic growth in the American states, the sclerosis theory appears to be reasonably well-supported. Younger states enjoy higher long-term economic growth rates. Older states have not grown as rapidly as younger states. But this relationship between age and economic growth is not as strong as implied by the sclerosis theory (table 6–4). The only period of growth closely related to age is the 1970s. This was the period studied by Choi (1983) and Dye (1980a), and the selection of this period

Table 6–4
Relationships between Economic Growth Rates and Age and Unionization

	Long Term Growth, 1952–1984	Growth by Periods				
		1952–1960	1960–1970	1970–1975	1975–1980	1980–1984
	Per Capita Personal Income					
Years	.34*	.29*	.06	.58*	.29*	−.35*
Unions	−.63*	−.41*	−.44*	−.10	−.21	−.42*
	Total Personal Income					
Years	.34*	.10	.19	.75*	.32*	.08
Unions	−.28*	−.13	−.18	−.18	−.29*	−.35*
	Nonagricultural Work Force					
Years	.47*	.42*	.24	.44*	.30*	.10
Unions	−.28*	−.36*	−.20	−.01	−.31*	−.10

Note: Figures are simple correlation coefficients. An asterisk indicates a statistically significant coefficient.

accounts for the initial strong support for the Olson theory. A very different picture emerges when age is correlated with growth in the early 1980s. In this most recent period, the older states outperformed the younger states.

Unionization of the work force turns out to be negatively related to economic growth rates in the states, in the fashion predicted by Olson's sclerosis theory. Labor organizations are said to resist innovation, push wage rates above marginal costs, and provide political support for regulation-restrictive and redistributional legislation. The absence of labor organizations is said to provide a more favorable climate for business expansion. And indeed long-term economic growth in the states is strongly and negatively related to the proportion of the work force that is unionized. Negative relationships between growth and unionization can be observed in every time period.

Age, of course, is a very crude measure of complex organizational developments. Unions are only one type of restrictive organization, and many other causal factors may impinge upon these simple associations. Gray and Lowery (1988) have specified several additional causal links between age and economic growth rates implied by Olson's sclerosis theory. They argue that empirical verification of the theory requires showing positive relationships among all of the following variables: age; growth in the number and power of organized interest groups; the adoption of collusive policies to restrict entry, fix wages and prices, and minimize competition; modified economic behaviors as a result of these policies; and adverse consequences for economic growth rates. They contend that any break in these linkages would invalidate Olson's theory. While theoretically valid, such a stern empirical test is difficult to construct and even more difficult to pass. We have only very crude proxies for the number and power of interest groups. It is difficult to assess the aggregate collusive effects of a wide range of state fiscal and regulating policies, and it is even more difficult to learn whether these policies significantly stunt economic growth. It is little wonder that Gray and Lowrey conclude that Olson's theory "remains an interesting but unproven account of varying economic growth rates" (p. 129).

Political scientists have made many attempts over the years to evaluate the power of interest groups within the states. All of these efforts have been of necessity very impressionistic and subjective. The first comprehensive effort was made by Belle Zeller (1954) based upon responses of political science instructors in the states to a mailed questionnaire. A more recent systematic ranking of state interest group systems was compiled by Sarah McCally Morehouse (1981) "based upon judicious consideration of the available evidence" (p. 112). Despite the subjectivity of these rankings, they are remarkably similar despite a lapse of nearly thirty years ($r = .76$).

The power of any single interest group within a state is inversely related to the number of groups in the state. Morehouse observes that "in rural, sparsely populated states, a large single company, corporation, or interest group may wield great amounts of power in that state's political system" (p. 112). And "interest groups appear to have somewhat less impact on public officials in systems containing a diversified economy and large numbers of groups and organizations" (p. 112).

These observations of the power of single interest groups in the states appear to run counter to Olson's argument that interest groups grow stronger in older, economically diversified states, while newer states are relatively free from their stultifying effects. However, the Morehouse measure of interest group strength is positively related to long-term economic growth ($r = .32$ for growth in per capita personal income), just the opposite of what might be expected from a superficial view of the Olson theory. And, indeed, others have reported this anomaly (Gray and Lowery 1988) and offered it as partial invalidation of Olson's work.

But the confusion occurs in the failure to differentiate between the power of single interest groups within the states (what is measured by political scientists) and the collusive powers of an aggregated complex interest group system (what concerns Olson). It is true that the oil and mining interests are very strong in Alaska and that no single interest group exercises comparable strength within the state of Massachusetts. Massachusetts has larger numbers of influential and diversified interest groups; no single interest dominates the state. But the cumulative activities of many different interests in Massachusetts, each seeking to obtain some privileges, protections, and subsidies for itself, create an interest group system that is more influential in the aggregate than the less developed interest group system in Alaska. By more influential we mean that the accumulated growth retardants of a large, complex, diversified interest group system will be greater than those of a less developed state. Clearly Olson's theory is directed at the cumulative growth retardants of a complex interest group system, not at the relative strength of a single interest group within a state's political system. Hence, measures of the strength of a single interest group are inappropriate for tests of the sclerosis theory.

Warmth and Sunshine

Most people consider warmth and sunshine preferable to cold and snow. If warmth and sunshine are considered nonpecuniary forms of income, then we might expect the migration of people to the Sunbelt, other things equal. Moreover, sunshine is nontaxable. It is the ultimate tax shelter. "As effective marginal income tax rates rose sharply in the seventies, the value of sunshine rose relative to other taxable forms of utility, and persons shifted into this location-specific tax shelter (Vedder and Galloway 1986).

Capital also flows to where people want to live. Economic growth over the last thirty years has occurred primarily in light industries, which are not closely tied to sources of raw materials or to river, railroad or sea transportation. Aerospace, computer, camera, electronics, business machine, and drug firms are more flexible in their choice of location than are steel, rubber, glass, or chemical firms. Managers of newer industries have greater personal discretion in locational choice. They can choose to maximize personal utilities—to live in warm, sunny climates.

Economic growth may be independently associated with TEMP (average daily mean temperature, reported for the largest city in the state) and SNOW (average yearly snowfall, reported for the largest city in the state). Of course, climate and region are inextricably related. In addition to these variables we can classify states by the familiar sunbelt-frostbelt regional dichotomy, where the sunbelt states are Hawaii, California, Nevada, Vermont, Colorado, Arizona, New Mexico, Texas, Louisiana, Arkansas, Mississippi, Tennessee, Alabama, Georgia, Florida, South Carolina, North Carolina, and Virginia; the other thirty two states are considered the frostbelt. And we can also employ the regional South–non-South dichotomy, where the eleven states of the Old Confederacy are the southern states: Alabama, Mississippi, Georgia, South

Table 6–5
Relationships between Economic Growth and Warmth and Sunshine

	Long-Term Growth, 1952–1984	*Growth by Periods*				
		1952–1960	*1960–1970*	*1970–1975*	*1975–1980*	*1980–1984*
	Per Capita Personal Income					
TEMP	.29*	.22	.52*	−.19	.14	.01
SNOW	−.30*	−.20	−.48*	−.17	.20	−.00
SUNBELT	.44*	.39*	.49*	−.00	−.07	−.05
SOUTH	.67*	.37*	.75*	.09	.07	.26
	Total Personal Income					
TEMP	.42*	.40*	.49*	−.01	.32*	.06
SNOW	−.31*	−.22	−.32*	−.16	−.02	.11
SUNBELT	.57*	.41*	.56*	−.24	.49*	.27
SOUTH	.29*	.37*	.40*	−.15	.20	.21
	Nonagricultural Work Force					
TEMP	.29*	.45*	.30*	−.09	.15	−.07
SUNBELT	.51*	.56*	.49*	−.04	−.22	.08
SNOW	−.27	−.35*	−.20	−.10	.06	.22
SOUTH	.18	.19	.31*	−.05	.07	.05

Note: Figures are simple correlation coefficients. An asterisk indicates a statistically significant coefficient.

Carolina, North Carolina, Virginia, Tennessee, Arkansas, Texas, Louisiana, and Florida.

Warmth and sunshine have indeed been associated with economic growth in the United States over the last three decades. Table 6–5 confirms other results of research (e.g., Dye 1980a; Vedder and Galloway 1986) about the importance of climate. But note that the climatic and regional variables were more important in the 1960s and 1970s than in the early 1980s.

Why would growth in the 1980s be unrelated to warmth and sunshine? It is not very plausible to suggest that people have changed their preferences and no longer value these amenities. Yet clearly the sunbelt growth phenomenon is time specific. We might speculate that world energy oversupplies in the 1980s, contrasted with a favorable energy market in the previous decades, explains this anomaly. The roller-coaster fortunes of the emerging rich states (especially Texas, Louisiana, Oklahoma, and Wyoming) may help to explain these time-specific findings.

Modern Mercantilism in the States

The mercantilists, against whom Adam Smith argued so eloquently, are still with us. Modern mercantilism operates under a pseudonym—"industrial policy." And it has been practiced more by the states than by the national government. In the context of the American states, modern mercantilism refers to direct government involvement in economic planning, job creation, capital formation, and other activities relating to industrial development. Like its historical predecessors, modern mercantilism requires government to select certain industries, activities, or regions as targets for tax incentives, capital infusions, and government expenditures. And like its historical predecessors, the costs of these activities are borne by consumer-taxpayers.

It remains a mystery, two hundred years after Adam Smith, why state economic planners believe their wisdom is superior to the judgment of the marketplace. But it is evidently true that state economic development officials, as well as governors, legislators, and local elected officials, believe that they can better direct the proper allocation of capital, labor, and technology to various economic enterprises than the market itself. It is unfair to argue that bureaucrats and politicians are simply rationalizing their own quest for power by extolling the virtues of an "industrial policy." Most believe in their own superior judgment. They believe they can act in the public interest despite abundant evidence that industrial policy decisions inevitably hinge on interest group pressures and the need to win political contributions and electoral votes. The consumer-taxpayer bears the burdens of these decisions, not only directly in the tax funds devoted to their implementation but also indirectly in the inefficiencies created by these market interventions.

Nonetheless, the competition among the states for industrial development is self-correcting over the long term. States that make bad deals with specific industries and corporations can learn from their mistakes. They can compare their growth and well-being with states that have avoided the burdens and inefficiencies of misguided interventions. (Indeed, there is some empirical evidence of a state learning process. For an examination of Pennsylvania's unhappy Volkswagen Rabbit experience, see Hansen 1984.) Without the corrective of intergovernmental competition, it is unlikely that the federal government would be able to learn from "industrial policy" mistakes. The corrective of international competition may come too late and prove too costly.

Types of Industrial Policy

The range of specific state and local government activities generally labeled as state industrial policy encompasses the following;

> Capital formation policies: State industrial development and pollution control bond financing, direct state loans, loan guarantees and venture capital programs.

Special tax treatment: Special tax treatments, including accelerated depreciation of industrial or pollution control equipment, tax reductions on manufacturers' inventory, tax reductions for new equipment or machinery, and property tax reductions, abatements, or moratoriums on land and capital improvements.

Labor force incentives: Incentives for building plants in high unemployment areas (enterprise zones), state-supported training of unemployed for work in new industries, and state incentives to industry to train the unemployed.

The first category focuses on capital formation. Many states and municipalities began these activities in the 1970s, during periods of very high interest rates. Both states and municipalities greatly increased their use of industrial development bonds (IDBs). From 1970 to 1985 IDBs grew from less than 2 percent of all municipal bond issues to 27 percent; private hospital bonds, student loan bonds, and housing bonds brought the total of private-purpose government bonds to 62 percent of the total municipal market (Dye 1985). This extensive use (or misuse) of IDBs led directly to corrective provisions in the Tax Reform Act of 1986, which phased out the interest exemptions of IDBs from federal taxable income. Some states also make use of direct low-interest loans, often to small business, or guarantees of private loans to new businesses. An even more controversial innovation is the state venture capital program, usually a quasi-public corporation that issues its own bonds to finance companies. Venture capital investments are by definition risky. As long as the venture capital corporation must compete in the bond market itself, it must exercise some prudence. Some states, however, allow these venture capital programs to tap into state pension funds (Hansen 1984).

The second category includes many traditional tax breaks, as well as some newer ones. Accelerated depreciation of new industrial machinery, as well as energy-conservation and pollution-control equipment, is common in state corporate income tax codes. In computing property taxes, many states have agreed to exempt manufacturers' inventory, as well as new equipment and machinery. Many states and municipalities exempt new business from property taxes for a certain number of years and sometimes extend these exemptions to new capital investments by older businesses.

The third category focuses on job-creation incentives. These activities may be politically more popular than industrial loans or tax breaks because the presumed beneficiaries are workers rather than corporations. Yet many of the direct benefits go to the businesses themselves. This is true in the federally assisted Job Training Partnership Act Program, as well as independent state-funded programs for training and retraining of workers. Businesses receive state funds to train the unemployed or tax incentives to locate in high unemployment areas.

This listing of state industrial development policies is by no means exclusive. State regulatory policies in air and water pollution, solid waste disposal, toxic wastes, and a wide range of environmental concerns might be considered in an overall industrial policy. State efforts to attract foreign investments should also be included. State right-to-work laws might be considered part of an industrial policy. And virtually all states use public funds to advertise their beauty, desirability, comfort, and attractiveness to business firms.

The Limited Effectiveness of Industrial Policies

Are state industrial policies effective in stimulating manufacturing or reducing unemployment? The literature on this topic to date has failed to identify significant growth effects for any of these direct industrial development activities. (ACIR 1967; Pierce Hagstrom and Steinbach 1979; Rasmussen Berdick and Ledebor 1984; Stutzer 1985; Rubin and Zorm 1985; Ambrosius 1986).

One of the best-designed tests of the effectiveness of various industrial development policies was undertaken by political scientist Margaret Ambrosius (1986). She identified states that had adopted various incentive policies and the year of their adoption. These policies included state bond financing; accelerated depreciation on equipment; tax exemptions for manufacturers' inventory; tax reductions on equipment, machinery, land, and capital improvements; and tax incentives for locating in areas of high unemployment and for training the hard-core unemployed. Pooled time-series analyses were performed on all adopting states with a dummy variable representing the intervention. The dependent variables were value added by manufacturing per capita and the unemployment rate. The results were uniformly negative. The study is noteworthy for demonstrating the absence of any significant intervention effects on either manufacturing or unemployment for any of the policies examined.

Another careful study by political scientist Susan Hansen suggests that industrial policies have some positive effects on the number of new firms coming into the state but negative effects on overall manufacturing and employment. She does not believe that industrial policy caused manufacturing and employment losses; rather she attributes this relationship to the pressures such losses place upon state governments to experiment with industrial policy. She speculates that "serious unemployment in a state is a compelling political reason to experiment with aggressive industrial policies" (Hansen 1984, p. 9).

The evidence to date, then, indicates that industrial development policies in the states have had limited economic success. But industrial policy follows a political rather than an economic logic. When a state confronts an economic downturn, politicians are pressured to do something, whether the something they do produces net economic benefits to their state or not. Hansen cites the political benefits of state-financed job training: "Business gets its work force trained cheaply, labor gets jobs, universities get more students and research monies, and politicians get the credit. But the costs per job . . . may be high" (Hansen 1984, p. 13).

It seems inevitable that state industrial development policy will sacrifice efficiency and growth to political expediency. State governments must respond to the political pressures of existing (old) industries, which wish to protect the status quo at the expense of consumers, taxpayers, and newly emerging industries. The tendency in state industrial development policy will be to protect large corporations and unions in especially depressed industries. As economist Herbert Stein explains: "To ask why our government would tend to protect the old established industries is like asking Willie Sutton why he robbed banks. Willie's answer according to the legend: 'Because that's where the money is.' In the case of our political leadership, the answer is, 'Because that's where the votes are.' The industries of the next generation have no votes or political action committees" (Stein 1983, p. 66). Stein was warning about the inefficiencies of a national industrial policy, but the same warning is appropriate for the states.

Over time states may learn to distinguish between industrial policy and economic growth policy. The distinction centers on the nature of public goods. Government activities can be described as public, quasi-public, or private. Pure public activities are supplied to all citizens, and each citizen's share of the marginal benefit is equal to his or her share of the marginal cost. Perhaps few government activities are purely public. Most government activities are quasi-public; that is, although all citizens may benefit to some degree from these activities, benefits flow disproportionately to some citizens, and costs fall disproportionately on other citizens. Some government activities are really private in nature; that is, only a few citizens benefit, and the costs are borne disproportionately by all other citizens. It is our argument that most of the governmental activities which are commonly designated as industrial policy are actually private goods. It is difficult to rationalize these activities in terms of the general welfare. In contrast, our notion of economic growth policy encompasses government activities that provide more general benefits and impose more proportionate costs across the citizenry.

Competition and Wealth

It is important to understand that economic growth is a function of many factors beyond the control of state governments. Changes in world demands, discoveries of new natural resources or exhaustion of existing resources, increasing or decreasing relative costs of labor, developments in transportation, changes in technologies, and development of new products all influence growth rates. None of these factors is easily manipulated by state governments. We can expect government policy to have at best only a marginal impact on economic growth.

The economies of the American states were "nationalized" in the first half of the twentieth century as capital, labor, and technology became increasingly mobile. While the relative positions of the states remained stable, the range of variation among the states was markedly reduced. Nonetheless, differences among the states in economic well-being remain significant; per capita personal income in some states is nearly twice that in other states. And convergence has been minimal since 1970.

Evidence indicates that economic growth in the states occurs in spurts and lags. States that are growing most rapidly in one time period are not necessarily the same states that are growing most rapidly at another time. Inferences about the causes of growth from time-specific tests must be made with caution.

Competition among the states offers protection against the prolonged continuation of inefficient policies. Comparisons of state economic performance give policymakers as well as scholars some general measures of evaluation. It is much more difficult to perceive and correct the error of monopoly government. Indeed, competition among the states may help explain why state growth rates change from one time period to the next and why no state remains on a downward trend for too long.

Competition encourages policy experimentation. Through experimentation and competitive evaluation, states can learn to distinguish between industrial policy—the attempt to intervene in markets with specific subsidies, exemptions, and special treatments, targeted at specific industries or corporations—and economic growth policy—the provision of truly public goods and services with the minimum burden in taxes and regulations.

7

Taxing, Spending, and Economic Growth in the States

> The labour of the English colonists is not only likely to afford a greater and more valuable produce, but in consequence of the moderation of their taxes, a greater proportion of this produce belongs to themselves, which they may store up and employ in putting into motion a still greater quantity of labour.
> ——Adam Smith, *The Wealth of Nations*, 1776

Adam Smith believed that it was government's moral responsibility to enrich the people. In the process, of course, government would also enrich itself. A government that sought to enrich itself at the expense of its people was not only immoral but would soon impoverish itself.

The mobility of capital, labor, and technology today adds force to Smith's lessons. Even in 1776 Smith recognized that heavy taxation would encourage "the owners of great capitals . . . to remove both their residence and their capital to some other country and industry and commerce would soon follow" (p. 858).

American state and local government officials generally understand that their own powers depend on the economic well-being of their jurisdictions. Growth in state and local budgets and public employment and the expansion of public services depend on growth of the local economy. The level of government activity is primarily a function of the level of economic resources. Rational governments can be expected to seek to maximize economic resources within their boundaries.

Competition among governments for mobile capital, labor, and technology is the best guarantee against oppressive taxation and regulation. State and local governments must make their jurisdictions attractive to productive workers, to owners of capital, and to managers of technology. They must endeavor to provide the most attractive packages of public services while imposing the lightest burdens of taxation.

Taxing and Economic Growth

Taxes lower the rate of return for individuals, families, and firms on their work, savings, and risks. Lowered rates of return reduce the incentive to engage in these economic activities.

The true burden of taxation for society is not only the personal income that is taken away from the private use of citizens but also the personal income forgone because of the tax disincentives to work, save, invest, and produce. Earlier we defined the tax burden as simply the proportion of personal income devoted to taxes. Measurement was a relatively easy task. But it is far more difficult to measure the costs of taxation in retarded economic growth. Indeed, at the national level, estimating the disincentive effects of taxation on economic growth has become a major pastime of both politicians and economists.

The effects of state and local taxes also deserve our attention. Estimating the true costs of these taxes is important, first, because they capture a significant portion of our personal income. In recent years, state and local taxes have amounted to almost 10 percent of personal income (see figure 3–1). The potential disincentive effects of such a burden should not be ignored. Another reason for focusing attention on state and local taxes is the opportunity provided for genuine comparative analysis. The states offer an excellent opportunity to explore the growth-retardant effects of various tax burdens and tax structures. Indeed, theoretically, economic growth in states should be more sensitive to changes in the tax policies of state governments than economic growth in the nation is to changes in federal taxes. This greater sensitivity should arise from the mobility of productive resources within the states.

Federalism, by providing the option of moving from one jurisdiction to another, should accentuate the disincentive effects of higher taxes in any one jurisdiction. People confronting high federal taxes have the options of working less and enjoying more leisure, saving less and consuming more goods and services, or avoiding new entrepreneurial endeavors that risk their time and money as a way of accommodating themselves to high taxes. People confronting high state and local taxes have an additional option: migrating to jurisdictions with lower taxes. It is certainly easier to move within the United States than between the United States and other countries. Thus, mobility should accentuate the growth-retardant effects of high taxes in any single jurisdiction.

It is not only the total tax burden that affects economic growth but the types of taxes governments choose. Consumption-based taxes, notably state sales taxes, may not have the same debilitating impact on productivity as corporate or individual income taxes. It is true that sales taxes must be paid out of personal income, but it is consumption that is being taxed directly, not work, savings, or investment. Indeed, by raising the costs of consumption relative to the costs of savings, sales taxes may have a modest beneficial effect on savings.

In contrast, individual income taxation directly taxes the return on earnings, dividends, interests, and rents. Progressive income taxation has the most harmful effect because it substantially lowers the rate of return on work and savings of the most productive people. Relatively modest aggregate tax burdens can have a very adverse effect on economic growth if these burdens are carried disproportionately by the most productive individuals and firms. Federalism accentuates the harmful effects of progressive state and local income taxation. The most productive people are usually the most mobile, and a highly progressive state income tax is a strong incentive to move.

State corporate income taxes are clearly a tax on capital. It is sometimes argued that corporate taxes are shifted to consumers, and this may be true with regard to federal corporate taxes. But corporations in any state, confronting a state corporate tax, cannot shift such a tax on to nationally traded products that are sold in many states. Competing corporations that do not confront the same state tax can underprice the product of the corporation paying the tax. Hence, a state corporate income tax must be borne by capital—that is, paid out of corporate profits and the return to stockholders.

Do State and Local Taxes Really Matter?

Despite good theoretical reasons for believing that state tax policies affect economic growth and despite widespread popular belief in state capitals that the tax climate directly affects industrial growth, many early studies failed to produce strong or consistent evidence that state and local taxes directly affected business locational decisions. Numerous statistical studies relating taxes to business location were summarized in two comprehensive review essays, one in 1961 (Due) and another in 1981 (Wasylenko). Apparently twenty years of research did not change the principal conclusion: "empirical evidence that taxes affect interregional business location decisions is almost nonexistent" (Wasylenko 1981, p. 196).

Early Studies

Most of the early statistical studies placed state and local taxes within a broader model of economic growth, one that included accessibility to markets and raw materials, wage rates and energy costs, labor force variables, and transportation facilities. Within such a model, state and local tax differentials were seldom found to have a significant independent influence on growth. This general conclusion from econometric studies was reinforced by results of survey studies of firms and managers. Only occasionally were taxes cited by firms or managers as an important determinant of locational decisions. Although business respondents might be expected to bias their answers to lobby for lower taxes, few actually cited tax burdens as an influential factor in their locational decisions. Many other factors were rated ahead of taxes in priority rankings (Kieschnick 1981). Economist Dennis Carlton found it "difficult to understand why taxes do not matter more strongly in influencing location choice especially in view of the frequent public clamor-ings of business against taxes" (Carlton 1983, p. 447).

Explaining the Limited Effects of Taxes

Several hypotheses might be advanced to explain why taxes do not seem to matter much in studies of locational decisions. First, tax differentials among the states may not provide a sufficient incentive to overcome other differences—for example in labor costs, energy costs, or access to markets. The ACIR estimates that state and local taxes represent only about 3 percent of the annual total costs of most business firms. Clearly the costs of labor, energy, and transportation amount to many times the cost of taxes for most firms.

Second, the benefits that business firms receive from higher taxes may offset the burdens. Some firms may desire high-quality educational systems, or improved highway and transit systems, or strong police and fire protec-tion, and they balance these benefits against higher taxes. If the tax burden is offset with valued public goods, then tax burdens may not necessarily re-tard growth.

Third, competition may prevent state taxes from having a major effect on business location and economic growth over the long term. The ACIR, in seeking to explain the absence of a clear relationship between tax burdens and industrial location decisions, suggested that

> this lack of relationship can be attributed in no small measure to the fact that states are constantly taking steps to insure that their taxes do not "get out of line" with those of their neighboring jurisdictions. A state usually moves into this competitive arena armed with many tax options and suffi-cient political support to enable it to go a long way toward neutralizing any tax differential advantage possessed by a neighboring state. (ACIR 1967, p. 70)

In other words, if a state were to get too far out of line with competing states, it would suffer adverse economic consequences. But all states know this, so none can long pursue tax policies that place heavy burdens on business. Tax burdens in the states may vary in cross-sectional comparisons for any given year. But states cannot afford over the long run to maintain high tax burdens. "Accordingly, competition can be expected to play a role in keeping state and local taxes close enough so that business firms will not be enticed to alter their locations and investment plans" (Benson and Johnson 1987, p. 413).

Recent Research

In contrast to earlier findings, some recent empirical research challenges the notion that taxes do not really matter. It is true that economic growth in the states is explained primarily by traditional market factors in virtually all of the existing economic research. However, Plaut and Pluta (1983) found that after controlling for these factors, state and local tax burdens had a significant negative effect on employment and capital stock growth. Benson and Johnson (1987) also found that state and local tax burdens had a significant negative effect on capital formation. Canto, Joines, and Laffer (1983) found that separate time-series analyses of each state, in contrast to cross-sectional analyses at particular times, revealed that changing state fiscal policies do in fact generate effects on after-tax incomes and economic performances. But the strongest argument to date that state and local taxes retard economic growth has been set forth by economist Richard K. Vedder (1982).

Neoclassical (supply-side) theory, according to Vedder, suggests the following hypotheses:

1. Economic growth varies inversely with the burden of state and local government taxes; the fastest-growing states should be the states with the lowest tax burdens.

2. Changes in tax burdens in any state vary inversely with economic growth; raising tax burdens in any state should slow economic growth.

3. States that structure their tax systems to rely heavily on income and capital taxation (through personal and corporate income taxes and property taxes) should grow more slowly than states that rely more heavily on consumption-based taxes (retail sales taxes).

4. States that spend more on direct and indirect forms of capital formation (education, highways, transit, and so forth) should grow more rapidly than states that spend more on redistribution (welfare).

5. States with steeply progressive tax rate structures should grow more slowly than states with flat-rate tax structures. Progressive income tax rate structures ultimately hurt both rich and poor.

Vedder finds empirical support for all of these hypotheses by focusing attention on the 1970–1980 period. All of his observations are cross-sectional: the high-tax states grew more slowly during this period than the low-tax states. For example, he reports a ten-year growth in real per capita personal income of 30.0 percent for sixteen low-tax states (Texas, West Virginia, Washington, D.C., Georgia, Missouri, Florida, Idaho, North Carolina, Indiana, Kentucky, New Hampshire, South Carolina, Tennessee, Arkansas, Alabama, and Mississippi), compared to a growth rate of 22.2 percent for sixteen high-tax states (Alaska, New York, Wyoming, Hawaii, Massachusetts, California, New Jersey, Minnesota, Maryland, Illinois, Michigan, Connecticut, Wisconsin, Delaware, Arizona, and Montana). He concludes that "the income generating effects of public expenditures financed by state and local taxes are more than offset by the income-destroying disincentive effect of the taxes" (Vedder 1982, p. 21). According to Vedder, "The optimal state and local fiscal policy would be one in which the overall tax burden is comparatively low, coupling high sales taxes with low income and property taxes" (p. 27).

Taxes and Growth Reexamined

Do states with high tax burdens suffer low growth rates? A reexamination of the growth-retarding effects of state and local taxes can begin with some simple cross-sectional observations of tax levels and burdens in the states and economic growth over various time periods. By observing long-term growth as well as growth in specific time periods, we can assess whether some of the disagreement among previous studies is a result of the time periods chosen. And by observing both tax levels (per capita total state and local taxes) and tax burdens (total state and local taxes as a percentage of personal income), we can determine whether conflicting findings are a product of the measures employed.

Total tax levels are negatively related to improvement in individual economic well-being in states—that is, to growth in per capita personal income. Growth in per capita income over all time periods is negatively related to tax levels at the beginning of these time periods (table 7–1). For example, long-term growth in per capita income (1960–1984) is negatively related to per capita tax levels at the beginning of the period—a significant – .63. Growth in per capita income over shorter time periods is not as closely related to tax levels, although all of the coefficients remain negative.

Growth in total personal income, however, does not appear to be closely related to tax levels, either over the long term or over shorter periods, so it makes a difference whether one is talking about aggregate growth in income, which is not closely associated with tax levels, or about growth in per capita income, which is associated with tax levels.

Perhaps more important, it makes a difference whether one is talking about tax burdens (per capita taxes) or tax levels (taxes as a percentage of personal income). In contrast to tax levels, tax burdens are not closely related to economic growth rates (table 7–2). It is true that most of the observed relationships between economic growth and tax burdens are negative, but few of these relationships are statistically significant.

Theoretically, it is the tax burden that ought to have the most significant growth-retarding effects. The tax burden defines the after-tax income or the real rate of return on work, savings, and risk. It is true that we have not yet controlled for other variables, which may be masking the effect of tax burdens, but these simple associations warn us that the problem of assessing the growth-retarding effects of state and local tax burdens is no easy task and

Table 7–1
Tax Levels and Economic Growth

Tax Levels (Per Capita) at Beginning of Each Time Period	Long Term, 1960–1984	1960–1970	1970–1980	1980–1984
Growth in Per Capita Personal Income				
State-local total taxes	−.63*	−.66*	−.41*	−.13
State only				
Total taxes	−.34*	−.29*	−.33*	−.08
Sales taxes	−.08	.07	−.11	−.21
Income taxes	−.18	−.13	−.33*	−.05
Corporate taxes	−.12	−.00	−.40*	.06
Growth in Total Personal Income				
State-local taxes	−.08	−.03	−.24	.15
State only				
Total taxes	−.27	−.26	−.31*	.37
Sales taxes	−.18	−.18	−.05	−.27
Income taxes	−.06	−.08	−.35*	.00
Corporate taxes	−.12	−.06	−.46*	.46

Note: Figures are simple cross-sectional correlataion coefficients for fifty states. An asterisk indicates a statistically significant relationship.

Table 7–2
Tax Burdens and Economic Growth

Tax Burdens (% Income) at Beginning of Each Time Period	Long Term, 1952–1984	1960–1970	1970–1980	1980–1984
Growth in Per Capita Personal Income				
State-local total taxes	−.01	−.02	−.20	−.06
State only				
Total taxes	−.26	−.36*	−.08	−.10
Sales taxes	.13	−.28	−.07	−.15
Income taxes	−.09	−.00	−.30*	−.05
Corporate taxes	.09	−.26	−.36*	.06
Top marginal rates	−.13	−.00	−.18	−.10
Growth in Total Personal Income				
State-local total taxes	.17	.00	−.10	.35
State only				
Total taxes	−.25	−.27	−.15	.34
Sales taxes	−.19	−.19	−.02	−.25
Income taxes	−.05	−.12	−.22	−.04
Corporate taxes	−.10	−.13	−.41*	−.47*
Top marginal rates	−.29*	−.15*	−.30*	−.05

Note: Figures are simple cross-sectional correlation coefficients for fifty states. An asterisk indicates a statistically significant relationship.

that these effects, if they are to be found at all, may turn out to be very modest. So far our results tend to confirm the traditional academic literature, which failed to find major adverse effects of state and local tax burdens.

Progressivity and Growth

Theoretically, the most harmful tax is a progressive personal income tax with high top marginal rates. High rates target the most productive individuals in society. They are given a strong disincentive to continue to work, to bear additional risks, to make more productive investments, to accept more demanding jobs, or to expend additional time and energy in generating taxable income. "Lawyers, doctors and other high income professionals spend more time on the golf course and consulting with their accountants and less time serving their clients. . . . Valuable resources are expended purchasing business and personal deductible items. . . . Similarly high marginal rates encourage investors to undertake projects that generate accounting losses. . . . Higher rate of return projects, generating taxable income, will be forsaken in favor of tax shelter investment" (Gwartney 1985, p. 429). High marginal rates also encourage tax evasion, an underground economy, and general disrespect for law. All of these results waste society's resources and retard economic growth. These costs to society, which are not reported in any government budget, weigh heavily on everyone.

The social and economic costs of high top marginal rates have been increasingly recognized by national governments, whether the party in power is conservative (Great Britain), socialist (New Zealand), or Republican (United States). The U.S. government reduced its top marginal tax on personal income in its 1981 and 1986 tax reforms from 70 percent to 28 percent (with a 33 percent hump range caused by the phase-out of deductions). The 1980s witnessed the longest sustained growth in GNP in the nation's history.

Theoretically, progressive state income taxes with high marginal rates should have a strong growth-retarding effect. This effect should be accentuated at the state level because of the opportunity for the most productive individuals to move to states with low marginal rates or no income tax at all. Thus, the growth-retarding effects of high rates would occur in two ways: disincentives to work and save within the state and strong encouragement to the most productive people to leave the state.

The growth-retarding effects of progressive income taxes and high top marginal rates may be moderated by interstate competition. Most states receive most of their revenue from sales taxes rather than income taxes. And most state personal income taxes have either flat or only moderately progressive rates (see table 3–7). Top marginal rates are excessive in only a few states: California (11 percent), Delaware (13.5 percent), Hawaii (11 percent),

Iowa (13 percent), Minnesota (16 percent), Montana (11 percent), New York (14 percent), and West Virginia (13 percent). Until the Tax Reform Act of 1986, states that based their taxes on federal taxes (Nebraska, 20 percent of U.S. tax; Rhode Island, 26 percent; and Vermont, 26 percent) were also levying excessively high marginal rates. Finally, an examination of the rate structure by itself does not completely inform us about incentives and disincentives to growth; it is possible that exemptions, exclusions, and special treatments in state income tax laws reduce the growth-retarding effects of high rates.

Perhaps as a result of these moderating influences, the empirical evidence of the growth-retarding effects of progressive state income taxes and high top marginal rates is weak. Income and corporate taxes retard growth only slightly more than sales taxes do. We can observe the relationships between each of these types of taxes and economic growth in table 7–1 and 7–2. In table 7–1 these taxes are expressed as per capita dollar amounts. The coefficients are generally negative but insignificant, except for the 1970–1980 period, when the states with high income and high corporate taxes grew more slowly than states with low income and low corporate taxes. Table 7–2 deals with tax burdens—income, sales, and corporate taxes expressed as a percentage of personal income. Here the evidence of growth-retarding effects of income and corporate taxes is very weak. Again only in the 1970–1980 time period do we encounter any significant negative coefficients. And in the 1980–1984 time period, the states with high corporate tax burdens actually grew faster than other states.

We can also observe the simple relationship between the top marginal income tax rates and economic growth in recent time periods. (Data on state rate structures for early time periods are elusive and unreliable.) We have coded the top rate of states with no personal income taxes as zero and recorded the top rate for other states from their official tables (*Book of the States*, various editions). It turns out that top marginal rates are negatively associated with economic growth, but the associations are very weak (table 7–2).

Again these results are similar to those reported in the earlier economic literature regarding the absence of strong relationships between tax structures and economic growth. In these cross-sectional studies, it is quite possible that interstate competition has a modifying effect on the adverse growth consequences of progressive taxation (Benson and Johnson 1987). We need to test for these effects in time-series analyses within states and learn whether changes in taxes have stimulated growth in individual states. We will undertake this task regarding tax burdens in the next section, but unfortunately we lack sufficiently detailed information on changes in rate structures, particularly top marginal rates, in all of the states, to allow us to inquire about the growth effects of changing top marginal rates. We can only speculate that lowering the top marginal rates in a few states with excessively high rates would have significant stimulative effects on their economies.

Tax Burdens and the Dynamics of Growth

Do changes in tax burdens within states affect their growth rates? Let us shift our attention from cross-sectional observations of the tax burdens and growth rates in the states to time-series observations of changes in these variables in each of the fifty states over time. We are no longer asking whether states with high tax burdens have low growth rates but whether growth rates within states are responsive to changes in their tax burdens. For example, is growth in per capita personal income in New York, California, Texas, and Florida (Figure 7–1) related to changes in tax burdens in these states. For policymakers this is the more important question: Can states increase economic growth rates by lowering tax burdens?

To test the responsiveness of growth rates to changes in tax burdens, time-series regressions were performed on each of the fifty states using lagged and unlagged procedures. Lagging implies that changes in tax burdens do not immediately affect growth but that some interval is required for the change in incentives to be recognized. It turned out, however, that results of contemporaneous regressions were virtually the same as results from two-year and four-year lagged regressions.

We are concerned with the effects of tax burdens on both individual economic well-being (per capita personal income growth) and the well-being of the state as a whole (total income growth). This means a total of one hundred

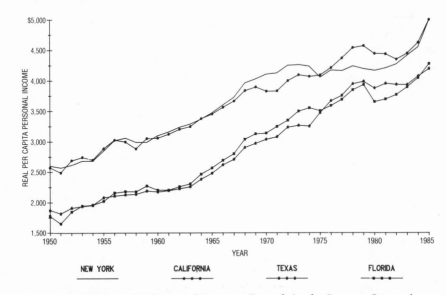

Figure 7–1. **Per Capita Personal Income Growth in the Largest States, in Constant Dollars**

separate regressions were performed for both per capita and total income for each state. The full results of these regressions are presented for New York in table 7–3. Note that in New York, the tax burden has a significant negative effect on growth in per capita personal income and a negative and close-to-significant effect on aggregate income. Inasmuch as the presentation of all of these statistics for each of the fifty states would numb the minds of most readers, we have condensed the results of one hundred regressions in table 7–4. This table presents only the T statistics for tax burden—total state and local taxes as a percentage of personal income—regressed on growth in per capita personal income and growth in total personal income.

Economic growth appears adversely affected by tax burdens in forty-six of the fifty states (table 7–4). All but four states show negative coefficients for the relationships between change in tax burdens and change in economic growth rates. These negative coefficients are statistically significant in only twenty states, however, so we can say with some confidence that increasing state and local government tax burdens in twenty states has had a significant growth-retarding effect in the periods under study (1957–1984). Nowhere do we find any significant growth-enhancing effects of raising tax burdens.

In order to confirm these results visually, we can plot changes in tax burdens and changes in per capita personal income over the years for any state. New York is a good example of a state whose economic performance was significantly increased by reductions in tax burdens in the late 1970s and 1980s. Figure 7–2 shows that tax burdens in New York were reduced in 1965 and per capita income responded favorably for several years. Tax burdens were reduced again in 1978 and 1979, and New York enjoyed its greatest income growth spurt in nearly three decades. Massachusetts is another example of a state whose economic performance was held back by high tax

Table 7–3
The Responsiveness of Economic Growth to Tax Burdens in New York

	Coefficient	Standard Error	T Statistic	Significance
Change in Per Capita Personal Income				
CONST	1942	561	3.45	.00
TAX BURDEN	−11069	4329	−2.56	.02
Number of observations = 27		R^2 = .99	Durbin Watson = 1.66	
Change in Total Personal Income				
CONST	28966	8463	3.4	.00
TAX BURDEN	−127151	65618	−1.94	.06
Number of observations = 27		R^2 = .99	Durbin Watson = 1.72	

Note: Time-series regression (Cochrane-Orcutt technique). Dependent variables are per capita and total personal income. The independent variable is taxes as a percentage of personal income.

Table 7–4
The Responsiveness of Economic Growth Rates to Tax Burdens in the States

	T Statistics (Coefficient + Standard Deviation)	
	Growth in Per Capita Personal Income	Growth in Per Capita Personal Income
Alabama	− .52	− .37
Alaska	− .09	− .17
Arizona	− .30	− .80
Arkansas	− .83	− .87
California	− 2.08*	− 2.00*
Colorado	− 2.01*	− 1.96*
Connecticut	− .26	− 1.36
Delaware	− 2.04*	− 3.18*
Florida	− .63	− .90
Georgia	− .66	− 1.44
Hawaii	− .44	− .30
Idaho	− .85	− .98
Illinois	− 2.12*	− 2.44*
Indiana	− 1.09	− 1.45
Iowa	− 3.97*	− 5.15*
Kansas	− 1.30	− 1.40
Kentucky	− 1.26	− 1.95
Louisiana	− .83	− .89
Maine	.51	.48
Maryland	− 2.81*	− 2.49*
Massachusetts	− .63	− 2.49*
Michigan	− .95	− .74
Minnesota	− 1.60	− 1.55
Mississippi	− .05	− 1.49
Missouri	− 2.50*	− 2.20*
Montana	− 2.06*	− 3.19*
Nebraska	− 2.95*	− 3.82*
Nevada	− 2.24*	− 2.18*
New Hampshire	− 2.92*	− 4.40*
New Jersey	− 2.56*	− 3.21*
New Mexico	− .52	− .20
New York	− 2.56*	− 2.24*
North Carolina	− .85	− 1.76
North Dakota	− 3.95*	− 5.27*

Table 7–4 continued

	T Statistics (Coefficient + Standard Deviation)	
	Growth in Per Capita Personal Income	Growth in Per Capita Personal Income
Ohio	−.89	−.73
Oklahoma	.54	1.45
Oregon	−.09	−.17
Pennsylvania	−2.16*	−2.10*
Rhode Island	−2.74*	−2.32*
South Carolina	−.07	−1.20
South Dakota	−3.08*	−3.50*
Tennessee	−.49	−.77
Texas	−.36	−.03
Utah	.50	.12
Vermont	−2.43*	−1.93
Virginia	−.87	−2.80*
Washington	−4.65*	−5.24*
West Virginia	−.07	−.76
Wisconsin	−3.10*	−3.48*
Wyoming	.03	.33

Note: Time-series regressions, 1957–1984 (Cochrane-Orcutt Technique). The dependent variables are per capita and total personal income. The independent variables are taxes as a percentage of personal income.

An asterisk indicates a significant T ratio.

burdens in the 1960s and early 1970s. After 1978, tax burdens were reduced each year, and Massachusetts experienced its "economic miracle" with sharply rising per capita incomes (figure 7.3).

In summary, the evidence of the growth-retarding effects of high state and local taxes is more persuasive when we examine the dynamics of growth. Time-series analyses in the separate states strongly suggest that changes in total tax burdens significantly affect economic growth rates. But not all states can increase growth rates by cutting tax burdens.

What distinguishes the states in which growth appears highly responsive to changes in tax burdens from states in which it does not? It turns out that the growth-responsive states are the high-tax states. This is not really surprising. The states that impose the heaviest taxes are those that can retard or accelerate economic growth by changing their tax burdens. California, New York, and Massachusetts were able to stimulate their economies with tax reductions in the late 1970s because they had hindered economic growth with

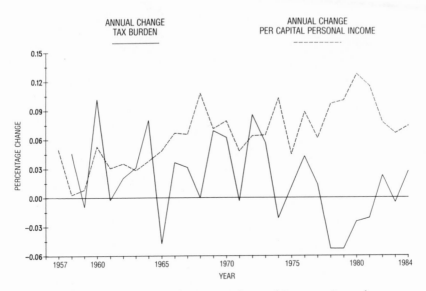

Figure 7–2. New York Tax Burden and Income Growth

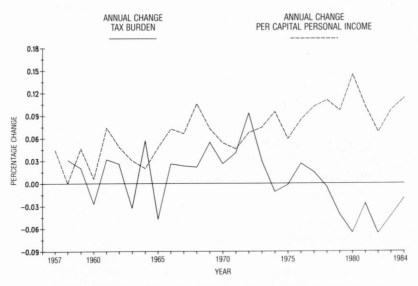

Figure 7–3. Massachusetts Tax Burden and Income Growth

high taxes in earlier years. We cannot expect that major tax reductions in low-tax states, such as Florida or Texas, would stimulate their economies in the same fashion as reductions in the high-tax states.

Spending and Economic Growth

Can states contribute to economic growth by spending for human and physical capital formation? Perhaps the reason that taxes do not have as much a growth-retarding effect as we might theorize is that some of the spending from higher taxes contributes positively to growth. The effect of taxes cannot be studied without considering how tax revenues will be spent. Some types of expenditures may offset the growth-retarding effects of taxation.

Theoretically government spending on capital infrastructure, especially transportation, should have a positive impact on economic growth. Most models of economic growth acknowledge that accessibility to markets is a major factor in industrial location. Reductions in transit costs for firms through government investment in highway, rail, water, and air transportation should improve the competitive position of a state's firms and contribute to economic growth. In commenting on growth in the Sunbelt, Watkins and Perry assert:

> Irrespective of the prevailing low wage levels, absence of unionization, availability of energy, and politically hospitable environment, no firm will locate in a region unless the requisite social and physical overhead capital has already been installed. . . . These infrastructural facilities . . . required massive public outlays for road construction and the expansion of auxiliary support services such as electric, sewage, and water facilities. (1977, p. 47–48)

Let us consider highway spending as a surrogate measure for state spending on the physical infrastructure of the economy. We know that infrastructure spending includes much more than highway spending, for example, for air, rail, and water transit, energy, water, sewer, and other public capital investments. But highway spending is clearly accounted for in state and local government reported expenditures. And it can also be argued that in a national economy in which growth is concentrated in light industries, highway transportation is more important than rail or water transportation.

Theoretically, educational spending should also contribute to economic growth. Families, including the families of corporate managers, may be concerned with the quality of education their children will receive in a state. High-quality educational systems may be especially attractive to families who place a high value on education, and these families are likely to be more productive as a result of their own commitment to improving educational capital. Empirical support for the proposition that educational spending attracts new residents has been found at the metropolitan level (Cebula 1977). Education should also add to the stock of human capital and increase the productivity of workers. There is an extensive literature estimating the impact of education on individual productivity and earnings. These effects may be muted, however, in our effort to study educational spending and state economic growth because people educated in one state can move to other states. The economic benefits of educational spending may not be fully reflected in improved productivity within a state if former students migrate to other states. Similarly, the adverse effects of poor educational systems may not be fully felt by a state if it can attract workers educated in other states. This is especially true of spending for higher education because the labor market for college-educated workers tends to be national. However, the quality of a state's elementary and secondary schools may have a more distinct impact on the productivity of its own work force.

In contrast to the stimulative effect of government spending on physical and human capital formation, redistributional spending can be expected to have a negative effect on growth. While it may be possible to view welfare expenditures as long-run investments in human capital, these investments would require a very long time span to reach fruition. Empirical observation suggests that welfare expenditures generally fail to contribute to productivity; they may even have the opposite effect (Murray 1984).

There is some limited evidence to support our theorizing about the stimulative effects of government spending for infrastructure. The simple cross-sectional relationships between state-local spending variables and economic growth in various time periods can be observed in table 7–5. The states that made the greatest efforts in highway spending were those that experienced the greatest growth in per capita personal income. This relationship between highway spending and economic growth occurred principally in the 1970s, however. Support for the notion that educational spending stimulates growth

Table 7–5
State-Local Spending and Economic Growth

Spending Burdens (Percentage of Income) at Beginning of Each Time Period	Growth in Per Capita Personal Income			
	Long Term, 1960–1984	1960–1970	1970–1980	1980–1984
Education	.11*	.11	.38*	.06
Highways	.31*	.07	.54*	−.13
Welfare	−.04	−.02	12	.21

Note: Figures are simple correlation coefficients for fifty stastes. An asterisk indicates a statistically significant relationship.

is even more limited. While the coefficients are positive for various time periods, only in the 1970s is the relationship significant. Finally, there is no convincing evidence in cross-sectional relationships that welfare spending retards economic growth. That is, the states with high welfare burdens were not necessarily the slowest-growing states.

Our inquiries as to whether changes in state spending for highways, education, and welfare affect growth produced weak and inconsistent findings. Time-series analysis for each state (300 separate regression problems, not shown, for each of three types of spending on both per capita and total income growth) failed to identify any strong or consistent stimulative effects for increased highway or educational spending or any strong or consistent adverse effects for increased welfare spending.

In summary, it is difficult to show that state and local government spending for human or physical capital contributes to economic growth. In the next section, we will examine the effects of redistributional (welfare) spending more closely. But in general the stimulative effects of state and local government spending are more difficult to identify than the growth-retarding effects of state and local government taxing.

Combined Effects: Sclerosis, Convergence, and Taxes

Economic growth is not easy for governments to achieve or scholars to explain. Economic development is a dynamic process in which changing relative prices, international competition, and subtle changes in motivation and incentives are not easily captured by empirical tests. It is not likely that we will ever explain most or all of the variation in economic growth rates in the American states.

Nonetheless, we might combine several of the theories already discussed and try to assess the combined effects of the various measures derived from them. We can combine the sclerosis theory, which postulates deterioration in the vitality of older economies that have accumulated many organizational retardants to growth; with convergence theory, which postulates that less developed economies can grow more rapidly than advanced economies at the technological frontier; with tax burden theory, which postulates that taxes reduce returns on work, savings, and risk and thereby discourage growth.

All three of these theories are complementary. The sclerosis view focuses on organizational constraints that reduce the rate of growth in an advanced economy, and the convergence theory focuses on accelerated growth in a less developed economy. Either phenomenon will result in a narrowing of income differentials over time. Tax burdens may be increased because of a greater needs for public goods in advanced economies or because of the claims of increasingly powerful bureaucracies and organized interests over time. Thus, tax burdens should be greater in more advanced economies and in economies with greater organizational and institutional development. All three theories, then, may combine to explain differentials in growth rates among the states. Our task is to assess their combined effect and to compare the contribution of each to economic growth.

To do so, we have pooled observations of various indicators of these theories, together with growth in per capita personal income, both cross-sectionally and longitudinally for the forty-eight coterminous states for the period 1961 through 1984. By pooling all of these observations—forty-eight states for twenty-four years—N is 1,152. We base the regression on this total. We can no longer examine separate states or particular time periods, but the increase in N allows us to introduce multiple regression techniques (see the Appendix).

As indicators of the sclerosis theory, we employ Olson's YEARS variable—the number of years since admission to statehood or readmission for the Confederate states—and a variable indicating whether a state has a right to work law, RTW. This is a proxy for the strength of unionism; annual data on unionization are not available. As an indicator of convergence theory, we include as an independent variable the 1957 level of per capita personal income, CONVERGE. The tax burden indicator is the ratio of total state and local own-source revenue to total personal income, TAX. Annual change in this ratio is employed in the pooled regression analysis to reduce autocorrelation effects. Finally, annual change in state and local per capita welfare expenditures, WELFARE, is employed as an indicator of redistributional spending.

Overall, the combined model explains about one-third of the variation in growth rates in all of the states (table 7–6). These modest results warn us that forces outside the states largely determine their economic fortunes. (Indeed, a separate econometric analysis of the same data that includes dummy variables representing national economic cycles and the oil shocks succeeds in increasing the explained variance to .66.) Nonetheless, these results lend support to all three general explanations of economic growth in the states.

The convergence theory is strongly supported by the experience of the states over the past three decades. The coefficient for CONVERGE, the 1957 level of personal income in each state, is significant. We might speculate, however, that this influence is time specific. At the end of World War II the southern and western states had a great deal of catching up to do. They were ripe for the relatively rapid growth predicted by the convergence theory. But now that per capita incomes among the states have narrowed, the convergence phenomenon will play a less important role in determining future state growth rates.

The sclerosis theory receives some limited support from these results. Although the coefficient for YEARS is not statistically significant, the coefficient for right to work laws is associated with growth. Perhaps the greater strength of the YEARS variable reported in previous research (Dye 1980a;

Table 7–6
Determinants of Growth of State Per Capita Income

Independent Variables	Coefficient (t values in parentheses)
Constant	7.246* (14.84)
RTW	.363* (2.53)
YEAR	.002 (1.16)
WELFARE	−.199* (−4.17)
CONVERGE	−.025* (−4.65)
TAX$_t$	−2.261* (−20.28)
R^2 = .31	

Note: Pooled regression analysis, forty-eight states, 1961–1984. An asterisk indicates a statistically significant coefficient.

Choi 1983) resulted from its association with the convergence phenomenon. When these influences are sorted out, convergence appears to have a stronger effect on state growth rates than sclerosis, at least insofar as these forces are captured by our measures.

Welfare spending appears to have a significant growth-retarding effect, independent of other factors. Perhaps welfare spending reflects the general growth of institutional retardants; that is, perhaps it should be considered an indicator of the sclerosis theory.

The most important finding in our search for the determinants of economic growth rates in the states centers on the result obtained with the TAX variable. Tax burdens have significant and independent growth-retarding effects in the overall experience of the states. Changes in tax burdens have a significant and negative effect on changes in per capita personal income. This may not be true for all states at all time periods, but the pooled experiences of all of the states over the 1961–1984 time period indicate that tax burdens do retard growth. Moreover, the growth-retarding effects of tax burdens are independent of the sclerosis and convergence explanations.

Competition and Taxation

A central problem in political economy is how to tax efficiently—that is, how to raise the revenues required for necessary public goods and services without creating disincentives to work, savings, risk, and creativity.

Monopoly governments have difficulty in estimating the developmental consequences of their tax policies. They can make no direct comparisons of the results of alternative levels and incidence of taxation. International comparisons are always flawed by vast cultural and historical differences, and the lessons of past policy decisions are often obscured by different contemporaneous conditions.

Competition among governments is very helpful in revealing the true consequences of public policy. Intergovernmental competition provides policymakers with direct incentives and evaluative standards—motives and measures—for greater efficiency in tax policy. Intergovernmental competition offers a rough market solution to the informational problems confronting public officials.

Of course, economic growth is in large measure a product of factors over which state and local governments have little control. Regional growth models must include accessibility to markets and raw materials, the costs and availability of factors of production, changing demands for regional exports, discoveries of new or exhaustion of old national resources, and changes in technology that alter a region's competitive position with other regions. Tax policies may have only marginal effects on economic growth in the states, yet these marginal effects are clearly important to citizen-taxpayers.

Competing governments have a greater incentive to strive for moderate tax burdens and proportional tax incidence than monopoly governments. Citizen-taxpayers, as well as public officials, can benefit from comparative information. They respond not only by voting against public officials who impose heavy taxes but also by leaving or threatening to leave the state or by not coming in the first place. Thus, the consequences of inefficient tax policies are accentuated in a federal system.

Admittedly empirical evidence linking tax policies with economic growth in the states is not as strong as the theoretical argument would suggest. The states with the heaviest tax burdens and highest top marginal rates are not always the slowest-growing states. The longitudinal evidence is somewhat stronger: raising or lowering tax burdens, especially in high-tax states, appears to have the expected growth-retarding or -accelerating effects.

But the linkage between taxes and growth in the states may be obscured by competition itself. Competition may prevent any single state from imposing heavy tax burdens or steeply progressive tax rates. We cannot directly observe the effect of these policies because no state could long afford to pursue them. Interstate tax competition has kept state tax burdens moderate and top marginal rates low relative to federal burdens and rates. Where would state tax burdens and rates be in the absence of such competition?

8
Toward Competitive Federalism

> In the compound republic of America, the power surrender by the people is first divided between the distinct governments, and then the portion allotted to each subdivided among distinct and separate departments. Hence a double security arises to the rights of the people. The different governments will control each other, at the same time that each will be controlled by itself.
>
> ——James Madison, *Federalist*, Number 51

Federalism and Competition

Creating "opposite and rival interests" within government itself was the distinctive contribution of the founders of our nation. Intergovernmental competition was structurally encouraged in the allocation of powers to the several branches of the national government and in the division of powers between the national government and the states. The focus of scholarly writings on American federalism throughout the nation's history has been on competition between the national government and the states. Competition among state governments and their local subdivisions has received less attention, yet this competition is a fundamental part of the idea of federalism.

Federalism—multiple, independent governments with significant and autonomous responsibility for the welfare of people living within their jurisdictions—offers protection for many important political values: individual liberty, pluralism, party competition, political participation, and the management of intense conflict. But it also provides an opportunity to develop the values of intergovernmental competition: (1) greater overall satisfaction of the preferences of citizens, (2) incentives for governments to become efficient and provide high-quality services at their lowest costs, (3) restraints on the size of the public sector and the tendencies of governments to over-supply goods and services, (4) greater responsiveness of state and local governments to the policy preferences of consumer-taxpayers, (5) restraints on the overall burdens of taxation and the imposition of nonproportional taxes, (6) encouragement of economic growth and individual economic well-being, and (7) encouragement of innovation and experimentation in public policy.

The Values of Federalism

The values of federalism itself have been well argued over the past two centuries, yet it is worthwhile to remind ourselves of them. First, federalism provides protection to individuals from the immense power of government. Even before the founders were in their graves, Tocqueville was warning against the dangers of centralized government to individual dignity:

> Above [the people] stands an immense and tutelary power, which takes upon itself alone to secure their gratifications and to watch over their fate. . . . After having thus successively taken each member of the community in its powerful grasp and fashioned him at will, the supreme power then extends its arm over the whole community. It covers the surface of society with a network of small complicated rules, minute and uniform, through which the most original minds and the most energetic characters cannot penetrate, to rise above the crowd. The will of man is not shattered, but softened, bent, and guided; men are seldom forced by it to act, but they are constantly restrained from acting. Such a power does not destroy, but it prevents existence; it does not tyrannize, but it compresses, enervates, extinguishes and stupefies a people, till each nation is reduced to nothing better than a flock of timid and industrial animals, of which the government is the shepherd. (Tocqueville 1835)

Federalism distributes power more widely throughout society. It encourages the development of multiple leadership groups. Pluralism among elites is believed to provide better protection for individual liberty than a single elite. The pluralist argument for federalism was expressed by political scientist Robert A. Dahl:

> States and local governments have provided a number of centers of power whose autonomy is strongly protected by Constitutional and political traditions. A governor of a state or the mayor of a large city may not be the political equal of a president (at least not often); but he is most assuredly not a subordinate. In dealing with a governor or mayor, a president rarely if ever commands; he negotiates; he may even plead. Here then is a part of the intermediate stratum of leadership that Tocqueville looked to as a barrier to tyranny. (Dahl 1967, p. 189).

Federalism facilitates party competition. State and local governments provide a political base of offices for the opposition party when it has lost national elections. In this way, state and local governments contribute to party competition by helping to tide over the losing party after electoral defeat so that it may remain strong enough to challenge incumbents at the next election. Moreover, state and local governments provide a channel of recruitment for national political leaders. National leaders can be drawn from a pool of leaders experienced in state and local politics.

Federalism stimulates political participation. Although fewer people vote in state and local elections than in national elections, more people run and win office at the state and local level. There are over eighty-three thousand governments in the United States: states, counties, townships, municipalities, towns, special districts, and school districts. Nearly a million people hold some kind of public office. The opportunity to exercise political leadership contributes to popular support of the political system. By providing more opportunities for direct citizen involvement in government, state and local governments contribute to the popular sense of political effectiveness and well-being. Public opinion studies consistently report that people believe that local government is more understandable, that they have greater confidence in it, and they feel more capable of affecting its policies.

Federalism assists in managing conflict. Federal forms of government, wherever they are found, have arisen in response to diversity and conflict within a society. Federalism allows diverse peoples, with conflicting policy preferences, to be brought together in a single nation, without placing un-bearable strains on the political fabric of the national government. Potential conflicts between geographically separated interests are mitigated by allow-ing each interest to enact its own policies within separate states. This arrange-ment seeks to manage traumatic and potentially nation-shattering conflicts, to avoid destructive battles over a single national policy, to protect the integ-rity and the very existence of the national government.

The Values of Intergovernmental Competition

The values of intergovernmental competition have been less well understood than the values of federalism itself. Yet it is our argument that one of the great strengths of federalism is the opportunity it presents for the develop-ment of intergovernmental competition.

Let us now develop the arguments on behalf of intergovernmental com-petition in the light of the empirical observations of the states presented in the previous chapters.

Efficiency

Competition, information, and mobility combine to offer protection against the oversupply of public goods and services. Monopoly government is far more vulnerable to the many supply-side forces inherent in governmental and political processes. It is possible, of course, that public goods are not really oversupplied—that the growth of government is "a misplaced concern of ideological conservatives." If so, we still have nothing to fear from intergovernmental competition. In our theory, competition will reduce the supply of public goods only if they are in fact oversupplied relative to citizen preferences.

The experience of state and local governments in the years since 1976 suggests that their growth can be halted. The modest yet significant contraction in the size of this sector over the last decade lends some empirical support to our argument. The growth pattern of the competitive state-local sector certainly contrasts with that of the monopoly federal sector. And it is important to note that the contraction of the state-local sector coincided with a decline in demand for the largest service function of state and local government, education. Thus, we have evidence that the state-local governmental sector contracts when demand for public service contraccts; we have no evidence to date that the federal sector can contract at all. We believe the real long-term constraint on the growth of state-local sector is competition. But we also acknowledge that some institutional features of state government—the popular initiative and constitutional prohibitions against debt—also contribute to restraint in state-local public sector growth.

The absence of good information about the true demand for public services, together with the natural tendencies of elected officials and bureaucrats to expand their functions, powers, and budgets, produces an oversupply of public goods—more than citizen-taxpayers would choose for themselves if confronted with full knowledge of their costs and benefits. But multiple governments, offering different packages of services and costs to citizens in their jurisdictions, provide information to citizens everywhere about what government services can be provided at what costs. This information is valuable to both citizens and officials because it allows them to compare governmental performances. Mobility is not absolutely essential to inspire efficiency; all that is necessary is comparative information for taxpayer-voters and competition for public office. Some public officials may welcome the challenge of comparison with other jurisdictions. Not all public officials consciously seek to obscure information in the fashion predicted by narrow models of bureaucratic behavior. Some want to do what is right but simply lack information. And voters who are informed about comparative costs—even if these voters are a very small proportion of the electorate—can influence governmental performance.

Information is an important product of intergovernmental competition, but the driving force in the competitive federalism model is mobility. Mobility, real and potential, of people, industry, and capital not only better satisfies the preferences of consumer-taxpayers but forces governments to become more efficient. There is good reason to believe that the United States is the most mobile society in the world. Approximately 40 percent of the population of the United States changes residence at least once in a five-year period; 18 percent move to a different county and 9 percent to a different state (table 8–1).

Table 8–1
Population Mobility in the United States

	Percentage of Total Population Moving over Five Years		
	1970–1975	1975–1980	1980–1985
Total movers	41.3	46.4	39.9
Different county	17.1	19.5	17.8
Different state	8.6	9.7	8.7
Different nation	1.6	1.8	1.8

Source: *Statistical Abstract of the United States, 1987*, p. 25.

Responsiveness

Governmental competition inspires policy responsiveness. Despite nationalization of the states over time in many economic and political dimensions, policy variations are not diminishing. States continue to exhibit significant differences in levels of public spending and taxation. Whatever the theoretical deficiencies of the median voter model, variation in the levels of public services provided in the states is closely associated with characteristics of the populations. For many years the determinants literature in state and local government provided good predictive models of taxing and spending based on income, education, urbanization, and other demographic characteristics of populations (Fisher 1964; Dye 1966; Hofferbert 1966a; Sharkansky and Hofferbert 1969). These early studies even identified the distortions in these relationships created by federal aid (Sachs and Harris 1964). We have shown how these cross-sectional relationships have persisted over the years. More important, we have shown that changes over time in public spending in most of the states can be attributed to identifiable changes in the demand for services, notably education. We acknowledge that bureaucracy, centralization, and institutional sclerosis are alive and well and influencing spending levels in states; many of our cross-sectional comparisons confirm the importance of these supply-side forces. But there is equally compelling evidence that the demands of consumer-taxpayers in the states also shape spending policies. In nearly all of the states, changes in state spending over time can be estimated well from a simple demand-side model, one in which school-aged population is the driving force behind the largest functional component of state-local spending, education.

Constraints

Competitive federalism places revenue constraints on policymakers. The range of variation in tax levels and burdens among the states is quite large and has persisted over time. Tax levels are closely associated with income levels; supply-side forces have only a modest impact. However, tax burdens—state-local tax revenue as a percentage of personal income—cannot be estimated very well from income levels or other demographic characteristic of state populations. Moreover, tax burdens tend to change over time, with some states imposing heavy burdens in some years relative to other states and then dramatically lightening their tax burdens to move toward the state median. The dynamics of these relative movements resemble the convoy analogy—with some ships moving out ahead of the convoy and then falling back and other ships trailing the flotilla and then moving up into the pack.

These revenue dynamics appear to conform to a competitive pattern—one likely to be produced by competition, information, and mobility among the states. But we also speculate that the constitutional mechanisms for initiative and referendums have a very important role in tax policy. These devices facilitate closer relationships between taxpayer preferences and public policies. We emphasize their facilitative role because referendum voting does not always lead to lower taxes. Indeed, the recent record of referendum voting shows as many defeats as victories for tax limitation initiatives, and even when these measures are approved, they are not always effective in lowering tax burdens.

Competition allows citizen-voters to compare revenue burdens among the states, and this comparative information itself constrains decision making. Citizen-taxpayers have the additional option of moving or threatening to move, and knowledge of this option also constrains decision making. Moreover, special institutional arrangements in state and local government—earmarked revenues, user charges, initiative and referendum voting, balanced budget requirements—place additional constraints on state and local taxing and spending, constraints that are largely absent in the federal government. The result is general moderation in the tax burdens imposed by state and local government rough proportionality in tax incidence and tax revenues linked more directly to demands for public services.

Finally, federalism helps combat fiscal illusion. Smaller units of government prevent the costs of public services from being dispersed over so large a jurisdiction that their burdens are unnoticed. We know that interest groups seek to concentrate benefits for themselves and to disperse costs over such a wide segment of society that individual citizens have little incentive to inform themselves, organize, and devote resources to counter these special interest claims. We know that voters tend to credit their elected representatives for special interest programs that benefit them directly, yet seldom do they blame their representative for the taxes they pay for special interest programs for others. Competitive federalism helps to counter these expansionist tendencies of interest group activity by reducing the size of taxpaying constituencies and thus limiting the dispersal of costs. The costs of special interest subsidies granted by state or local government cannot be dispersed over the entire nation in the fashion of federal government subsidies. By more closing matching costs with benefits, state and local governments are held to greater accountability by voter-taxpayers.

Distortions

The principal distortion in public policy in the states arises from the effects of the federal grant system. Consumer-taxpayers in the states cannot accurately make benefit-cost calculations because of the financial intervention of the federal government. Although the federal proportion of state-local revenue has declined slightly in the 1980s, it is still over 18 percent. Federal aid reduces the responsiveness of state-local spending to characteristics of state populations. The overall effect of such transfers is to create an oversupply of public goods; citizens and officials in the states provide higher levels of public services than they would if they had to pay their full costs from their own tax revenues. Our calculations show that federal aid has had a major stimulative effect on state-local spending. This effect appears in both cross-sectional observations (states with higher levels of federal aid spend more total and own-source money than state with lower levels of federal aid) and in time-series observations of individual states (in virtually all of the states' federal aid has been a major determinant of change in spending levels).

The expansion of the federal grant system over the years has not been driven by fiscal federalism arguments. That is, federal intervention has not come in response to concerns about "externalities"—spillover benefits and costs of state and local government activity. Rather centralization is the result of nationally organized interests' substituting their own policy preferences for those of citizens and officials in states and communities. We have explained the success of nationally organized interests by our rent-seeking theory of centralization. It is more efficient to seek subsidies, privileges, and protection at a single central location than to do so at fifty or eighty-three thousand subnational locations. Moreover, the larger national arena permits interests to disperse the costs of their specialized and concentrated benefits over a broader constituency. This reduces the burden of any single subsidy on the individual citizen and thus weakens potential opposition.

The Need for Auxiliary Precautions

Policy responsiveness in the states is clearly not a product of competitive, policy-relevant party politics. We would not have to concern ourselves so much about competition, information, and mobility if we were certain that democratic processes within the states would ensure policy responsiveness. But party competition and policy-relevant electoral politics are rarely found in the American states. The responsible party model—competitive policy-oriented parties whose election to office brings about significant policy changes—is notably absent from state politics. It is true that differences among the states in levels of party competition and voter participation have diminished over time, primarily as a result of increased competition and participation in the southern and border states. But these changes have not been accompanied by any notable increase in policy-relevant party politics. When we observe changes in welfare and tax policies in each of the states over time, we find that these changes are largely unrelated to changes in party control of state government. The party system in most states fails to give citizen-voters a means of influencing these policy directions. The weakness of the responsible party model in the states, the absence of competitive parties, and the irrelevance of party control of state government to policy reinforce the need for auxiliary precautions for popular control of government.

Economic Development

Competition inspires the states to be concerned with the impact of their taxing and spending policies on economic growth and to become directly involved in economic development activities. Only recently has international competition begun to inspire similar concern in Washington. Prior to 1981, discussion of federal tax policy almost always centered on redistributional issues. Scholars and politicians who raised questions about the growth-retarding effects of federal tax policies were ignored or ridiculed. But developmental issues have long been central to debates over taxing and spending in state capitols and city halls, and it is competition that has kept developmental concerns in focus.

Monopoly governments have no direct way of estimating the growth-retarding effects of their tax policies. Cross-national comparisons are confounded by vast cultural differences, and longitudinal examinations of the effects of past tax policies are obscured by historical circumstances. Competing governments are in a better position to observe the economic consequences of their policy decisions. Competition provides both motives and measures for policymakers to achieve efficiency.

Over the longer term, economic growth rates in the states have been affected by the nationalization of the economy. The convergence theory helps explain why states that began at relatively low levels of economic development grew more rapidly than states that began at higher levels. It is easier for less developed states to attract the transfer of existing technology than to invest new technology. And capital and labor tend to flow to where output can rise more rapidly. But these convergence or catch-up forces may not play an important role in the future. Convergence has slowed since 1970. There is no longer enough variation among regions to permit diffusion itself to determine growth rates.

The sclerosis theory remains intriguing. Explaining growth rates by reference to the accumulated growth-retarding effects of interest group activity is intuitively satisfying. And it is true that younger states have enjoyed higher long-term economic growth rates than older states. But there has been a reversal of this pattern in the 1980s; older states have recently outperformed younger states. Specific tests of the sclerosis model have been unsatisfying. Political scientists have become confused over the difference between the relative strength of single interest groups in states (which may accelerate growth) and the aggregated influence of complex interest group systems in states (which may retard growth).

Growth-Retarding Effects of Taxes

Economic growth rates in the states are only marginally influenced by state and local government. So many other forces affect state economic development—among them changes in world demand for specific products, changes in technologies, changing energy and labor costs, discoveries of new natural resources, and developments in transportation—that it is difficult to sort out the independent effects of state tax and spending policies. Moreover, economic growth in the states occurs in spurts and lags. States that experienced the most impressive economic growth rates in the 1970s are not the same states that were growing most rapidly in the 1980s. This complicates the search for general explanations of regional economic growth.

The growth-retarding effects of heavy tax burdens and high marginal rates in the states are significant. It is true that cross-sectional observations indicate that the states with the heaviest burdens and highest rates are not always the slowest-growing states, depending on the time period examined. But the time-series evidence is somewhat stronger: raising or lowering tax burdens, especially in high-tax states, appears to retard and accelerate growth as expected.

Innovation

Competitive federalism inspires policy innovation. Perhaps the most noteworthy state policy innovations in recent years have come as a result of state efforts to improve their economic position (Osborne 1988; Fosler 1988). Just as entrepreneurs compete with new ideas in the marketplace to find an advantage over their rivals, so also public officials in states and communities have been inspired by intergovernmental competition to seek innovations in public policy.

We have distinguished between economic growth policy and state industrial policies. Economic growth policy is the provision of truly public goods and services with minimum burdens in taxes and regulations. State industrial policies generally involve special treatments—loans and subsidies, guarantees and exemptions—that in the long run contribute to economic inefficiency. But the effects of various industrial policy decisions are not easy to identify. The literature to date has failed to observe any significant aggregate growth effects for any direct state industrial development activities (ACIR 1967; Pierce, Hagstrom, and Steinbach 1979; Rasmussen, Bendick, and Ledebor 1984; Rubin and Zom 1985; Ambrosius, 1986).

There are good theoretical reasons for predicting that direct state involvement in capital formation, as well as special tax treatments, will inevitably produce inefficiencies. But competition among the states in industrial policies is self-correcting in the long run. States will gradually learn from their mistakes as they compare their progress with other states. Consider how much worse a national industrial policy would be—a monopoly government allocating capital, dispensing subsidies, and granting special privileges and protections. (Not that the federal government does not already do so in innumerable tax code provisions and subsidy programs, but a national industrial policy would legitimate and enlarge the scope of these subsidies, privileges, and protections.) The only corrective to a national industrial policy would be international competition, and far more damage would be done to the nation before global competition would exert its correcting influence. Perhaps the results of the industrial policy experiments currently being conducted in America's "laboratories of democracy" will succeed in discouraging the federal government from pursuing national industrial policy.

Competition and Public Policy

Most debates over federalism are only lightly camouflaged debates over policy. Philosophers and economists (Rawls 1971; Buchanan and Tullock 1962) may assert a distinction between constitutional issues—deciding how issues should be decided—and policy issues—deciding the issues themselves. They may argue that constitutional rules should be decided behind a veil of ignorance about the immediate policy consequences of these rules; that the decision-making process should be established before policy choices are fed into the process; that individuals should be uncertain about the policy consequences of selecting a particular constitutional process before they do so.

But in politics, constitutional decisions are never separated from policy outcomes. People do know what the policy consequences of various constitutional arrangements will be. Citizens as well as political leaders consistently subordinate constitutional questions to immediate policy concerns. Indeed, history is replete with examples of the same political leaders arguing one notion of federalism at one time to achieve their immediate policy goal and then turning around and supporting a contradictory notion of federalism later when it fits a new policy goal. No American politician, from Thomas Jefferson onward, has ever so strongly supported a view of federalism that he or she ended up conceding a policy battle.

If competitive federalism is to be politically viable, it must be discussed in a policy context. Abstract debates about federalism or competition, devoid of policy implications, hold little interest for most citizens or politicians. "Most people have little interest in abstract debates that argue which level of government should be responsible for a given task. What most people care about is getting the policies they want" (Nice 1987, p. 24). Wise politicians are familiar with the wisdom expressed by political scientist E.E. Schattschneider years ago: "The outcome of all conflict is determined by the scope of its contagion. The number of people involved in any conflict determines what happens; every change in the number of participants, every increase or deduction in the number of participants affects the results" (Schattschneider 1942, p. 2). Thus debates about federalism must acknowledge policy consequences.

Let us consider the impact of the competitive federalism model for different types of policy decisions. Policies have been usefully classified as allocational, developmental, or redistributional (Lowi 1964). Allocational policies produce and distribute public goods and services to consumer-taxpayers. These policies encompass the provision of a broad range of state and local government services—education, health, welfare, streets and highways, police and fire protection, sewers, water and utilities, garbage disposal, parks and recreation, and so on. Developmental policies are those that directly add to the economic well-being of the state or community. These policies are directed toward economic growth; they include attracting industry, building transportation facilities, providing utilities, renewing urban areas, training the labor force for work, and so on. Redistributional policies are designed to redirect wealth to benefit particular segments of society and thus satisfy equity concerns. These policies include traditional welfare services, health care for the poor, unemployment compensation, low-income housing, as well as progressive taxation. Note that these are analytical distinctions among types of policies; any specific government activity may have allocational, developmental, and redistributive elements within it.

Allocational Policy

Competitive federalism directly strengthens the allocative functions of government. Decentralization permits governments to match services with variations in demand. Greater overall citizen satisfaction can be achieved with multiple governments' offering different packages of public services at different prices. Competition forces governors to become more efferent in its allocative activities, providing better services at lower costs. Competition forces government to be more responsive than monopoly government to citizen preferences. This has been the major thrust of our argument for competitive federalism.

The value of competition in allocative policies has not been seriously challenged. Paul E. Peterson, one of the few political scientists to incorporate the notion of competition into a coherent theory of federalism, appears to agree:

> Allocation is the function that local governments can perform more effectively than central governments, because decentralization allows for a closer match between the supply of public services and their variable demand. Citizens migrate to those communities where the allocation best matches their demand curve. (Peterson 1981, p. 77)

Developmental Policy

Competitive federalism also directly strengthens the developmental policies of government. States and communities have strong incentives to compete for capital investment, skilled labor, and advanced technology. We have argued that economic growth policies are much broader than industrial development policies. States and communities may find that special concessions to particular firms and industries are not an efficient way to increase the economic well-being of their citizens. Rather economic growth policies encompass the provision of public services—high-quality schools and universities, good highways, adequate utilities and infrastructure, police and fire protection, pleasant parks, and even effective and humane welfare services—that make states and communities attractive to managers of firms and their most productive employees. Of course, economic growth also requires that these services be purchased at the lowest possible cost. Competition increases the likelihood that state and local governments will operate efficiently, so that their taxes will remain competitive with other states and communities providing comparable levels of service.

The state's role in economic development has traditionally centered on the provision of physical infrastructure, especially transportation. Indeed for many years economic growth in the states correlated closely with state expenditures for transportation (Dye 1980a). But it is likely that economic growth in the future will depend more upon state investment in intellectual infrastructure. Economic growth is always and everywhere a function of human creativity. In practical terms, investment in education at all levels—elementary and secondary schools, trade and vocational schools, community colleges and state universities, research institutions and parks—is likely to become the key to competitive advantage in the economy of the future. Fortunately for the future of the United States, education is largely a function of competitive state and local governments rather than monopoly centralized government. Economic competition among the states can become the driving force behind improvements in education and research.

In addition to improvements in physical and intellectual infrastructure, competition can also drive states and communities to improve the quality of life in their locales. A skilled, educated, creative work force can neither be recruited to a state nor retained if the general quality of life is considered unattractive. It is difficult to assess systematically the economic effect of public investment in parks and recreation, cultural and sports facilities, leisure activities, historical preservation, charm, and pleasant surroundings. But there are innumerable journalistic accounts of the importance of quality of life factors in industrial location decisions, particularly for newer high-tech industries. The following quotation is representative:

> Unlike smokestack industries that need access to raw materials, energy, and transportation, high-tech plants located where the quality of life is high enough to draw a skilled work force. You don't locate plants for cheap labor or even taxes. You locate where people want to live. (Osborne 1988, p. 6; see also Schemenner 1982)

It is hard to imagine a more beneficial competition among governments than competition to improve the quality of life in America's states and communities.

Thus, development policies are well served by federalism. Paul Peterson argues convincingly that the federal government would be wise to leave economic development policy to state and local governments:

> Since state and local governments are well equipped to pursue developmental objectives, most public efforts of this type should be left to them. By delegating responsibility for most developmental programs to state and local governments, the federal government would frankly admit its incapacity to use those programs to help populations with special needs. (Peterson, Rabe, and Wong 1986, p. 230)

Even strong proponents of state industrial policies warn against federal intervention. Osborne reasons that

> the American economy—indeed the world economy—is made up of a series of regional economies, each of which radiates out from a city or network of cities. Each regional economy is unique. Each has a different mix of industries, a different labor market, a different set of educational institutions, and different capital markets. In this country, the governmental unit that most

closely matches the regional economy is the state. (Osborne 1988, pp. 283–284)

Redistribution Policy

The most serious challenge to the competitive federalism model arises in redistributional policy. Can multiple competing government undertake redistributive policies without creating unbearable free-rider problems for themselves? Will states and communities be restrained from providing the welfare services they would otherwise prefer because of the threat of an inundation of poor people from less beneficent free-riding jurisdictions? Will tax burdens to support generous welfare services encourage the nonpoor—both households and business—to migrate to jurisdictions that impose lighter tax burdens because they provide frugal welfare services?

The empirical evidence to support the view that the poor will move to high welfare benefit states is very weak. Sociologist Larry H. Long in a review of the relevant literature in 1974 concluded that "no study has presented empirical evidence for the hypothesis that welfare payments themselves have attracted large numbers of persons to states and cities with high benefit levels" (Long 1979, p. 46). Long reached similar conclusions in his own research. However, Paul E. Peterson and Mark C. Rom (1987) argue that there is a significant, albeit sluggish, response of poor people to welfare benefit levels in the states. He concentrates his attention on migration patterns after 1969 when the U.S. Supreme Court ruled (in *Shapiro* v. *Thompson*) that states could not constitutionally deny welfare benefits to new residents. He calculates that increasing welfare benefits in a state increases its poverty population. He assumes that increases in the poverty population are "almost certainly due to migrations rather than welfare-induced changes in labor force participation rates" (Peterson and Rom 1987, p. 54). But the poor are not very mobile, and when they do move, they are more likely searching for job opportunities rather than higher welfare benefits.

The wealthy are more mobile than the poor. The argument that capital investment and productive labor will migrate to states with lower welfare spending rests on somewhat stronger empirical support. Underpinning this argument is the hidden assumption that individuals, families, and firms seek only to maximize their after-tax personal income; that is, they place little or no value on public services, especially welfare services from which they receive no direct financial benefit. But neither our competitive federalism model nor its antecedent Tiebout model is so narrow in its assumptions. The "utility functions" of individuals, families, and firms include their physical, social, and cultural environment, as well as their after-tax income. Few of us want to see poverty, hunger, homelessness, ill health, or deprivation in our society, even if we do not expect to suffer these maladies ourselves. States or communities that aggravate these hardships would hardly look attractive to families or businesses seeking places to locate.

Competition encourages policy responsiveness. Welfare policies, like all other policies, are more responsive to citizen demands when undertaken by multiple competitive governments rather than monopoly government. The effect of competition is neither to lower nor to raise welfare spending but to bring it into line with citizen demands. Competitive governments must seek to match their welfare policies with both the compassion and the prudence of their citizens.

Welfare policies rest primarily on the equity preferences of middle-class Americans rather than the poor themselves. We have observed that welfare spending in the states is not associated with proportions of poor, aged, or minority persons in their populations. Welfare policies reflect the economic prosperity of the states. We have already demonstrated that variations in welfare spending among the states are largely a function of income: welfare spending is higher in high-income states than low-income states, and welfare spending goes up with increases in income. The best hope for the poor lies in economic development—not only more job opportunities but also raised welfare spending.

In short, while we acknowledge that competitive federalism raises some theoretical concerns about redistributional policy, we remain convinced that the equity preferences of society are better served by multiple competing governments than centralized monopoly government. Welfare policies depend more on the equity preferences of middle-class voters than on the voting power of the poor. Welfare spending correlates with wealth not poverty. It is the wealthy who are mobile, not the poor. Whatever adverse effects competition may have on welfare policies, these effects are more than compensated for by the opportunities provided for policy diversity, responsiveness, and comparative experimentation.

Conditions for Competitive Federalism

Competitive federalism is more a theoretical model than a description of the American federal system. The model depends on a series of assumptions that are not fully realized in the real world of government. Just as various "market failures"—externalities, monopolies, immobilities, and imperfect information—reduce the efficiency of the competitive market model, so also do various imperfections limit the utility of the competitive federalism model. To summarize, competitive federalism depends on the following assumptions:

1. Autonomous state and local governments with significant independent responsibility for the welfare of the people living in their jurisdictions;

governments that offer a wide range of public policies and vary the level of public goods and services.

2. Costs of government goods and services that are equal to the revenues collected from taxpayers in each jurisdiction.

3. Limited externalities, or spillovers, of either costs or benefits among jurisdictions and no collusion among state and local governments to restrain competition.

4. The availability of good information to consumer-taxpayers about the services and costs offered by state and local governments throughout the nation.

5. Mobility of consumer-taxpayers and a propensity to consider governmental services and costs as important criteria in locational decisions.

The failure of the American federal system to realize these assumptions fully does not destroy the model. Reality is seldom perfectly consistent with models. The relaxation of these assumptions leads to various inefficiencies (see Pestieau 1984). But the model remains important for analytical purposes to the extent that it describes behavior under specified conditions, and it is important for normative purposes to the extent that it identifies conditions to be changed to bring about desired results.

The competitive federalism model, like all economic models, depends on marginal choices. Marginal choices always involve net additions or subtractions from the current state of affairs. Analytic models that depend on marginal choices are always certeris paribus; they describe and predict behavior when all else is equal. State and local decision makers, as well as consumer-taxpayers, always confront decisions involving changes given the current state of affairs. The model does not depend on the behavior of every family and firm or even most families and firms. Just as prices are set by a small group of active bidders, the policies of state and local governments can be shaped by a very small proportion of families, businesses, and inventors who are making locational decisions at the margin. All that is required is that a significant portion of consumer-taxpayers meet the specifications of the model.

The competitive federalism model is useful in directing attention to the real-world conditions that obstruct its function. If we view the model as normative as well as analytical, then we are provided with a guide to action—to recommendations for constitutional and policy changes that will shape real-world conditions to fit the model better and reap its benefits.

Constitutional and Policy Implications

Competitive federalism, viewed as a normative model, generates some clear constitutional and policy prescriptions:

1. State and local governments must be constitutionally encouraged and protected in the exercise of significant and autonomous responsibilities for the welfare of their citizens.

2. State and local governments must be free to compete against one another in the kinds of public goods they provide, in the kinds of regulations of private activity they enact, and in the nature and burden of the taxes they impose.

3. National government interventions in the domestic policy responsibilities of state and local governments must be constitutionally limited.

4. The national government must seek legislatively to reduce fiscal interventions that relieve state and local governments of the responsibility to tax their citizens fully for public services provided.

5. Families and firms must be constitutionally unhampered and legislatively encouraged to move about the country with a minimum of relocational costs.

6. The national government and the states must endeavor to provide comparative information on the quantity, quality, and costs of public services offered by the states.

Strengthening Federalism

Certainly competitive federalism requires at a minimum a constitutionally recognized federal system of government. And a federal system must mean something more than "procedural safeguards . . . inherent in the workings of the National Governments itself" (majority opinion in *Garcia v. San Antonio Metropolitan Transit Authority*). Rather, federalism must mean constitutionally recognized separate and autonomous national and state governments, both with significant and independent responsibility for the health, safety, and welfare of their citizens, protected by a constitution that neither can change without the consent of the other.

Recent proposals to restore federalism have sought to do so not by trying to restore the notion of a national government of enumerated powers but rather by constitutionally recognizing substantive state powers and expressly prohibiting the Congress from interfering with these powers. The ACIR endorsed a series of constitutional amendments designed to instruct the courts to determine constitutional limits to congressional power over the states, give substantive meaning to state powers under the Tenth Amendment, prohibit congressional mandating of state actions, prohibit general congressional preemptions of state powers, especially with regard to interstate commerce, and restrict congressional conducting of grant monies (table 8–2). The ACIR also recommended consideration of a constitutional amendment giving two-thirds of the states the power to declare null and void an act of Congress. The White House Working Group on Federalism produced a series of legis-lative rules proposals that generally sought to accomplish these same goals without resort to constitutional amendments (table 8–2).

There are many eminently sensible recommendations for reforming the federal grant-in-aid system. There are hardly any commentators on the fed-eral grant system, whatever their political persuasion, who do not call for some simplification of that system. Illustrative of these recommendations are the principles set forth for grant reform by the former chairman of the Coun-cil of Economic Advisers, Murray Weidenbaum (table 8–2).

But we must recognize that the political landscape is littered with pro-posals to strengthen federalism. Whatever the merits of these proposals, it is difficult to develop much political support for restraining national power. Abstract theories of federalism are largely irrelevant to the general public. Most national surveys reveal general support for the notion of federalism, generally favorable evaluations of state and local government, and general concern about the concentration of power at the federal level (table 8–3). But paradoxically many Americans want the federal government to assume even greater responsibility in specific policy areas, including some traditionally thought to be state or local government responsibilities. For example, major-ities favor having a national policy for registration and voting, setting pen-alties for murder, establishing factory safety standards, and setting minimum wages.

Moreover, it is not likely that presidents, or Congress members, or can-didates for these national offices will ever be moved to restrain national power. People expect federal officials to "do something" about every virtually every problem that confronts individuals, families, communities, or the na-tion. Politicians gain very little by telling their constituents that a particular malady is not a federal problem.

Thus, the restoration of federalism, if it is to come at all, will depend upon what state and local government officials do to make it happen. The future of federalism depends not on restraining national power but rather reinvigorating state and local government.

In recent years the states have experienced a healthy resurgence. They have reformed their own constitutional structures, granted greater indepen-dence to their local governments, and performed especially well in educational policy (see Bowman and Kearney 1986). It has even been argued that the state are recruiting better politicians (Sabato 1983). But the real question is how to encourage this resurgence and continue to strengthen the states. The answer is through competition.

Strengthening Competition

Federalism should mean competition, not merely decentralization. The national government itself should undertake to strengthen competition among the states. It can do so in prosaic yet effective fashion by acting to improve information and mobility. Economist Charles Tiebout described the policy implications of his original "pure theory" of local expenditures: "Policies that promote residential mobility and increase knowledge of the consumer-voter will improve the allocation of government expenditures in the same sense that mobility among jobs and knowledge relevant to the location of industry and labor improve the allocation of private resources" (Tiebout 1956, p. 423).

The federal government's role in collecting and disseminating information on the performance of state and local government is seldom recognized for its real value. Information leads to comparison, and comparison leads to pressure for better performance. Informed comparisons can assist in sharpening political processes: voters can compare the costs they pay and the benefits they receive with the treatment of voters in other states. If the comparisons are unsatisfactory, public officials have some explaining to do when they run for reelection. Informed comparisons can also assist individuals, families, and firms in locational decisions. The threat of losing investment, jobs, and productive citizens can motivate public officials to improve governmental performance. In other words, information facilitates both voice and exit options of citizens.

The federal government's role in facilitating mobility is seldom explored. The nation's founders seem to have been more interested than contemporary statesmen in ensuring interstate mobility. They explicitly provided for a common market throughout the new republic (Article III, section 10: "No state shall . . . lay any Imposts or Duties on Imports or Exports "), thus constitutionally ensuring the mobility of market goods. They also acted in a way that protected the flow of capital by preventing the states from "impairing the obligation of contracts" (Article II, section 10) or devaluing the currency ("No state shall . . . make anything but gold and silver Coin a Tender in Payment of Debts," Article II, section 10). The founders were interested in constitutionally protecting citizen mobility. They declared in the original document that "the citizens in each state shall be entitled to all privileges and immunities of citizens in several states" (Article IV, section 2) and that "Full Faith and Credit shall be given in each State to the public Acts, Records and judicial Proceedings of every other States." While the U.S. Supreme Court has

Table 8–2
Proposals to Restore Federalism

Legislative Actions	Constitutional Amendments (Additions to Tenth Amendment)	Grants-in-Aid Reforms
1. Urge Congress to require a statement of constitutional authority and a federaliam assessment for all federal legislation.	1. The judicial power of the United States shall be used to decide questions of jurisdiction that may arise between the United States and the respective states, as defined by this Constitution.	1. Substitute, to the maximum extent possible, the states for the federal government in dealing with local governments.
2. Seek limitations on federal regulation of the states that interferes with state sovereignty.	2. Congress shall make no law abridging the freedom of the people of the several states to govern their own affairs, provide for a constitution and laws, raise revenue, secure public employees, regulate commerce within the state, or exercise all other powers necessary and proper to promote the general welfare. Nothing in this article shall be construed to restrict the power of the Congress to enforce the provisions of this Constitution.	2. Substitute state and local governments for the federal government in dealing with private institutions and individual citizens.
3. Seek congressional restrictions on the use of grants to regulate the states indirectly.	3. Congress shall make no law, nor shall the courts make any ruling, requiring any state to take any action that is not otherwise required expressly and explicitly by this Constitution. This section shall not be construed to limit the power of Congress or the courts to prohibit any specific action by any state that violates the Constitution or the laws of the United States.	3. Cap open-ended federal grant-in-aid matching programs (to limit federal dollar contributions to subgovernment grant recipients).
4. Discourage federal grants that authorize local expenditures that are not authorized by the states.	4. Congress shall make no law, nor shall the courts make any ruling, pursuant to Article 1, Section 8, Paragraph 3 of the Constitution, restricting the power of any state unless such law is expressly and explicitly for the purpose of regulating the free flow of commerce among the several states or with foreign nations, or preserving or strengthening national markets of exchange.	4. Combine and move to the states (and localities) categorical federal grand-in-aid programs through a block grant process.
5. Seek establishment of federaliam subcommittees of the judiciary committees and revision of parliamentary rules.	5. Congress shall make no law, nor shall the courts make any ruling, pursuant to Article 1, Section 8, Paragraph 18 of the Constitution restricting the power of any state unless in the absence of such law it would be impossible to carry into execution the powers delegated to the Government of the United States by this Constitution.	5. Provide maximum state discretion and minimum federal constraints in all block grants.

Table 8–2 continued

Legislative Actions	Constitutional Amendments (Additions to Tenth Amendment)	Grants-in-Aid Reforms
6. Promote optional state consolidation of federal programs.	6. No law enacted pursuant to Paragraph 3, Article 6, of this Constitution shall be construed to restrict the powers of any state unless such restriction has been expressly and explicitly stated in such law or unless in the absence of such a construction it would be impossible to carry such law into execution.	6. Place planning, audit, and review functions at the state level for grants programs, utilizing regular state agencies wherever possible.
7. Seek a requirement that Congress's intent to preempt be explicit.	7. (a) Congress shall make no laws, nor shall the Courts make any ruling, placing conditions or restrictions on the expenditure of funds by any state or legal subdivision thereof on the basis of the source of such funds, unless such funds are paid directly by the United States into the treasury of such state or legal subdivision pursuant to a contractual agreement between the United States and such state, or in the case of a legal subdivision such state and legal subdivision. (b) Conditions and restrictions placed upon the expenditure of funds of any state or legal subdivision thereof enacted pursuant to subsection (a) shall apply only to those funds paid under a program authorized in law enacted after the date of enactment of such conditions and restrictions.	7. Move regulatory authority from the federal to the state level of government where such shifts are appropriate.
8. Seek a prohibition on agency preemption by rulemaking or a requirement that congressional authorization of agency preemption be explicit.		8. Remove, where possible, spending mandates on state and local governments from federally financed programs.
9. Reform federal court jurisdiction to limit diversity of citizenship jurisdiction.		9. Give serious examination to replacing federal funding with a movement of revenue sources from the federal government to state and local governments.

Sources: For column 1, White House Working Group (1986); for column 2, ACIR (1986); for column 3, Weidenbaum (1982).

Table 8–3
Public Opinion and Federalism

Trust and confidence: "In which of the following people in government do you have the most trust and confidence?"
  Federal government, 19
  State government, 22
  Local government, 37

Power: "Overall do you feel that the federal government has too much power, the right amount of power, or too little power over the activities of state and local government today?"
  Too much power, 46
  The right amount of power, 37
  Too little power, 7

Efficiency: "From which level of government do you feel you get the most for your money—federal, state or local?"
  Federal, 28
  State, 22
  Local, 29

Waste: "Which government do you feel wastes the most of your tax money—federal, state or local?"
  Federal, 66
  State, 14
  Local, 8

Fairness: "Which do you think is the worst tax—that is, the least fair?"
  Federal income tax, 30
  State income tax, 12
  State sales tax, 21
  Local property tax, 24

"Should there be one national policy set by the federal government or should the 50 states make their own rules . . .

	Federal	States
. . . in controlling pollution	49	46
. . . in setting penalties for murder	62	34
. . . on the issue of registration and voting	64	31
. . . in selecting textbooks for public schools	35	61
. . . in establishing safety standards for factories	65	31
. . . in setting highway speed limits"	42	56

Sources: The first five questions are from ACIR (1967). The last question is from *New York Times*, May 26, 1987, p. 10
Note: All figures in percentages of U.S. public in national opinion surveys. "No opinions" and "don't know" not shown.

not given these provisions the scope and force of other sections of the Constitution, it has, by and large, protected interstate mobility. It has struck down state laws requiring a year of residence for eligibility to vote (*Dunn* v. *Blumstein*, 1972), eligibility for welfare (*Shapiro* v. *Thompson*, 1969), and eligibility for public medical care (*Memorial Hospital* v. *Maricopa County*, 1974).

Clearly Congress has a constitutional mandate to protect and encourage mobility. States and communities ought not to be permitted to place obstacles in the way of citizens or firms wishing to leave their jurisdictions. State laws restricting plant closing should be closely scrutinized. Fair notice laws ought not to become legal devices for obstructing mobility. (Nor should federal courts permit states or cities to claim that a business franchise, such as the Baltimore Colts football team, is public domain.) If firms contractually obligate themselves to remain in a particular jurisdiction, then that is their own burden, and the market will eventually reward or penalize them for their decision. But state and local governments must not be permitted by law to interfere with the mobility of capital.

Congress should also consider legislative approaches to facilitate the mobility of labor. It might begin by reviewing unemployment compensation, welfare, and food stamp programs to determine what immobilities have been induced by these programs and how these immobilities might be corrected. Congress might review the Federal Employment Service Program to encourage interstate transfer of information to job seekers. Greater mobility might be sought through the federally funded Job Training and Partnership Act program. In general labor ought to be encouraged, rather than discouraged, to move about the country in search of the most productive, highest-paying employment.

American Values and Competitive Federalism

American federalism cannot be sustained without underlying support for the values of individualism, competition, and opportunity. The linkages between these cultural values and federalism are not always explicit. Yet the survival of federalism depends not so much on efficiency arguments as it does on the values it embodies for the American people.

Markets are decentralized, voluntary, and competitive. To the extent that federalism creates a quasi-market in public goods and services, it embodies these same values. In contrast, centralization entails coercion and uniformity. Efficiency, if it is achieved at all, comes about through coercion—central authorities that can "audit, investigate, threaten, encourage and most important cultivate professional support [among bureaucrats] to bring about the desired level of compliance." The competitive features of federalism are more consonant with the underlying values of the American people than the coercive features of centralized government.

Mobility too is highly valued in American culture. It is not only vertical social mobility that is so highly valued by Americans but also movement about the country. Mobility is an individual response to unhappiness with conditions in a particular place. It does not require the organizational or political resources necessary to effect change within a community or society. The individual can act independently, packing up the family and going elsewhere. Indeed, escape from oppressive economic or political circumstances has played a unique role in the formation of the United States. The nation was populated by people who acted individually or in families to leave behind them seemingly intractable economic or political problems of their homelands. Movement provided Americans with a paradigm for problem solving, relocation, rather than submission or revolution.

American ambivalence toward equality may be the most vulnerable aspect of federalism. Different meanings attached to equality shape attitudes toward federalism just as they shape many other political attitudes. People are ambivalent about what kind of equality they want: equality of opportunity (to make of oneself what one can to develop one's talents and abilities and to be awarded for one's efforts and achievements) or equality of results (with everyone sharing in the economic well-being of the nation and no great disparities in income or life-style).

Clearly federalism is at odds with the idea of equality of results. Independence, diversity, and competition all mean inequality. In contrast, centralization and uniformity are better suited to achieve equal results. Virtually every recommendation for federal intervention in any policy issue is accompanied by an appeal to equality of results standards. These appeals are frequently successful because Americans do apply equality of results standards to the public, political spheres of life. In the private economic spheres of life, they are more likely to invoke equality of opportunity, but not when it comes to public goods and services. The idea that governments might provide individuals with different levels and types of public services in different locations throughout the nation is not as easily accepted as the idea that markets provide individuals with different amounts and types of goods.

The importance of attitudes toward equality to federalism was well stated by political scientist Aaron Wildavsky in an essay appropriately entitled "Federalism Means Inequality":

> Uniformity is antithetical to federalism. The existence of states free to disagree with one another and with the central government inevitably leads to differentiation. Yet states must differ if they are to do more than obey central directives. Were there to be a change in values toward equality of condition, the political culture that undergirds federalism would fall apart. You can have a belief in equality of opportunity to be different, but you cannot have a belief in equality of results to be the same and still have a federal system. (Wildavsky 1985 p.7)

In short, the struggle over federalism is linked to important value conflict in American society. Federalism is more than an argument between national elites and their state and local counterparts over who should govern. It is more than a strategic positioning of interest groups seeking more easily to concentrate benefits for themselves and more widely disperse costs to others. And it is more than disguised policy conflicts with participants seeking the most favorable decisional arena. It is all of these, but it is also an expression of contrasting social values: hierarchy, collectivism, redistribution, and equality of results versus individualism, competition, efficiency, and equality of opportunity. The erosion of federalism over the past half-century reflects the nation's changing values—its greater concern for redistribution and equality of results. The preservation of federalism depends on a resurgence of national interest in economic development and equality of opportunity.

Appendix: Studying Public Policy In the American States

The American states provide an excellent opportunity to develop and test propositions about political economy. Indeed, from the perspective of systematic scholarship, federalism is a great asset. It allows variations in public policy that permit us to develop and test propositions about their causes and consequences. States can truly be laboratories in helping us to understand why governments do what they do and what differences they make in our lives.

Public policies—the activities of government—can be viewed as dependent or independent variables in research design, depending upon whether one is interested in learning about their causes or consequences. Public policies are viewed as dependent variables when we are trying to determine why states do what they do—that is, when we are trying to explain these policies. Public policies are viewed as independent variables when we are trying to assess their effects on economic conditions in the states—that is, when we are trying to explain economic development in the states.

Throughout this book, we explored a variety of theories that offered explanations of public policy and economic growth. We developed and tested models derived from these theories—models that included propositions about relationships among popular preferences, government policies, and economic outcomes.

Models are simplified representations of reality. Model building is an art as well as a craft. We build models to simplify and order our thinking so that we can better understand the complexities of the real world. A model must not be so simple or abstract that it fails to reflect reality, yet it must not be so complex and complicated that it fails to clarify our thinking. It must be congruent with reality and have real-world empirical referents. It must be creditable not only in terms of its own internal logic but also in terms of the real-world relationships it mimics. Models must be insightful; they must identify truly significant relationships in the real world and screen out the irrelevant. But what is "significant" or "irrelevant" is a function of our purposes and values.

Models reflect the purposes of the model builder. The models developed in this book focused on the causes and consequences of the activities of state and local governments. Our purposes were to assess the responsiveness of these governments to the preferences of their citizen-taxpayers and to estimate the effect of their policies on the economic well-being of their states.

The models we used were very simple. We opted for simplicity and clarity, perhaps at the sacrifice of more complete explanations. Our object was usually to test the explanatory power of a model, not to predict values of the dependent variable. Often explained variance (total R^2) was quite low. Of course, the ideal would be to develop simple models with great explanatory power. But our primary purpose was to test simple explanatory models, not to increase explained variance.

Simplicity is a virtue. We tried to avoid atheoretical impulses to throw large numbers of variables into giant regression cauldrons. Our explanations are seldom independent of each other and cannot be treated as additive. Most measures are only crude surrogates for the concepts they represent. We expected large error terms. But we wanted to observe simple associations to help inform our theories.

We employed several research strategies throughout this book in testing propositions about the cause and consequences of state policies. Each of these strategies answers separate types of questions:

Cross-sectional analyses: Cross-sectional analyses compare conditions across the states at particular period in time. Traditional studies of the "determinants" of public policy in the American states (Dye 1966; Sachs and Harris 1964; Fisher 1964) compared public policies, usually expressed as taxing and spending levels, in all fifty states at various periods in time. Cross-sectional studies ask such questions as: Why are the policies of some states different from those of other states? Are differences among the states in public policy associated with differences in conditions hypothesized to explain these policies?

Consecutive cross-sectional analyses: Examining relationships between public policies in the states and conditions hypothesized to explain these policies at different points in time permits us to ask additional questions: Do the conditions that appear to explain policy differences at one time succeed in doing so at other times as well? Are the policies associated with economic well-being at one time also associated with economic well-being at other times? In other words, do our explanations of political efficiency hold up over time? Are our explanatory models weakening or strengthening over time?

Time-series analyses: Neither cross-sectional nor consecutive cross-sectional analyses deals with dynamic processes. These modes of analyses are essentially static in nature, analogous to snapshots at particular moments. In contrast, time-series analyses allow us to examine relationships between changes in public policies over time and changes in political, economic, or demographic variables. We can ask: Are changes in public policies responsive to changes in economic conditions? Does economic activity increase or decrease in response to changes in taxing or spending policies?

Separate state time-series analyses: By undertaking fifty separate time-series analyses—testing the explanatory models on each of the fifty states—we can ask whether the models apply to all of the states or only to some of them. If it turns out that a model explains conditions in some states and not others, we can ask what distinguishes the states in which the model works from those in which it does not. By undertaking fifty separate time-series analyses rather than pooling all observations at all periods of time, we are able to specify the states in which the models are successful.

Pooled analysis: Because of the small number of observations (N) available on the American states over the time span studied (a maximum of fifty in cross-sectional analyses and thirty-five in time-series analyses), we are limited in the number of independent variables we can use in any regression problem. In certain instances, however, we have undertaken to pool observations from all states at all times in order to expand the N and thereby permit the introduction of multiple control variables. Unfortunately, the trade-off for this expanded N is an inability to specify which states or which time periods are conforming to the hypotheses. But the pooled technique is useful in resolving some problems of interdependencies among independent variables. It allows us to ask such questions as the following: Overall, among all states and all time periods, what generalized effects do tax burdens have on economic growth? Do tax burdens have any general effects on economic growth independent of other forces affecting state economies?

Clarity of understanding is preferred over methodological elegance throughout this book. Methodology is an aid in explanation, not an explanation itself. We believe that knowing what we are talking about in substantive terms at each step in the analyses is preferable to talking about statistical artifacts. Thus, for example, we chose explanatory variables with real-world referents, such as per capita personal income, rather than artificially constructed factors. And we preferred simple bivariate correlations and regression analyses so that we learned what relationships existed among the variables before we proceeded to test multivariate explanatory models. Our cross-sectional regression problems were all linear least-square estimates of interval measures. Correlation coefficients (r) and standardized regression coefficients (β) were reported in the tables rather than regression coefficients (b), because in model building, we are concerned primarily with the strength of relationships rather than estimates or predictions of the dependent variables. We used an asterisk to indicate whether the F-test permits rejection of the null hypothesis at the .05 level of confidence. Our time-series regression problems employed the Cochrane-Orcutt procedure for first-order serial-correlation correction. We reported R^2s and T statistics for each problem. T statistics are simply the b values divided by their own standard deviations; T statistics of 2.0 or above permit rejection of the null hypothesis at the .05 level of confidence.

The data base for this inquiry, $TATE$, consisted of fifty separate state data sets of fiscal and economic variables, together with an aggregated national data set. Each data set included state government revenue, total and by source, and expenditures, total and by function; combined state and local government revenue, total and by source, and expenditures, total and by function; total personal income and personal income by type and industry source; and total employment and unemployment and employment by industry group. These measures were combined with a wide variety of population characteristics; indicators of economic resources and social needs; party competition, voter participation, and partisan control of state government; bureaucracy, centralization, unionization, and interest group activity; and region and climate. Observations for most fiscal and economic variables extended from 1952 to 1985 for all states (except Alaska and Hawaii which extend from 1957 to 1985). $TATE$ was constructed to facilitate cross-sectional analysis at any point in time and time-series analysis for any individual state.

The principal sources of the data for $TATE$ were the various editions of U.S. Bureau of the Census, *Governmental Finances*; U.S. Bureau of Labor Statistics, *Employment and Earnings*; U.S. Bureau of Economic Analysis, *Survey of Current Business*; and U.S. Bureau of Census, *Statistical Abstract of the United States*. Unless otherwise noted in tables or text, the source of the data presented in this book is $TATE$.

References

Adelman, Irma, and Cynthia Taft Morris. 1973. *Economic Growth and Social Equity in Developing Countries*. Stanford: Stanford University Press.

Advisory Commission on Intergovernmental Relations (ACIR). 1963. *Industrial Development Bond Financing*. Washington, D.C.: ACIR.

———. 1967. *State-Local Taxation and Industrial Location*. Washington, D.C.: ACIR.

———. 1981. *Regional Growth: Instate Tax Competition*. Washington, D.C.: ACIR.

———. 1986. *Reflections on Garcia and Its Implications for Federalism*. Washington, D.C.: U.S. Government Printing Office.

———. 1987.*Changing Public Attitudes on Governments and Taxes*. Washington, D.C.: ACIR.

Ambrosius, Margery M. 1985. "Olson's Thesis and Economic Growth in the States." Paper presented at the Midwest Political Science Association, Chicago.

———. 1986. "Effects of State Economic Development Policies on the Health of State Economies." Paper presented at the Midwest Political Science Association, Chicago.

Aranson, Peter, and Peter C. Ordeshook. 1977. "Incrementalism, Fiscal Illusion, and the Growth of Government in Representative Democracies." Paper presented at the Fourth Interlaken Seminar on Analysis and Ideology, June.

Aronson, J. Richard, and John L. Hilley. 1986. *Financing State and Local Government*. 4th ed. Washington, D.C.: Brookings Institution.

Bahl, Roy W. 1965. "Determinants of Changes in State and Local Government Expenditures." *National Tax Journal* 18 (March): 50–57.

Bahl, Roy, Marvin Johnson, and Michael Wasylenko. 1980. "State and Local Government Expenditure Determinants: The Traditional View and a New Approach." In *Public Employment and State and Local Government Finance*, pp. 65–119. Edited by Roy Bahl, Jesse Burkhead, and Bernard Jump. Cambridge, Mass.: Ballinger Publishing Company.

Baumol, William J. 1967. "Macroeconomics of Unbalanced Growth: The Anatomy of an Urban Crisis." *American Economic Review* 57:415–426.

———. 1986. "Productivity Growth, Convergence, and Welfare." *American Economic Review* (December): 1072–1085.

Beam, David R., Timothy J. Conlan, and David B. Walker. 1983. "Federalism, the Challenge of Conflicting Theories and Contemporary Practices." In Ada Finifter, ed., *Political Science: State of the Discipline*. Washington, D.C.: American Political Science Association.

Beck, Paul Allen, and Dye, Thomas R. 1982. "Sources of Public Opinion on Taxes." *Journal of Politics* 44(February): 172–182.

Benson, Bruce L., and Ronald N. Johnson. 1987. "Capital Formation and Interstate Tax Competition." In Dwight R. Lee, ed., *Taxation and the Deficit Economy*. San Francisco: Pacific Research Institute.

Berry, William D., and David Lowery. 1987. "Explaining the Size of the Public Sector: Responsive and Excessive Government Interpretations." *Journal of Politics* 49:401–440.

Bird, R.M. 1970. *The Growth of Government Spending in Canada.* Toronto: Canadian Tax Foundation.

Bish, Robert L. 1987. "Federalism: A Market Economics Perspective." *Cato Journal* 7:377–397.

Black, Duncan. 1958. *Theory of Committees and Elections* Cambridge: Cambridge University Press.

Borcherding, Thomas E. 1977a. *Budgets and Bureaucrats: The Sources of Government Growth.* Durham, N.C.: Duke University Press.

———. 1977b. "One Hundred Years of Public Spending, 1870–1970." In *Budgets and Bureaucrats: The Sources of Government Growth,* pp. 19–44. Edited by Thomas E. Borcherding. Durham, N.C.: Duke University Press.

———. 1977c. "The Sources of Growth of Public Expenditures in the United States, 1902–1907." In *Budgets and Bureaucrats: The Sources of Government Growth,* pp. 45–70. Edited by Thomas E. Borcherding. Durham, N.C.: Duke University Press.

Bowman, Ann O'M., and Richard C. Kearney. 1986. *The Resurgence of the States.* Englewood Cliffs, N.J.: Prentice-Hall.

Brazer, Harvey. 1959. *City Expenditures in the United States.* Occasional Paper No. 66. New York: National Bureau of Economic Research.

Brennan, Geoffrey, and James M. Buchanan. 1980. *The Power to Tax.* New York: Cambridge University Press.

Brenner, Reuven. 1987. *Rivalry: In Business, Science, Among Nations.* Cambridge: Cambridge University Press.

Breton, Albert. 1974. *The Economic Theory of Representative Government.* Chicago: Aldine.

Buchanan, James M. 1977. "Why Does Government Grow?" In *Budgets and Bureaucrats: The Sources of Government Growth,* pp. 3–18. Edited by Thomas E. Borcherding. Durham, N.C.: Duke University Press.

———. 1979. "The Potential for Taxpayers Revolt in American Democracy." *Social Science Quarterly* 59(March): 691–696.

Buchanan, James M., and Gordon Tullock. 1962. *The Calculus of Consent.* Ann Arbor: University of Michigan Press.

Buchanan, James M., and Richard E. Wagner. 1977. *Democracy in Deficit.* New York: Academic Press.

Cameron, David R. 1978. "The Expansion of the Public Economy: A Comparative Analysis." *American Political Science Review* 72 (December): 1243–1261.

Canto, Victor, Douglas H. Joines, and Arthur B. Laffer. 1983. "Persistent Growth Rate Differentials Among States in a National Economy." In *Foundations of Supply-Side Economics.* New York: Academic Press.

Carlton, Dennis. 1983. "The Location and Employment Choices of New Firms." *Review of Economics and Statistics* 65 (August): 440–449.

Cebula, Richard J. 1977. "An Analysis of Migration Patterns and Local Government Policy Toward Public Education." *Public Choice* (Winter): 113–121.

Chamberlin, John. 1974. "Provision of Collection Goods as a Function of Group Size." *American Political Science Review* 68 (June): 707–716.

Cherney, Hollis. 1975. *Patterns of Development*. London: Oxford University Press.

Choi, Kwary. 1983. "A Statistical Test of Olson's Model." In Dennis C. Muller, ed., *The Political Economy of Growth*. New Haven: Yale University Press.

Chubb, John E. 1985. "The Political Economy of Federalism." *American Political Science Review* 79 (December): 944–1015.

Citrin, Jack. 1979. "Do People Want Something for Nothing." *National Tax Journal* 32 (June): 112–118.

Cnudde, Charles, F., and Donald J. McCrone. 1969. "Party Competition and Welfare Policies in the American States." *American Political Science Review* 63:858–66.

Copeland, Gary M., and Kenneth J. Meier. 1984. "Pass the Biscuits Pappy: Congressional Decision-Making and Federal Grants." *American Politics Quarterly* 12 (January): 3–21.

Council of State Governments. 1984. *The Book of the States 1984–85* Lexington, Ky.: Council of State Governments.

———. 1986. *The Book of the States 1986–87* Lexington, Ky.: Council of State Governments.

Cuccitti, Peggy. 1978. *The Role of Equalization in Federal Grants*. Washington, D.C.: U.S. Government Printing Office.

Cutright, Phillips. 1967. "Inequality: A Cross-National Analysis." *American Sociological Review* 32 (August): 562–577.

Dahl, Robert A. 1967. *Pluralist Democracy in America*. Chicago: Rand McNally.

Davis, Otto A., M.A.H. Dempster, and Aaron Wildavsky. 1974. "Toward a Predictive Theory of Governmental Expenditure: U.S. Domestic Appropriations." *British Journal of Political Science* 4 (October): 419–452.

Dawson, Richard E., and James A. Robinson. 1963. "Inter-Party Competition, Economic Variables, and Welfare Policies in the American States." *Journal of Politics* 25:265–289.

Dennison, Edward. 1962. *The Sources of Economic Growth in the United States*. Washington, D.C.: Committee on Economic Development.

Downs, Anthony. 1957. *An Economy Theory of Democracy*. New York: Harper & Row.

———. 1960. "Why the Government Budget Is Too Small in a Democracy." *World Politics* 20 (March): 541–563.

Due, John F. 1961. "Studies of State-Local Tax Influences on Location of Industry." *National Tax Journal* 14 (June): 163–173.

Dunn v. Blumstein. 405 U.S. 330 (1972).

Dye, Thomas R. 1966. *Politics, Economics, and the Public*. Chicago: Rand McNally.

———. 1980a. "Taxing, Spending and Economic Growth in the American States." *Journal of Politics* 42 (November): 1085–1107.

———. 1980b. "State Energy Policies." *Texas Business Review* 54 (September–October): 245–249.

———. 1984. "Party and Policy in the States." *Journal of Politics* 46 (November): 1097–1116.

———. 1985. "The Impact of Federal Tax Reform on State-Local Finances." *The CATO Journal* 5(Fall):597–608.

———. 1987. *Understanding Public Policy*. 6th ed. Englewood Cliffs, N.J.: Prentice-Hall.

Dye, Thomas R., and Thomas Hurley. 1978. "The Responsiveness of Federal and

State Government to Urban Problems." *Journal of Politics* 40 (February): 196–207.

Easton, David. 1965. *A Framework for Political Analysis.* Englewood Cliffs, N.J.: Prentice-Hall.

Elazar, Daniel J. 1962. *The American Partnership: Intergovernmental Cooperation in Nineteenth Century United States.* Chicago: University of Chicago Press.

———. 1966. *American Federalism: A View from the States.* New York: Thomas Y. Crowell.

———. 1980. "Is the Federal System Still There." In Advisory Commission on Intergovernmental Relations, *Hearings on the Federal Role.* Washington, D.C.: U.S. Government Printing Office.

———. 1981b. "States as Polities in the Federal System." *National Civic Review* (February): 77–82.

———. 1981a. "The Evolving Federal System." In Richard M. Pious, ed., *The Power to Govern.* New York: Academy of Political Science.

Eulau, Heinz, and Kenneth Prewitt. 1973. *Labyrinths of Democracy.* Indianapolis: Bobbs-Merrill.

Fabricant, Solomon. 1952. *The Trend of Government Activity in the United States Since 1900.* New York: National Bureau of Economic Research.

Fenton, John H. 1966. *Midwest Politics.* New York: Holt, Rinehart and Winston.

Field, Melvin. 1978. "Sending a Message: Californians Strike Back." *Public Opinion* 1 (July–August): 5.

Firoina, Morris, and R.G. Noll. 1978. "Voters, Bureaucrats, and Legislators: A Rational Choice Perspective on the Growth of Bureaucracy." *Journal of Political Economy* 9 (June): 239–253.

Fisher, Glenn W. 1961. "Determinants of State and Local Government Expenditures." *National Tax Journal* 14 (December): 349–355.

———. 1964. "Interstate Variation in State and Local Government Expenditures." *National Tax Journal* 17 (March): 57–74.

Fosler, R. Scott. 1988. *The New Economic Role of the American States.* New York: Oxford University Press.

Fossett, James W. 1983. *Federal Aid to Big Cities: The Politics of Dependence.* Washington, D.C.: Brookings Institution.

Friedman, Milton. 1980. *Free to Choose.* New York: Harcourt Brace Jovanovich.

Friedreich, Carl J. 1963. *Man and His Government.* New York: McGraw-Hill.

Fry, Brian R., and Richard D. Winters. 1970. "The Politics of Redistribution." *American Political Science Review* 64 (June): 508–527.

Garcia v. San Antonio Metropolitan Transit Authority. 469 U.S. 528 (1985).

Gist, John R. and Carter H. Hill. 1981. "The Economics of Choice in the Allocation of Federal Grants." *Public Choice* 36(February):63–73.

Goodwin, R. Kenneth, and W. Bruce Shepard. 1976. "Political Processes and Public Expenditures." *American Political Science Review* 70:1127–1135.

Gramlich, Edward M. 1969. "The Effect of Federal Grants on State-Local Expenditures." *Proceedings of the National Tax Association,* 569–573.

———. 1977. "Intergovernmental Grants: A Review of the Empirical Literature." In Wallace E. Oates, ed., *The Political Economy of Fiscal Federalism.* Lexington, Mass.: Lexington Books.

Gramlich, Edward M., and Harvey Galper. 1973. "State and Local Fiscal Behavior and Federal Grant Policy." *Brookings Papers on Economic Activity* 1:15–58.

Gray, Virginia, and David Lowery. 1988. "Interest Group Politics and Economic Growth in the U.S. States." *American Political Science Review* 82 (March): 109–132.

Grodzins, Morton. 1966. *The American System*. Chicago: Rand McNally.

Gwartney, James. 1985. "Is the Flat Tax a Radical Idea?" *Cato Journal* 5 (Fall): 407–432.

Hansen, Susan B. 1983. *The Politics of Taxation*. New York: Praeger.

———. 1984. "The Effects of State Industrial Policies on Economic Growth." Paper presented to the American Political Science Association, Washington, D.C.

Haveman, Robert Henry. 1970. *The Economics of the Public Sector*. New York: John Wiley.

Heidenheimer, Arnold J., Hugh Heclo, and Carolyn Adams. 1975. *Comparative Public Policy*. New York: St. Martin's Press.

Hibbs, Douglass A., Jr. 1977. "Political Parties and Macroeconomic Policy." *American Political Science Review* 71 (December): 1467–1487.

Hirsch, Werner Z. 1970. *The Economics of State and Local Government*. New York: McGraw-Hill.

Hirschman, A.O. 1970. *Exit, Voice, and Loyalty*. Cambridge: Harvard University Press.

Hobbes, Thomas. 1651. *Leviathan*. Edited by Michael Oakeshott. New York: Collier Books, 1962.

Hofferbert, Richard. 1966a. "The Relation Between Public Policy and Some Structural and Environmental Variables in the American States." *American Political Science Review* 60 (March): 73–82.

———. 1966b. "Ecological Development and Policy Change." *Midwest Journal of Political Science* 10 (November): 464–483.

———. 1981. "Communication." *American Political Science Review* 75:722–725.

Holcombe, Randall G. 1986. *An Economic Analysis of Democracy*. Carbondale: Illinois University Press.

Holt, Robert T., and John E. Turner. 1966. *The Political Basis of Economic Development*. New York: D. Van Nostrand.

Horowitz, Ann R. 1968. "A Simultaneous Equation Approach to the Problem of Explaining Interstate Differences in State and Local Government Expenditures." *Southern Economic Review* 34 (April): 459–476.

Jackman, Robert W. 1975. *Politics and Social Equality: A Competitive Analysis*. New York: John Wiley.

Jennings, Edward T. 1979. "Competition, Constituencies, and Welfare Policies in American States." *American Political Science Review* 73:414–429.

Kemp, Kathleen A. 1978. "Nationalization of the American States." *American Politics Quarterly* 6 (April): 237–247.

Key, V.O., Jr. 1949. *Southern Politics in State and Nation*. New York: Random House.

———. 1958. *Politics, Parties and Pressure Groups*. 4th ed. New York: Thomas Y. Crowell.

Kieschnick, Michael. 1981. *Taxes and Growth: Business Incentives and Economic Development*. Washington, D.C.: Council of State Planning Agencies.

Kurnow, Ernest. 1963. "Determinants of State and Local Expenditures Reexamined." *National Tax Journal* 16 (September): 57–74.

Kuznets, Simon. 1955. "Economic Growth and Income Inequality." *American Economic Review* 45 (March): 1–28.

———. 1957. "Quantitative Aspects of the Economic Growth of Nations." *Economic Development and Cultural Change* 5 (July): 1–57.

———. 1966. *Modern Economic Growth*. New Haven: Yale University Press.

Ladd, Carl. 1979. "The Polls: Taxing and Spending." *Public Opinion Quarterly* 43(Spring): 126–135.

Larkey, Patrick D., Chandler Stolp, and Mark Winer. 1981. "Theorizing About the Growth of Government: A Research Assessment." *Journal of Public Policy* 1 (May): 157–220.

Lasswell, Harold D., and Abraham Kaplan. 1970. *Power and Society*. New Haven: Yale University Press.

Lasswell, Harold D., and Daniel Lerner. 1952. *The Comparative Study of Elites*. Stanford: Stanford University Press.

Levy, Frank. 1979. "On Understanding Proposition 13." *Public Interest* 56 (Summer): 66–89.

Lewis, I.A. 1980. "California's Stamp Tax Act." *Public Opinion* 7 (June–July): 54–55.

Lewis-Beck, Michael S., and Tom W. Rice. 1985. "Government Growth in the United States." *Journal of Politics* 47 (February): 2–20.

Long, Larry H. 1979. "Poverty States and Receipt of Welfare Among Migrants and Nonmigrants in Large Cities." *American Sociological Review* 30 (February).

Lowery, David. 1986. "After the Tax Revolt: Some Positive, If Unintended, Consequences." *Social Science Quarterly* 67 (December): 736–750.

———. 1987. "The Distribution of Tax Burdens in the American States: The Determinants of Fiscal Incidence." *Western Political Quarterly* 40 (March): 137–158.

Lowery, David, and William D. Berry. 1983. "The Growth of Government in the United States: An Empirical Assessment of Competing Explanations." *American Journal of Political Science* 27 (November): 664–694.

Lowery, David, Thomas Konda, and James Garand. 1984. "Spending in the States: A Test of Six Models." *Western Political Quarterly* 37 (March): 48–66.

Lowery, David, and Lee Sigelman. 1981. "Understanding the Tax Revolt: Eight Explanations." *American Political Science Review* 75 (December): 963–974.

Lowi, Theodore J. 1964. "American Business, Public Policy and Political Theory," *World Politics* 16 (July): 677–715.

Lyons, William. 1977. "Per Capita Index Construction: A Defense." *American Journal of Political Science* 21 (February): 177–182.

Lyons, William, and Michael R. Fitzgerald. 1987. "Intergovernmental Aid and Ratio Measurement." *Social Science Quarterly* 68 (September): 478–486.

McDowall, David et al. 1980. *Interrupted Time Series Analysis*. Beverly Hills: Sage Publications.

Madison, James, Alexander Hamilton, and John Jay. 1787. *The Federalist*. New York: Modern Library, 1937.

Maitland, Ian. 1985. "Interest Groups and Economic Growth Rates." *Journal of Politics* 47 (February): 44–58.

Memorial Hospital v. Maricoba County 415 U.S. 250 (1974).

Miller, Gary, and Terry M. Moe. 1983. "Bureaucrats, Legislators, and the Size of Government." *American Political Science Review* 77 (June): 297–232.

Mitchell, William C. 1983. "Fiscal Behavior of the Modern Democratic State: Public Choice Perspectives and Contributions." In Larry Wade, ed., *Political Economy*. Boston: Klujwer-Nijhoff.

Morehouse, Sarah McCally. 1981. *State Politics, Parties, and Policy*. New York: Holt, Rinehart and Winston.

Mueller, Dennis C., ed. 1983. *The Political Economy of Growth*. New Haven: Yale University Press.

Murray, Charles. 1984. *Losing Ground: American Social Policy, 1950–1980*. New York: Basic Books.

Musgrave, Richard A. 1969. "Theories of Fiscal Federalism." *Public Finance* 24:521–532.

Nardinelli, Clark, Myles S. Wallace, and John T. Warner. 1987. "Explaining Differences in Growth Rates: Catching Up versus Olson." *Public Choice* 52:201–213.

National League of Cities v. Usery. 1976. 426 U.S. 833.

Nelson, Michael A. 1987. "Searching for Leviathan: Comment and Extension." *American Economic Review* 77 (March): 198–205.

Nice, David C. 1987. *Federalism: The Politics of Intergovernmental Relations*. New York: St. Martins Press.

Niskanen, William A. 1971. *Bureaucracy and Representative Government*. Chicago: Aldine-Atherton.

North, Douglass C. 1955. "Location Theory and Regional Economic Growth." *Journal of Political Economy* 63 (June): 243–258.

Norton, R.D. 1986. "Industrial Policy and American Renewal." *Journal of Economic Literature* 24 (March): 1–40.

Nutter, G. Warren. 1978. *Growth of Government in the West*. Washington, D.C.: American Enterprise Institute.

Oates, Wallace E. 1972. *Fiscal Federalism*. New York: Harcourt Brace Jovanovich.

———."Searching for Leviathan: An Empirical Study." *American Economic Review* 75 (September): 748–757.

O'Brien, Thomas O. 1971. "Grants-in-Aid: Some Further Answers." *National Tax Journal* 24 (March): 65–78.

Okun, Arthur M. 1975. *Equality and Efficiency: The Big Trade Off*. Washington, D.C.: Brookings Institution.

Olson, Mancur. 1965. *The Logic of Collective Action*. Cambridge: Harvard University Press.

———. 1982. *The Rise and Decline of Nations*. New Haven: Yale University Press.

Osborne, David. 1988. *Laboratories of Democracy*. Boston: Harvard Business School.

Ostrom, Charles W., Jr. 1978. *Time Series Analysis: Regression Techniques*. Beverly Hills: Sage Publications.

Palmer, John L., and Isabel V. Sawhill. 1984. *The Reagan Record*. Washington, D.C.: Urban Institute.

Peacock, Alan, and Jack Wiseman. 1967. *The Growth of Public Expenditures in the United Kingdom*. Princeton, N.J.: Princeton University Press.

Pechman, Joseph A. 1985. *Who Paid The Taxes*. Washington, D.C.: Brookings Institution.

Peirce, Neal R., Jerry Hagstrom, and Carol Steinbach. 1979. *Economic Development: The Challenge of the 1980's*. Washington, D.C.: Council of State Planning Agencies.

Pelissero, John. 1984. "Statistical and City Needs." *Journal of Politics* 46 (August): 916–935.

———. 1985. "Welfare and Education Aid to Cities." *Social Science Quarterly* 66 (June): 444–452.

Pelissero, John, and David R. Morgan. 1987. "State Aid to Public Schools." *Social Sciences Quarterly* 68 (September): 466–478.

Pestieau, Pierre. 1984. "The Optimality Limits of the Tiebout Model." In Wallace Oates, ed., *The Political Economy of Fiscal Federalism*. Lexington, Mass.: Lexington Books.

Peterson, Paul E. 1981. *City Limits*. Chicago: University of Chicago Press.

———. 1988. "The Case for a National Welfare Standard." *Brookings Review* (Winter): 24–32.

Peterson, Paul E., Barry G. Rabe, and Kennneth K. Wong. 1986. *When Federalism Works*. Washington, D.C.: The Brookings Institution.

Peterson, Paul E. and Mark C. Rom. 1987. "Federalism and Welfare Reform." Discussion paper. Washington, D.C.: Brookings Institute.

Phares, David. 1980. *Who Pays State and Local Taxes*. Cambridge: Oegleschalager, Gunn and Hain.

Plaut, Thomas, and Joseph Pluta. 1983. "Business Climate, Taxes and Expenditures, and State Industrial Growth." *Southern Economic Journal* 50 (July): 99–119.

Preston, Samuel H. 1984. "Children and the Elderly: Divergent Paths for America's Dependents." *Demography* 21 (November): 435–457.

Pryor, Frederick L. 1968. *Public Expenditure in Communist and Capitalist Nations*. London: Allen and Unwin.

———. 1983. "A Quasi-Test of Olson's Hypotheses." In Dennis C. Mueller, *The Political Economy of Growth*. New Haven: Yale University Press.

Ranney, Austin. 1971. "Parties in State Politics." In Herbert Jacob and Kenneth M. Vines, eds., *Politics in the American States*. Boston: Little, Brown.

Rasmussen, David, Bart Bendick, and Larry Ledebor. 1984. "A Methodology for Selecting Economic Development Incentives." *Growth and Change* 15 (January): 18–25.

Rawls, John. 1971. *A Theory of Justice*. Cambridge: Harvard University Press.

Reese, Charles. 1979. *State and Community Governments in the Federal System*. New York: John Wiley.

Rostow, Walt W. 1961. *The Stages of Economic Growth* New York: Cambridge University Press.

Rubin, Barry M., and C. Kurt Zom. 1985. "Sensible State and Local Economic Development." *Public Administration Review* 45 (March–April) 333–339.

Sabato, Larry. 1983. *Goodbye to Goodtime Charlie*. 2d ed. Washington, D.C.: Congressional Quarterly Press.

Sachs, Seymour, and Robert Harris. 1964. "The Determinants of State and Local

Government Expenditures and Intergovernmental Flow of Funds." *National Tax Journal* 17 (March): 75–85.

Saltzstein, Alan. 1977. "Federal Categorical Aid to Cities: Who Needs It versus Who Wants It." *Western Political Quarterly* 30 (September): 377–383.

Schattschneider, E.E. 1942. *Party Government*. New York: Rinehart.

Schmenner, Roger. 1982. *Making Business Location Decisions* Englewood Cliffs, N.J.: Prentice-Hall.

Sears, David O., and Jack Citrin. 1982. *Tax Revolt*. Cambridge: Harvard University Press.

Shannon, John. 1987. "The Return to Fend-for-Yourself Federalism." Paper presented to the American Political Science Association, Chicago, 1987.

Shapiro v. Thompson. 394 U.S. 618 (1969).

Sharkansky, Ira. 1968. *Spending in the American States*. Chicago: Rand McNally.

Sharkansky, Ira, and Richard I. Hofferbert. 1969. "Dimensions of State Politics, Economics and Public Policy." *American Political Science Review* 63:869–879.

Smith, Adam. 1776. *The Wealth of Nations*. New York: Modern Library, 1937.

Stein, Herbert. 1983. "Don't Fall for Industrial Policy." *Fortune*, November 14, 1983, 64–66, 85–86.

Stein, Robert M. 1981a. "The Allocation of Federal Aid Monies: The Synthesis of Demand-Side and Supply-Side Explanations." *American Political Science Review* 75 (June): 334–343.

———. 1981b. "The Targeting of State Aid." *Urban Interest* (Special Issue): 47–60.

———. 1982. "The Allocation of State Aid to Local Governments." In Advisory Commission on Intergovernmental Relations, *State and Local Roles in the Federal System*. Washington, D.C.: ACIR.

Stein, Robert M., and Keith E. Hamm. 1987. "A Comparative Analysis of the Targeting Capacity of State and Federal Intergovernmental Aid Allocations." *Social Science Quarterly* 68 (September): 447–465.

Stutzer, Michael J. 1985. "The Statewide Economic Impact of Small-Issue Industrial Revenue Bonds." *Quarterly Review* 9 (Spring): 2–14.

Sundquist, James L. 1969. *Making Federalism Work* Washington: Brookings Institution.

Tarbel's Case. 1872. 13 Wall. 397.

Temin, Peter. 1967. "A Time Series Test of Patterns of Industrial Growth." *Economic Development and Cultural Change* 15 (January): 174–182.

Texas v. Wade. 1869. 7 Wall. 700.

Thompson, W.R. 1965. *A Preface to Urban Economics*. Baltimore: Johns Hopkins Press.

Thurow, Lester. 1980. *The Zero-Sum Society*. New York: Basic Books.

Tiebout, Charles M. 1056. "A Pure Theory of Local Expenditures." *Journal of Political Economy* 64 (October): 416–424.

Tocqueville, Alexis de. 1835. *Democracy in America*. Edited Richard D. Heffner. New York: New American Library, 1956.

Tucker, Harvey J. 1982a. "Interparty Competition in the American States." *American Politics Quarterly* 10:93–116.

———. 1982b. "It's About Time: The Use of Time in Cross-Sectional State Policy Research." *American Journal of Political Science* 26 (February): 176–196.

Tufte, Edward R. 1978. *Political Control of the Economy*. Princeton, N.J.: Princeton University Press.

Tullock, Gordon. 1971. "The Charity of the Uncharitable." *Western Economic Journal* 9 (December): 379–392.

U.S. Department of Commerce. Bureau of the Census. 1987. *Census of Governments*. Washington, D.C.: U.S. Government Printing Office.

U.S. Department of Commerce. Bureau of the Census. 1988. *Statistical Abstract of the United States 1988*. Washington, D.C.: Government Printing Office.

U.S. Office of Management and Budget. 1987. *Special Analysis of the Budget of the United States 1988*. Washington, D.C.: Government Printing Office.

Uslander, Eric M. 1976. "Pitfalls of Per Capita." *American Journal of Political Science* 20(February) 125–133.

Uslander, Eric M. 1976. "Pitfalls of Per Capita." *American Journal of Political Science* 20(February) 125–133.

Vedder, Richard. 1982. "Rich States, Poor States: How High Taxes Inhibit Growth." *Journal of Contemporary Studies* (Fall): 19–32.

Vedder, Richard, and Lowell Galloway. 1986. "Rent-Seeking, Distributional Coalitions, Taxes, Relative Prices and Economic Growth." *Public Choice* 51:93–100.

Wagner, Richard E. 1971. *The Fiscal Organization of American Federalism*. Chicago: Markham.

———. 1976. "Revenue Structure, Fiscal Illusion, and Budgetary Choice." *Public Choice* 25:45–61.

Ward, Michael D. 1978. *The Political Economy of Distribution*. New York: Elsevier.

Wasylenko, Michael. 1981. "The Location of Firms: The Role of Taxes and Fiscal Incentives." In Roy Bahl, ed., *Urban Government Finance*. Beverly Hills: Sage.

Watkins, Alfred J., and David C. Perry. 1977. *The Rise of the Sunbelt Cities*. Beverly Hills: Sage.

Weidenbaum, Murray. 1982. "Strengthening Our Federal System." In *American Federalism*. Edited by Robert B. Hawkins. San Francisco: Institute for Contemporary Studies.

White House Working Group on Federalism. Domestic Policy Council. 1986. *The Status of Federalism in America*. Washington, D.C.: U.S. Government Printing Office.

Wildavsky, Aaron. 1964. *The Politics of the Budgetary Process*. Boston: Little, Brown.

———. 1985. "Federalism Means Inequality." *Society* 22:5–14.

Wilde, James A. 1968. "The Expenditure Effects of Grant-in-Aid Programs." *National Tax Journal* 21 (September):340–348.

Wilensky, Harold L. 1975. *The Welfare State and Equality*. Berkeley: University of California Press.

Winters, Richard. 1976. "Party Control and Policy Change." *American Journal of Political Science* 20:597–636.

Wright, Deil S. 1978. *Understanding Intergovernmental Relations*. Belmont, Calif.: Wadsworth.

Zeigler, Harmon. 1983. "Interest Groups in the States." In Virginia Gray, Herbert Jacob, and Kenneth Vives, eds., *Politics in the American States*. 4th ed. Boston: Little, Brown.

Zeller, Belle. 1954. *American State Legislatures*. New York: Crowell.

Index

About the Author

Thomas R. Dye is McKenzie Professor of Government and Policy Sciences at Florida State University. He received his B.S. and M.A. degrees from Pennsylvania State University and his Ph.D. degree from the University of Pennsylvania. He is the author of numerous books and articles in American government and public policy including *The Irony of Democracy* (with Harman Zeigler), *Politics in State and Communities, Understanding Public Policy, Who's Running America?, American Politics in the Media Age, Power in Society,* and *Politics, Economics, and the Public.* His books have been published abroad and translated into many languages, including Russian and Chinese. He has served as president of the Southern Political Science Association, president of the Policy Studies Organization, and secretary of the American Political Science Association. He is a member of Phi Beta Kappa, Omicron Delta Kappa, and Phi Kappa Phi, and listed in most major biographical directories including *Who's Who in America.*